METHODS OF TEACHING EDUCATIONAL PSYCHOLOGY

METHODS OF TEACHING EDUCATIONAL PSYCHOLOGY

By

M. Alice Raj Kumari
M.A., M.Ed., (Ph.D.)
Principal
Tarlupadu College of Education
Tarlupadu, Prakasam Distt., A.P.

D. Rita Suguna Sundari
M.Sc., M.Ed.,
Principal
St. Paul's College of Education
Giddalur, Prakasam Distt., A.P.

General Editor
Dr. Digumarti Bhaskara Rao
M.Sc., M.A., M.A., M.Ed., Ph.D.
Reader
R.V.R. College of Education
Srinivasa Nagar Colony
Guntur–522 006
Andhra Pradesh
India

DISCOVERY PUBLISHING HOUSE
NEW DELHI-110002

First Published - 2004

Reprinted - 2018

ISBN: 978-81-7141-820-6

Methods of Teaching Educational Psychology

Published by:

DISCOVERY PUBLISHING HOUSE PVT. LTD.
4383/4B, Ansari Road, Darya Ganj
New Delhi-110 002 (India)
Phone: +91-11-23279245, 43596064-65
Fax: +91-11-23253475
E-mail: discoverypublishinghouse@gmail.com
sales@discoverypublishinggroup.com
web: www.discoverypublishinggroup.com

Printed at:
Infinity Imaging Systems
Delhi

Foreword

Teacher education is quantitatively marching ahead towards quality education. The central and state governments through the NCTE and the Directorates of School/Higher Education are rendering their legitimate service in improving the quality of teacher education by formulating and implementing various academic policies and educational programmes. Along with these policies and programmes, the teacher educators and the prospective teachers teaching and studying in teacher education institutions need good curriculum and quality books.

The methods of teaching each subject play a pivotal role in enhancing the efficiency of their practitioners. Identifying the very importance of the methods of teaching and the quality of books, a series of books on the methods of teaching different subjects have been developed by experienced teacher educators for the benefit of teachers in making in teacher education institutions. Thanks to the authors.

Valuable suggestions for the improvement of these books are welcome from fellow teacher educators, prospective teachers and other academicians involved in the arena of teacher education.

The authors and the editor dedicate this series of books on the methodology of teaching to Mr. Tilak Raj Wasan, Proprietor, Discovery Publishing House, New Delhi, for taking up this commendable task of publication to meet the felt needs of teacher education faculty and clientele.

Dr. Digumarti Bhaskara Rao
Research Director in Education
Nagarjuna University
br_digumarti@rediffmail.com

Preface

The movement of modern education in India is almost two century old. It has come of age now. Over the decades, great educationists have contributed towards the development and evolution of education, as a discipline. Thus, education in India has been enriched a lot.

As a result, the Indian education system can be placed at par with any advanced education system in the modern world. In fact, education is a vast sea and Teachers' Training is a stream in it. So, it makes it essential that the responsibilities of the faculty members are focused on the task of providing better training to the future teachers, for their better learning and proper development. And this responsible exercise can only be undertaken, if the trainers are equipped with all the needed skill and knowledge of the subject, they are supposed to teach. Hence, it becomes essential for making adequate provisions, for each course to the teacher-trainees. Methods of Teaching are very important for the successful training of teachers and for their career in future.

In order to provide all related material in one cover, here is this book, on this important subject. Of course there are several books on the subject in the market, but, every book has its own style and way of presentation. Similarly, the present one, too has its own merits and advantages.

During the course of the preparation of this book, the undersigned has done his best for the accomplishment of the job. He would be pleased and feel contented, if this book is acknowledged, as a textbook and a reference tool for the teachers and students, alike.

Author

Contents

1

Introduction

In modern times, during this age of science and technology, psychology has been considered as one of the youngest; yet one of the most influential sciences. It has influenced education in different ways and practically given a new turn, a psychological turn to the human mind. For a skilful teacher of the present-day society, knowledge of the child has been considered to be more important than the knowledge of the subject matter. Therefore, teachers in the modern society should be equipped with those psychological skills and competence, which are badly needed for the successful guidance of learning, adjustment and the growth of the child.

The subject 'Psychology' has two aspects-pure and applied. Pure psychology formulates broad principles brings out theories and suggests tecniques for the study of human behaviour, which finds in its applied aspect, i.e. branches of Applied Psychology, Clinical Psychology, Crime Psychology, Industrial Psychology, Occupational Psychology and Educational Psychology. Therefore, Educational Psychology is nothing but one of the branches of Applied Psychology in the practical shape It is an attempt to apply the knowledge of Pure Psychology to the field of education. It consists of application principles and techniques to human behaviour in educational situations. In other words. Educational Psychology is a study of the experiences and behaviour of the learner in relation to educational environment. In order to develop a clear understanding of the term 'Educational Psychology', it is necessary to understand the meaning of psychology and education separately.

About 2000 years ago, Psychology appeared as a separate branch of study. It was the genius of Aristotle that gave birth to this science. Yet, in its modern form, it is one of the latest of all disciplines. It has been changing its meaning from time to time. According to Rudolf Goeckel the term psychology has been derived from two words, "Psycho" and "Logos", Psycho means soul and Logos means "Science of" or "Talk about". Thus psychology means "The science of soul". Goeckel named it as Psychologia. Soul is a being which dwells in the body and at the end of life it leaves the body. Since soul is a metaphysical entity, scientific investigation is not possible. Therefore psychology as the science of soul has been discarded by the modern psychologists. Therefore, the definition of psychology as the science of soul was discarded.

The philosophers again developed another definition of psychology as the "Science of Mind". After sometime controversy arose on the nature of mind. People began to feel that like soul, it is equally impossible to define mind scientifically. Ultimately this definition was discarded.

Psychology was again defined as the science of consciousness or immediate experiences. Ultimately, it was observed that consciousness forms only a very negligible part of the personality of an individual and the scope of psychology goes much beyond the study of consciousness. It also studies the sub-conscious and unconscious states of human mind. On this ground, the psychologists rejected this definition.

The above definitions given by philosopher-psychologists before the beginning of experimental psychology were considered to be very much inadequate and were rejected. Now it is defined as "the science of behaviour". To understand this definition, let us now discuss in brief the meaning of the science and behaviour.

Science has been defined as "systematic study of knowledge" concerning the relationship between the cause and effect of a particular phenomenon. In order to collect the scientific data and systematised material, science employs various kinds of methods of enquiry such as observation, classification, formulation of hypothesis, analysis of evidence, etc. It also organises and develops our knowledge of the world, we live in. Psychology too aims at the same thing. It uses scientific methods to study human behaviour. It also helps us to understand, control and predict human behaviour.

Behaviour is a specific response which can be seen and observed in an active way. Psychology as the science of behaviour also aims at studying the behaviour of the individual and groups. We can study the behaviour of an individual in social mileu. As a social science it studies scientifically the socio-cultural problems of particular society. Hence it is the science of behaviour.

"Education is an activity, which goes on in the society." It attempts to develop the personality of an individual and then prepares him for membership in a society. "Man without education would still be living just like an animal. It is education, which transforms man from a mere two legged animal into a human. It helps him to behave like a man and prevents him from behaving like an animal. Any modification brought about in the behaviour of an individual as result of his interaction with the environment constitutes learning." Thus modification of behaviour of an individual for healthy social adjustment in the society is education.

The term Educational Psychology is the combination of two words. Education and Psychology. So far, we have discussed the meaning of Psychology and Education separately. Let us now focus our attention to the meaning of Educational Psychology.

Psychology is the science of behaviour. It aims at studying the behaviour of individual and the group. Besides, this it also helps us to control the behaviour of the organism as a whole. Education on the other hand, implies the modification of the behaviour of an individual. In order to modify the behaviour of an individual, the teacher must study the behaviour of the individual first. To study the behaviour of the child the teacher must take the help of true Psychology and to modify the behaviour of the child he must take the help of Education. Thus, Education and Psychology are interrelated. Pure Psychology helps to study behaviour and Educational Psychology as an applied branch of psychology applies psychological principles of Education to modify human behaviour.

Educational Psychology as outlined above is a branch of psychology concerned with human learning and development in educational settings. It involves scientific study of techniques that can be used to enhance learning. Studies conducted by the Educational Psychologists generally deal with the following three important areas.

It includes teaching methods, styles, management techniques etc.

It includes application of principles of cognitive and developmental Psychology, taking into account individual differences and learning styles.

2

Educational Psychology

It includes social context of the classroom or home environment.

Sl.	Education		Psychology
1.	Modern education is a group phenomenon. Hence some of the group psychological laws can be applied to the process of education viz. group dynamics.	1.	Psychology also deals with groups.
2.	Modern education is defined as for behaviour, of behaviour and by behaviour. Hence psychological laws, processes and findings can be applied to education.	2.	Psychology is surely a behavioural science.
3.	Educational goal today is all round psychology development of the individual. Hence psychology aids teachers in affording better educational development of children.	3.	Developmental psychology gives required insight into human development in all of its aspects.
4.	Modern education caters to the needs, interests and abilities of children. Hence knowledge of psychology of needs and of interests enables teachers to plan educational programmes in a desirable manner.	4.	Psychology enables understanding of needs, interests and abilities of children.
5.	Education involves proper organisation learning of teaching learning situation. Hence it is a common meeting group of both the subjects.	5.	Psychology of learning gives into these areas.

6. Education aims at the development of personality and character. Hence there are psychological aspects in this area also.	6. Psychology analyses these aspects of development minutely.

According to Arthur Coladarci of Stanford University, Educational Psychology is the empirical foundation of education. It consists of those aspects of education which can be observed, tested and experimentally verified and as such Educational Psychology is the scientific foundation of Education. But effectiveness of Educational Psychology is proved only when its methods and findings become a part of educational practices, when the teachers apply psychological methods and when they develop and experiment attitudes towards their efforts.

Judd describes Educational Psychology "as a scientific study of the life stages in the development of an individual from the time he is born until he becomes an adult."

Charles E. Skinner states, "Educational Psychology is the branch of psychology which deals with teaching and learning."

According to Walter B. Kolesnik "Educational Psychology is knowledge of the study of those facts and principles of psychology which helps to explain and improve the process of education. Educational Psyhology thus is the body of scientific knowledge about two activities-Education and Psychology."

The Discipline

We often put a question-What is the Nature of Educational Psychology? The answer to this question becomes almost clear when we try to examine the meaning and definitions discussed earlier. Its nature is scientific as it has been accepted that it is a science of education. Its relation with education and educational psychology is also to throw light on its nature. We can summarise the nature of educational psychology in the following way.

(i) Educational Psychology is a positive and not a normative science: Usually normative sciences like Ethics and Philosophy decide the aims of education. It is not the function of Educational Psychology to decide the same.

But once it is decided Educational Psychology will help us in telling whether aims are attainable or intangible. As a positive science, Educational Psychology will be concerned with the discovery of techniques, by which the educational goals can be attained out of scientific study. When psychology declares that a particular aim is unattainable, philosophers will then rethink and modify the goals of education.

(ii) Educational Psychology is a Behavioural Science: As noted earlier, the scientific study of how learning and other human behaviour have relevance to education is the principal concern of Educational Psychology. Thus Educational Psychology may be thought of as a behavioural science with two main referents-human behaviour and education. In the educative process human beings are the objects of investigation about whom generalisations are developed and knowledge is sought. The second important referent of education, Educational Psychology is concerned with behavioural questions that are related to the objectives and practices of education.

(iii) Educational Psychology is an Applied Science: The action of Educational Psychology is to be found not only in the nature of the subject itself but rather in its application in the classroom. Teachers primarily deal with groups of children not with psychological theory or experimental results, but their learning is constantly being applied to a unique set of circumstances. That is why teaching is a profession and not a trade.

Educational psychology is just an application of psychological principles in the field of education and also changing the behaviour of the individual. It is to predict behaviour, control and influence it. Thus it becomes an applied branch of Psychology.

(iv) Educational Psychology is a Social Science: Social psychologists study humans who interact frequently, if not continually, with each other and live in groups ranging from the family to the society. Social psychologists are not only concerned with the effect of the groups (whether family, peer, professional, cultural or social) upon the individual and vice versa, but are also interested in a wide variety of other personal interactions.

(v) Educational Psychology is a Counselling Psychology: We use the word counselling to refer to the functions of psychologists whose principal job is to deal with people who are in need of help or advice but not primarily who have emotional difficulties. A branch of psychology closely related to counselling is to be found in the work of the school psychologists—planning, teacher training, problem of parents, and the like. Educational Psychology thus encompasses counselling psychology.

(vi) Educational Psychology in an Educational Science: General psychology may be considered as the primary behavioural science. The domain of psychology is very broad, including the study of collective behavioural problems of individuals in educational situations. Educational Psychology collects necessary knowledge from general psychology to apply the same in educational setting. For example, to discover what makes teaching effective and what makes learning effective. We need the help of several special areas of general psychology. In Developmental Psychology the teacher learns about human growth from infancy (and even before) to maturity-how physical, intellectual, emotional, and social potentials mature and change as a child grows; what conditions foster healthy growth, and what conditions block it. Many changes in teaching methods and curriculum have come about as more has been learned about the ways in which children typically develop and how their needs change. Another focal point of attention has been the special problems of the child who is "different" in some way.

The Psychology of learning is concerned with acquisition and change of our patterns of behaviour, how those processes take place most efficiently, how learning of different kinds can be measured, what conditions help us retain what we learn and use it appropriately in new situations, and how learning varies with different levels of ability. Many kinds of learning "content" are involved in school work from simple muscular responses to highly complex intellectual process. A teacher's need for studying the psychology of learning is obvious.

It becomes evident that modern psychology offers a great deal of help to educational psychology to apply scientific principles to educational settings and thus educational psychology becomes an educational science.

(vii) Educational Psychology is concerned with Human Factor in Learning: *The Encyclopedia of Educational Research* (1960) defined the nature of Educational Psychology as follows:

Educational psychology is concerned with human factor in the learning. It is a field in which concepts derived from experimental work in psychological laboratories are applied to education, but is also a field in which experimentation is carried out to test the applicability of such concepts to education and to round out the study of topics of crucial interest to teachers. It is the study of the learning teaching process in its various ramifications.

(viii) Educational Psychology is a Growing Science: Historically, Educational Psychology began with William James and Edward Thorndike in the USA in 1808. Since then the field of educational psychology has been influenced by works in related fields such as developmental psychology, educational measurement, cognitive psychology, personality theory, counselling, individual differences, and most recently computer science researchers, who are involved in scientific study of techniques that can be used to enhance the teaching learning process are contributing many new ideas to be applied in the field of education.

(i) Not the Nature of Subject but its Application in the Classroom is its Real Nature: The nature of Educational Psychology is in no way concerned with the nature of the subject matter itself but with its application in the classroom situation. Knowledge of psychological theory alone cannot help the classroom teachers to deal with the students. Their knowledge in theory should be connected with classroom practice.

(ii) Psychological Foundations of Education cannot be Educational Psychology: Psychological foundation of education cannot be considered as deeper a science as Educational Psychology. It is to be considered as intermediary discipline that attempts to orient the students into the realms that are common between education and psychology. It is more concerned with the applicational aspect and not so much with the theoretical aspect of Educational Psychology. It aims at the application of the psychological knowledge to the field of education. It mainly emphasises on understanding the psychological aspects that serve as the educational foundation.

(iii) Educational Psychology is not Mysterious: Many people imagine that Educational Psychology is something magical or mysterious and that somehow educational psychologists have a superior or almost super human way of looking into the thoughts and feelings of the students. The notion is in other words, that there is a psychological method or approach, and that any one who knows how to use this and uses it successfully has an advantage over anyone who lacks it but in a true sense Educational Psychology is no more mysterious today. It is an ordinary applied science. It has no magic, no mysterious ways and no dark or hidden routes by which it gets its knowledge. Whatever educational psychologists have learned, they have learned through observation, and through careful observation in the classroom. Hence, Educational Psychology is neither magical nor mysterious.

(iv) Educational Psychology is not Common Sense: Some people go to the opposite extreme and assume that Educational Psychology is essentially nothing more than common sense. To them, Educational Psychology is nothing but what wise people have discovered from their experience, whether they have ever had formal training in the subject or not.

It would of course, be overstating the case to say that educational psychology has a monopoly of knowledge of human behaviour and its modification. The fact remains that application of scientific psychological principles in educational settings and the psychology of common sense in educational setting are different. For one thing there are statements that are accepted by common sense but not accepted by pyschology. One example of this is the common notion that those who are insane or seriously mentally ill have "lost their minds." In the other words, insane people are considered to be unable to reason adequately or accurately. This common-sense idea of insanity is far from the truth. Although intellectual abilities are sometimes disturbed in mental illness, a great, many individuals who are insane are not suffering for lack of ability to reason. If given an intelligence test, they do as well as others. In such cases, the difficulty is not in the intellectual realm at all but rather in the field of emotion. Thus, psychology must insist that insanity cannot be regarded as the "loss of mind".

On the other hand, a good many things that are accepted by psychology are not accepted by common sense. An example relates to the phenomenon of colour. The common sense view of colour is that the colour is in the object which we see. Thus, if we see yellow flowers and blue flowers in a vase on our desk, common sense says the yellowness and the blueness are actually in the flowers themselves. From the standpoint of modern science this view is entirely unacceptable. We have every reason at present to believe that the colour is not in the object but rather in the perceiver.

The Sphere

Scope means, the limits of a particular subject in the field of its operation. What is to be included in its study or what subject-matter does it contain comes under its scope. Educational

Psychology, as discussed so far, deals with the behaviour of the learner in educational settings and should limit itself within the four walls of the teaching-learning process and educational environment. It must try to solve the problem evolving in actual teaching-learning situations and help the individuals involved in this process.

The psychologists who deal with the problems of education are concerned with what to teach, when to teach and how to teach. A famous psychologist, Lindgren points out that Educational Psychology is concerned with understanding the learner, the learning process and the learning situation. The scope of Educational Psychology may be discussed under the following heads.

(i) The learner (student)

(ii) The learning process

(iii) The learning situation

(iv) The learning experience

(v) The teacher

(i) The Learner: The term 'learner' applies to students who individually or collectively participate in the educational programmes. These students taken collectively constitute the class. In fact, the behaviour of the class is none other than the behaviour of the students. There can be no teaching without there being a learner. Therefore, Sir John Adams once remarked "Teacher teaches John Latin. Teacher must have the knowledge of John's psychology; therefore, the teacher must study psychology."

The teaching of Latin without the knowledge of John will not be effective. John (the learner) thus becomes the center of the teaching-learning process.

From psychological point of view, John is a child and he should consider, not his needs, ambitions, fears and other emotions are not the same as those of an adult. Treat him, therefore, as a developing organism which is unique and not as a small model adult.

Two learners of the same age differ from one another in a number of ways. When one has a liking for music and dislike for mathematics and science another may have, dislike for music and for mathematics and science. Hence, while preparing the curriculum for the learners we must take into consideration the dual differences that exist among the learners.

However, intelligent a learner may be, he cannot become successful in life if he lacks motivation. Hence motivating the learner is very important. In the classroom, situation from the psychological view, not only motivation but also the developmental characteristics of personality, mental health, individual differences intelligence, etc, of the learner come under the scope of educational psychology.

(ii) The Learning Process: Learning is the process by which we acquire and retain attitudes, knowledge, understanding, skills and capabilitiesand these cannot be attributed to the inherited behaviour patterns or his physical growth. Capacity for learning is related to innate physiological factors. Rate of learning depends on both inherited environmental factors.

(a) Affective learning has to do with feelings and values and therefore influences our attitudes and personalities.

(b) Cognitive learning is achieved by mental processes such as reasoning, remembering and recall. It helps in the problem of remembering and recall. It helps in problem solving, developing new ideas and evaluation.

(c) Psychomotor learning has to do with the development of skills which require efficient coordination between our brains and muscles, as when we read or write or carry out physical skills such as balancing, skipping or jogging.

A number of other processes have been put forward to explain how we learn. All of them have conceived of learning as a process that progresses in stages.

(iii) The Learning Situation: It is difficult to imagine any period of our life situations, when we are not learning some-thing, even though we are not always aware that we are learning. While walking down a street on any ordinary day, we continually modify our behaviour. Learning is commonly through experiences in response to environment. Thus learning situation covers all life experiences that modify our behaviour.

From academic point of view a learning situation refers to the classroom setting, which is composed of students, a teacher and a room. All have unique characteristics. In addition to these features we also have the behaviour of teacher and students. Behaviour includes not only overt physical activity such as talking, and doing, but also cognitive process like cognizing, thinking and evaluating. In the classroom and the school, the teacher is to help bring about desirable changes in student behaviour. Through the teacher's interaction with students and the students' interaction with one another, many desired interests, motives, social skills and several outcomes in the cognitive and psychomotor domains are acquired more efficiently than if there was no practical interaction.

(iv) The Learning Experience: Although Educational Psychology does not connect itself directly with the problem of what to teach or what learning experiences are to be provided for the learner, yet it has the full responsibility of suggesting techniques of acquiring the learning experiences. Once the task of deciding the aims and objectives of a piece of instruction at a particular stage is finished the need of of Educational Psychology is felt. At this stage, Educational Psychology helps in deciding what learning experiences are desirable, at stage of growth and development of the learner so that these experiences can be acquired with a greater ease and satisfaction. In this area, Educational psychology has the subject matter which deals with the knowledge and principles of psychology which facilitates the selection of the desirable learning experiences for the learner.

(v) The Teacher : It is not enough for a carpenter to be good at sawing and polishing wood because every kind of wood has different characteristics and behaves in different ways under his tools. The skilled carpenter need to know about trees, their variety, their characteristics and how to make the best use of them, so it is with teaching. Teaching skills alone are not sufficient. He must understand the children as learners. He must try to recognize those characteristics that are significant in helping each child to learn more effectively.

Any teacher who knows anything about the learners is aware that growing up is more than growing bigger. Children are not little adults nor are adults big babies. It is essential, therefore, that teachers who are closely concerned with children during that period of life some of the most important developments take place should know as much as possible about the process of growing and developing.

One of the first things we notice when we try to understand the learners is how differently they are, how each develops at his pace and along his own path of progress. No child is typical. He is in his own way unique. Yet like the doctor who must recognise which symptoms are serious and which are trivial, the teacher must distinguish between those variations that are normal and those that may indicate a child's need for special attention.

Understanding the learner from psychological point of view is an attempt to find out as much as possible about a particular learner by spending some time with him and learning about his physical, mental and personality characteristics and relevant facts about the environment in which he is growing up. Recording of such child studies is important so that the information can be used in wider studies or, where necessary for helping a child with problems.

In an important sense, it is not desirable to limit the scope of Educational Psychology to the above five areas only. Educational Psychology is a developing and a fast growing science. Like any other developing branch of science it multiplies itself every year. New ideas are coming into picture because of the results of new researches and experiments in the field. Society is dynamic in nature. So also is education. The new problems in the process of education and their solution are coming with a faster rate. Educational Psychology is trying harder and harder with the result of the development of new concepts, principles and techniques. For example, traditionally developmental psychologists were concerned with the study of the child development, but in recent years adolescence, adulthood and old age have drawn increasing interest. A major concern of developmental psychologists has been the process of socialization - how the immature, and relatively helpless infant is transformed into a functioning member of society. An important part of socialization is the process whereby language is acquired and this is an area of vigorous research activity. Although developmental psychology has been with us since the very beginning of psychological study, its current popularity is increasing. This example proves that it is unwise to fix the boundary of Educational Psychology by defining its scope. It will not only harm the progress of Educational Psychology but also prove as a great obstacle in the progresses of education.

The boundaries of Educational Psychology, therefore, must be left free for its future expansion so as to facilitate the inclusion of all that is created in this field. As a result of which we can solve most of the problems of education and help the teaching-learning process to meet the demands of exigencies.

Teacher's Role

The contemporary age has witnessed an ever-growing interest in the welfare and education of children. Because of the recognition of the significance of the period of childhood, the present age has been called "the children's century". Modern education is also described as child-centered. Besides this paedocentric knowledge and understanding of children, the teacher should have knowledge of Educational Psychology. It will give him larger awareness of the nature, abilities and needs of the students he teaches, of the processes involved in his work and his own capacities and limitations.

Teachers in modern schools, whether primary or secondary, are often amazed at children's eagerness to learn, their creative problem solving, persistent efforts in self-development and their academic, athletic and artistic accomplishments. Trained teachers who are curious and scientifically oriented often wonder why and how children learn as much and even more effectively. The answers to these questions are relevant to the knowledge of psychological principles. The teachers can obtain positive results, if they can apply psychological principles in the classroom, laboratory, on the playground and in any learning situation.

Teachers and prospective teachers at the secondary stage of education, therefore should try to enhance their understanding of their students by studying Educational Psychology. Thus they can provide proper guidance for effective learning.

Education Psychologists have much to offer the secondary school teachers in understanding the learners, because they have extensive resources at their disposal. In their research, they have access to children of all ages and ability groups in ongoing complete learning situations. They also help the teachers in their understanding of the principles of teaching, especially in the field of learning, in understanding developmental tasks of adolescents, individual differences and mental health. In all these fields, the teachers and prospective teachers become successful in understanding the learner.

Students' Growth

Modern education is concerned with the development of both the individual and society. It is the duty of the Teacher to develop the constructive potentialities of every learner as fully as possible. At the same time he should aim to preserve and enhance the conditions of constructive living in society. In additior to these, he should turn to the accumulated and continually expanding knowledge which makes up our cultural heritage and he should see that it is rich in curriculum resources. For the teacher should believe in a subject-child - community-centered education. When the teacher seeks the development of the learner, he should look to the following aspects.

(i) The teacher should enable the learners to achieve an inquiring mind, skills for effective communication, knowledge for maintaining, protecting and improving his health and for satisfying interests and skills and ethical character.

(ii) The teacher should enable the learners to achieve comfortable, useful and happy social relationships in their families, with friends and with other people at work and play. The learner should develop respect for humanity in general.

(iii) The teacher should enable the learners to attain economic efficiency by becoming an intelligent consumer and by preparing material suited to his talents and interests and to the needs of his society.

(iv) The teacher should enable the learners to develop civic responsibility, which involves a sense of social justice, an understanding of his society, participation as a citizen, tolerance, interest in conservation and devotion to the ideas of democracy.

In summarizing the role of the teacher in the development of knowledge of the learners, we can say that the teacher should look to the development of a community of individuals enjoying an increasingly satisfying constructive way of life. They involve the attainment of intellectual proficiency, occupational competence, effective group participation and leadership.

Besides the above areas, the teacher also gets help from Educational Psychology for the development of the learners in the following areas as well.

(i) Physical development, health and body care, including individual health, and elementary aspects of public health, grooming and understanding of growth.

(ii) Individual, social and emotional development, including mental health, emotional stability, growth of personality, and self-understanding and evaluation.

(iii) Ethical behaviour standards, and values, including observance of moral and civil laws, observance of the customs and mores of the culture, and the development of such characteristics as sportsmanship, kindness and helpfulness.

(iv) Social relations, a category which grows out of the preceding two and is devoted to the individual as a person in his personal, and social relations with others with whom he associates in home, community, and place of work.

(v) The social world, which considers the behaviour of the child in relation to the broader social setting of community, state and nation and includes geography, civics, economics, government, and the traditional Indian way of life.

(vi) The natural environment, as revealed by the physical and biological sciences, which emphasize learning to think scientifically and the use of scientific methods both as scientists and for solving problems in everyday living.

(vii) Aesthetic development, including both appreciation of the arts and personal participation in art, music, crafts and other creative activities.

(viii) Communication, including an understanding of the language, effective use of language skills in reading, handwriting, composition, usage, spelling, punctuation, speaking and listening.

(ix) Quantitative relationships, consisting mainly of arithmetic, including understanding our number system, knowledge of how it is widely used in solving quantitative problems in society, and the development of problem-solving skills.

Experts and Scholars

Within each of these nine broad and interrelation areas, objectives are further classified as indicative of four "types of behavioral change".

(1) Knowledge and understanding, which would include the objective of learning " how to use table of contents of a book".

(2) Skills and Competence, under which we would place such objectives as " skill in untangling unfamiliar words."

(3) Attitudes and Interests, under which we would include "enjoyment of a wide variety of reading materials," and

(4) Action Patterns, which "refer to broad generalized ways of behaving" such as ways of responding to problem situa-

tions through the union of intelligence with good working habits and scientific methods of thinking. According to Campbell-Stewart, Educational Psychology helps the teachers in the following ways:

(i) To outline aspects of the learning process: Teaching methods rest fundamentally upon the psychology of learning. A teacher aims at modifying the experience and responses of his students in many ways. He should, therefore, know the conditions of the learning process thoroughly. Psychology helps him by rendering a most systematic and exhaustive analysis of the learning process.

(ii) To outline the main phases in psychological growth from infancy to maturity: The infant, the boy, the adolescent and the young man have different outlooks and attitudes. A systematic study of the characteristics of each one of these developmental phases will not only be interesting but also rewarding for a teacher who desires to be successful and effective in the classroom. Detailed information regarding these stages of growth is furnished by psychology.

(iii) To match subject matter and processes to be learned to labels of development and psychological principles: A practical outcome of the study of development stages is the equipping of the teacher with the skill to match the class instruction with the mental levels of the learners. Educational Psychology also helps in the formation of the guiding principles which are the bases of this correlation of the curriculum and teaching to the psychological growth level of the learner.

(iv) To give some training in assessing and making allowance for the social matrix beyond the school in which the child and the teacher live: As the child leaves the school he is exposed to many social influences, a large number of which are only too often adverse, nullifying the healthy socio-cultural effect of the education received at the school. Streets, cinemas, cafes, etc, are few instances of the sources of these undesirable influences in the beyond-the -school social matrix. In order to assess their pernicious or non-pernicious effect and in order to counteract their undesirable influence on the child. Educational Psychology aims at training the teacher in adopting suitable remedial measures. Some of these measures are: organization of sports and games, conducting of psychological test, guidance of the students and their parents, etc.

(v) To give the teacher insight into his own psycho-logical process and his own role as teacher: A teacher should learn to control his own conflicts before he starts teaching. If he does not do so the students merely serve as more or less suitable materials on which "to react his unconscious and unsolved difficulties," Knowledge of Educational Psychology helps the teacher to know himself.

Some of our teachers develop an undesirable attitude towards their students due to poverty, ill-health, insecurity of service, incompetence to do the allotted work, emotional tensions, inability to get on amicably with colleagues, etc. These and host of other unfortunate factors affect the teaching-learning situation adversely.

Our society, on the other hand is unfavourable towards the teaching profession. Teaching has been accepted as a 'failure belt'. It is the refuge of the "unproductive men and unmarriageable women". Because of such an attitude of the society towards teaching profession, our teachers do not feel for their profession. If this is re-inforced by an already existing painful tension in the mind, of the teacher, his plight becomes all the more miserable because of this additional inner enemy.

Educational Psychology which helps a teacher to know his own inner nature. He also understands the mechanism of the factor leading to his failure as a teacher. The knowledge of his own self and his profession helps him to improve both as a person as well as a teacher.

Educational Psychology also helps the teacher in proper management of the classroom to promote learning and minimize disruption. It teaches him how to present his lessons to both large and small groups-and when to do which. It also teaches him how to predict certain learning patterns of students of different ages and from different backgrounds to comprehend the importance and limitations of the theories employed in teaching strategies, and to utilize the many tools and techniques that are available to him. Besides, studying. Educational Psychology will remind a teacher how challenging teaching can be, and how gratifying it is when a teacher devotees his time and energy to this work.

Educational psychologists incorporate knowledge of the teaching process, the learning of the teaching process, and the learning environment in strategies that are designed to enhance learning. They study topics such as cognitive and developmental psychology, principles of measurement and classroom management. Educational psychologists also conduct experiments, some in the classroom and some in laboratories to find their own answers to unresolved questions and so on.

3

Role of the Teacher

For the development of social traits in the child and to build him as a good citizen, the school, family and society are to play a very crucial role. In all these environments social development of the child is well-directed and well-shaped by teaching learning process. Education in very valuable for the child. Parents and elders should teach their children how to co-operate and keep good relation with all family members. Direction, advice and above all encouragement are basic for the development of the child. They should not be neglected but be given love and affection. Otherwise his social growth is retarded. He becomes autocratic and selfish. Selflessness, tolerance and co-operativeness are the qualities which should be inculcated in the child. Hard and rigid behaviour, sometimes causes mental instability. Many parents out of fear of danger, do not give their children independence to do any work and they themselves do that work for the child. By this, the quality of self-independence is hampered.

In case of schools or other educational institutions proper environment should be created to facilitate social growth of the children. School can arouse in the children qualities like friendship leadership, co-operation, responsibility, pity, unity, etc. This cannot be achieved only by advice. For this co-curricular activities should be encouraged. Sports and games, staging of drama, discussion, excursion, scouting, Red Cross, etc, are helpful for the child in the development of social traits. Human relation-ship is the foundation of sociability. So it is the first and foremost duty of the teacher and school to see how best students can keep direct relation among themselves and engage in constructive work.

Special Qualifications

1. Sympathy: It is a social quality. One should not only express explicitly sympathy in the sorrow of others, rather he should cooperate in order to do away with the misery of others. This is true sympathy. Sympathy should be active but not passive. It starts from home. Its learning cannot be rendered simply by means of advice. If the child receives sympathy from his family members and gets required help in the time of need, he develops exactly the same quality for others. These qualities may not be explicit in the child, for the child's power of observation, imagination, thinking and gathering experience may not be enriched. So he fails to express sympathy for others. For this reason the elders, by means of concrete examples should eradicate qualities like hate and jealousy from the child's mind. The child first applies these qualities to his own people. This is extended to others at a later stage.

2. Friendliness: Sympathy and sentiment for one and all creates friendship. A child of two or three years can make contact with other children of his own age if they are left together at a particular place. This contact develops into friendship. Generally similarity in interest, age, height, social and economic status serves as foundation of friendship, selflessness, co-operation, etc. It has been observed by examining the students of a class that many students are interested to create new friends and some others lead isolated life. This happens due to individual differences in the personality. The child with whom others become interested to mix and make friendship with are called 'stars' and friendless students are called 'isolates'. Apart from this, there are some students who become intimate with only one friend and there are others who have many intimate friends. The former is called 'paid' and the later is called 'friendship gang'. This difference should be marked by the teacher and he should steer them in the right way. He should take steps to facilitate the isolate child to enlarge his circle of friends and become sociable.

The followings are some reasons for the isolation of the student.

(a) Anti-Social: Some children show rough behaviour. They show anti-social behaviour like disturbing others at the time of study, quarreling frequently, beating others, stealing books and money, tearing up of the books and notes, etc. For such reasons other children are not interested to keep relation with him and finally he is isolated.

(b) Socially Indifferent: Some children are always thoughtful, inattentive and shy. They are introverts. Thought, imagination and attention of such students are always self-directed. They are not hopeful in creating friendship and lead a busy life. Their mental health needs to be restored. For, the teacher should apply principles of love, sympathy and consolation and engage them in responsible work by which they can be brought back to social mainstream. Sometimes the suggestion of psychologists proves useful in such cases.

(c) Underdeveloped: The students whose social and moral maturity does not keep tune with their growth in chronological age lie behind other general students and feel isolated.

The students who are friendly with all and with whom others want to make friendship show some distinct qualities. The qualities that make a student popular and friendly to all are his patience, good health, efficiency, responsibility, dependability, co-operation, service and help to others, and love for all, etc. Again good adaptability and emotional balance make him popular among friends.

Cooperation-vs-Competition

Cooperation is one of the finest social traits. When the child, for the first time leaves his family and enters into the other environment his span of social relations widens. He develops group behaviour. After becoming the member of a group, he tries to be co-operative. Group co-operation gives birth to group competi-tion. One group of children compete with another group for which all members of a group are to be united. It is difficult to say which of the two qualities—co-operation and competition starts first in human life, because during infancy and early childhood brothers and sisters in a family compete among themselves to be nearer and dearer to their elders. This type of competition is also possible in a classroom.

It should not be misunderstood that family only serves as a ground for competition. It also facilitates co-operation. Experience and moral educations makes competition change into co-operation. Competition cannot be blamed, since without competitive attitude, the child cannot continue his endeavour for development and perfection. But both co-operation and competition have their own limits. They should respond to the needs of the society. Though competition is helpful for the child, it has some drawbacks, because at times such a competitive mentality makes the child jealous and he undergoes tension. So proper balance should be maintained between these two qualities and that is the duty of the teacher. Apart from these if the competition is fair and constructive, social health is restored.

For the all-round development of the child, good social moral upliftment should be given proper attention in the school curriculum. The behaviour of the child should be closely and intensely observed by the teacher which will guarantee the healthy development of the child social and moral.

The whole series of anatomic and physiological changes taking place between the beginning of pre-natal life and the close of senility may be considered as the physical growth. The study of physical growth of both children and the adolescents is very interesting and helpful also. Ordinarily, people make an estimate of the age of the children from their size and treat them accordingly. They also expect them to behave in a manner appropriate to the level of their physical growth. But the basic growth of the child is determined by two factors: heredity and environment. The hereditary factor refers to the characteristics of their family and race and environmental factors refer to healthy or unhealthy surroundings in which the children live, their nutritional and climatic factors, etc.

The behaviour of the child gets influenced by physical development in two ways: direct and indirect. Directly, it determines what children can do. For example, a child, who is developed according to his chronological age, can compete with his peers in games and sports on equal terms. If not, he fails to compete with them and gets himself isolated from the peer group.

Indirectly, physical development influences the attitude of the child towards self and others. In other words, it is his adjustment to the human environment. For example, children who are overweight cannot adjust with their thinner-mates. As a result of which they develop a feeling of personal inadequacy. If, on the other hand, their friends refuse to play with them because they are too slow, they develop a feeling of "martyrdom" in addition to the feeling of inadequacy. Such a feeling creates a havoc in the personality development of the children and the adolescents.

Growth and Development

Physical growth brings bodily and physiological changes (internal as well as external) in an organism from the conception till death. These changes take place in the following dimensions.

(i) Changes in Physical Structure: Changes in terms of height, weight, body proportions and general physical appearance are considered as changes in the gross physical structure of an individual.

(ii) Change in Internal Organs: Changes in the functioning of glands, nervous system and other body systems like circulatory, respiratory, digestive, muscular, lymphatic and reproductive are known as changes in internal organs.

Physical growth does not occur at a regular rate. It occurs in periods, phases or waves. Sometimes it appears slowly and sometimes rapidly.

Researchers are recognizing more and more that a child's physical development has a strong influence on his personality. Researcher Tanner, put it this way:

"All the skills, aptitudes, and emotions of the growing child are rooted in or conditioned by his bodily structure. Behind each stage of learning lies the development of essential cell assemblies in the brain; behind each social interaction lies a body image conditioned by the facts of size and other features....... How fast a child grows and what type of body structure he has can exert a crucial influence on the development of his personality. The child's sense of identity is strongly linked to his physical appearance and ability."

Children's Growth

The period of infancy covers knowledge of the entire pre-school age, from birth to about 5 to 6 years. In the first few weeks the human embryo and foetus grow at an extremely rapid pace both in size and structure through the multiplication of cells. Within a period of nine months, from the time of conception, the human organism grows from an almost weightless cell to about seven to eight pounds. By the time the human infant is born the rate of growth shows an enormous decrease as compared with that of the foetus. Even then the most rapid physical changes and the most striking growth of the whole post-natal life takes place during the first year. This early period of rapid growth is uniquely significant for education.

Significant Elements

(i) Rapid Growth and Development: Infancy is the period of growth and development. Inner as well as outer organs, develop rapidly at this stage. There is rapid growth in terms of height, weight and size. There is rapid development of emotions and almost all the emotions are developed in the child during this stage. This stage is marked by intensive motor activity and restlessness.

(ii) Dependence: An infant depends upon his mother, father and other family members for the satisfaction of his basic needs. He is a helpless creature and can move and function only with the help of others. Even for the emotional satisfaction, he depends upon others. He expects that everybody around him should love him and give him his entire affection and attention. He wants to love and to be loved and in this exchange he totally depends on the mercy of others. In this way the child at this stage is dependent but as he moves into the later years of his infantile behaviour he slowly proceeds towards independence.

(iii) Self-Assertion: Although the child is a helpless one and depends upon others for the satisfaction of his needs, he is quite self-assertive. He tries to dominate his superiors and elders. His wishes must be fulfilled. He thinks he is always right and those all around him should obey him. He is the prince without a crown.

(iv) Period of Make-believe and Fantasy: Infants live in the world of their own creation. This is a period of rich but baseless imagination. As at this stage the infant has limited potentialities and aspires more than what he can actually get in actual life. He compensates himself in fantasy and make-believe.

(v) Selfish and Unsocial: In infancy the child is almost completely ego-centric and selfish. He does not want to share his toys or give any of his possessions to anyone else. He wants to have all the things, even love, admiration and affection reserved for him. He does not care for the social and moral codes and principles and places his self-interest at the premium.

(vi) Emotionally Unstable: Infancy is the period of violent emotional experiences. The emotions at this stage are marked by intensity, frequency and instability. They are spontaneous and the infant is hardly able to exercise control over them. He is not able to hide his feelings and in this way, the emotional expression of the infant is generally in the overt form.

(vii) Sexual Development: Although the sex organs at this stage are not developed, yet the sex tendency is in a continuous stage of development. The findings of psychoanalysts like Freud and others have clearly shown that the sexual life of the infant is as rich as that of an adolescent. The infant passes through the three stages, sexual development stages of self-love, homosexual and heterosexual. At the initial stage, the child-derives pleasure from his own body by sucking his thumb or touching the sex organs. Later on he seeks the satisfaction of his sex impulse outside and develops sentiments of love for the mother or father depending upon his sex. Finally the child develops heterosexual tendency and in this respect the male child gets attached to the mother and the female child to the father.

(viii) Respiration and Circulation: During infancy, the lungs develop rapidly and breathing capacity is increased. The heart also grows in size and its action becomes stronger but slower than at the embryo stage. The pulse rate which was one hundred and thirty for boys and one hundred forty for girls at birth drops gradually so that it is ninety-five for boys and ninety for girls. Parents and teachers must realise that the developmental rate of the heart varies with children. Recognition of this fact can help us to prevent tragedies resulting from too great a strain laid on this organ.

(ix) Muscular Development: The very slow development during infancy shows a slight acceleration at age three. Development proceeds from the bigger to the smaller muscles. Thus, an infant thrusts out his arms in play, but immaturity of the smaller muscles of his wrists and fingers prevent their manipulation.

This is determined by maturation of necessary muscles. A child will sit up, stand or walk only when the necessary muscles have matured. But this process of muscle maturation is very slow during infancy and these motor skills are acquired very slowly. Prior to this maturation, actions are awkward and they involve many unnecessary movements. In trying to grasp an object, an infant will exhibit several unnecessary movements of the shoulders, upper arms and elbows. The use of the thumb occurs only after the ninth month. As the infant advances in age, greater maturity of the muscles results in the unnecessary movements being dropped and action being refined. There is also greater strength and speed in the movements.

When the human infant is born, he weighs about 7 to 8 pounds. In length, he is about 20 inches. In the very first year the weight triples and the length increases by about 40%. The rate of growth slows down considerably during the next three years and after that it becomes steady.

Growth in weight is influenced to a great extent by nutrition. Infants from poorer families are weightless and are shorter in stature as compared with infants from rich families. There is also variation in growth rate due to sex-difference. The male infants are larger than female infants of the equal age.

Childhood begins with the school going age round of about 5 or 6 years and ends with the beginning of adolescence, i. e. about 12 years in case of the girls and 14 years in case of the boys.

During childhood period, height and weight progress at a fairly uniform rate. But, motor development including posture, motor skills, co-ordination, locomotion, etc, which begin from infancy, go on unchecked.

Physical Health

The rate of physical growth continues to be slow. Between the ages of six and nine years, children grow about three to four pounds annually. This slow trend continues during the next phase also. Between the ages of nine and twelve years, increase in height is only an inch per year. Weight increases by about two or three pounds per year but this increment varies from month to month. This slow period of growth is called the pre-puberty lag. The growth is slowest for girls between the ages of nine and ten years, while boys grow slowest between ten and eleven years.

An average six year old is about three feet tall and thirty-five to forty pounds in weight. As the growth rate is slow at age nine, the child is about three and half feet tall and nearly fifty-five to sixty pounds in weight. Girls are generally shorter and lighter than boys. The most significant physical change occurring during this period is the lengthening of the limbs. The legs especially grow vary fast and children appear long-legged. Though children are generally healthy, postural defects are likely to appear now. In our efforts to correct this, we must try to find out the causes which may be infection, malnutrition, fatigue or even emotional disturbance.

The lungs continue to grow and the breathing capacity increases. The heart has not yet attained its full growth. Between the ages of nine and twelve these organs are almost, but not fully developed. Hence we must prevent children from exerting themselves too much.

The slight acceleration in muscular development that had set in after age three, still continues. Muscle tissue increases and coordination improves. By age six, a child has reasonable mastery over the basic skills. Hence the child is very active, and enjoys games that involve much physical activity. But his imperfect muscle-co-ordination makes him prone to falls. Since the muscles of the orbit are not developed fully, long reading sessions are prohibited for the six year olds. Between the ages of nine and twelve, muscle growth increases and co-ordination also improves. The child's actions are more refined and skillful. Reading sessions can also become longer now.

Children between the ages of six and nine have a reasonably good mastery over the basic motor skills of sitting, standing, walking and simple finger manipulation. Improving muscle co-ordination helps the child to acquire new skills and improves the already acquired ones. Thus, the six and seven year olds may be seen trying to climb a stairway by taking two steps at a time. They also try climbing and jumping down from high places. By age twelve, muscle co-ordination is almost perfect. At this stage improved co-ordination of hand and finger muscles helps the child to produce good handwriting.

A child at this stage is full of energy and action. The school authorities, therefore, should take care that the early education of the child takes cognizance of this significant physical factor. Consequently, primary education should be predominantly informal. It should have ample provision for interesting and diversified activities.

Most of children grow according to the average pattern of development characteristic of their age level. Some children however, differ markedly from the average in many respects. Some of them go through the whole developmental process more rapidly. Others more slowly, than the average growth rate typical of their age. Some children show striking individual peculiarities in the trend and speed of growth at various levels of development. They may thus be advanced at one stage of their development and retarded at another. Throughout these developmental variations however, every child keeps on undergoing almost ceaseless growth in various parts of its body .

During the first ten years, the boys are slightly superior to girls in most of physical growth. The tempo of physical development, however, is faster on the whole in girls than in boys.

On the average, the period of rapid growth, following the onset of puberty, starts two years earlier in girls than boys. The significant year in which most rapid growth usually occurs is the 12th in the case of girls (about one year before the first menstruation) and the 14th or 15th for boys. Between the age of 11 and 15 years the girls usually excel the boys in weight and height. Growth in girls, however, stops abruptly after the menarche. The average girl reaches her mature stature by 16 1/2 (sixteen and half) years. The average boy, on the contrary, continues to grow until he is almost 19.

The body proportions of young boys and girls are very similar in general. Boy's skeletal frames become broad at the shoulders. Their general growth is characterized by heavy muscles and greater strength. In girls the pelvis widens and the hips broaden. Pads of thicker fat in certain areas of the body result in the typical softness of the female figure.

These developmental proportions are typical for the two sexes. Nevertheless, there are a great many children whose course of growth does not fit in with the average pattern of physical development described above.

Many attempts have so far been made to classify individual children into physical types. The most commonly recognized racial and familiar traits usually forming the basis of such classification are variations in skin colour, form and colour of hair, shape of head, ear and nose, colour and shape of eyes, general structure, span and weight. It may be pointed out that these variations are more or less permanent. They persist in the individuals from family to family and from generation to generation. In changed environments, these physical traits may undergo some modifications but their general nature remains fundamentally unchanged on the whole.

Scholars' Views

One classification of physical types is presented by Scammon. His four types of children based on their physical growth are as follows:

1. The Lympoid: This is a physical type in which the rate of growth of the child increases rapidly until 11 to 12 years and then decreases almost as rapidly to the adult level.
2. The Neural: It is the type of rapid early growth at 3 or 4 years gradually slowing down and reaching almost adult level by 12 to 14 years.
3. The General Type: It is characterized by a rapid rise in growth in early infancy followed by another rise around puberty.
4. The Genital Type: It is marked by a slow growth in the early years which becomes very rapid at puberty.

Another interesting classification based on physical peculiarities, is presented by Kretschmer. His physical types are also four in number. Their salient features are:

1. Pyknic Type: This is characterized by round trunk and short extremities.
2. Asthenic Type: Small trunk and long extremities are the distinctive features of this type.
3. Athletic Type: This type shows a moderately proportional development of the body.
4. Dyspalastic: This is a mixed type of physical growth.

A thorough knowledge of physical typologies might not be very helpful for a teacher in his actual school work though it proves very insightful for the school medical officer. Some general information regarding the salient characteristics of physical growth among children, however, is almost indispensable for any successful teacher because obviously proper guidance in the field of physical health is as essential for a child as any other help and guidance.

Impacts and Implications

It is not possible to have watertight compartments between physical, cognitive, emotional, social and moral development. They are closely interlinked. The growth and development of any one of these aspects affects the growth and development of the other. Therefore, physical growth is not an exception to it. It influences the other aspects of growth and development in other directions also. For example, growth and development of the nervous system influences the growth and development of intellectual powers. Emotional and social adjustment is also linked with physical growth and development. While the children having normal physical growth and development are accepted by their age group, the physical deviates, who are very small, very large, too fat, etc, remain isolated. They are often nicknamed, ridiculed and denied participation in the play and recreational activities enjoyed by childran of the same age. It brings serious maladjustment and personality problem. The young child, if intelligent enough, becomes aware of the fact that he differs in appearance and physical abilities from other children. His attitude towards self is injured and self-confidence is shaken. In this case either he becomes shy and timid or becomes aggressive in order to compensate for his inferiority feeling. Besides this, the balanced growth and development of the internal as well as external organs depends on the balanced functioning of the body systems. The functioning of the body systems decides the interest, attitude and the total behaviour of an individual. For example, glands and their functioning affect his emotional behaviour to a great extent. Similarly his anato-mical development, the development of circulatory, respiratory system, etc, give the persons the required abilities for partici-pating in various motor activities.

Thus physical development has a great impact on the total make-up of an individual. Therefore, it needs a very careful attention. It can help the teachers to achieve one of the most impor-tant aims of the educational process to bring an all round balanced development.

Children between the ages of three and five years are too young to cope with the work of the primary school. But they are mature enough to start preparing for it. Kindergarten training is therefore, very important. It is here that the child gets the first experiences of school life. He memorises short nursery rhymes, sings with others, learns to obey simple commands and follows directions. He gets accustomed to being separated from his mother and learns to adjust to a fixed schedule. He is also taught to work and play with other children of his age. Hence, the song-dance-and-play atmosphere of the nursery school is just a happy place where learning is a joy.

Activity must form an integral part of nursery training. As the children acquire new motor skills, they have an innate urge to practice them. Action songs, games that involve varied activities like running, skipping and jumping are enjoyed by them. As repetition and drill are also enjoyed, the same action or drill can be repeated profitably.

Children between ages six and nine years have a keen desire to read and write. But their muscle coordination is still imperfect. Hence the teacher must not over-emphasise reading and writing. Handwriting also cannot be expected to be very good at this stage. Between age nine and twelve, reading can be encouraged. The teacher can also help the child to improve his handwriting.

4

Methods of Teaching

For purposes of study, it is convenient for us to isolate the aspects of the learning process. But we must remember that knowledge about the learning process is not an end in itself. Our real goal is to learn how to apply our knowledge so that children will learn in the most effective way possible.

The old saying that teachers are born and not made no longer holds true. As a modern, well-trained teacher, you must first have learned what and how to teach each child. You must know the material that you are to teach, the nature of the child, and the best methods of instruction. True, much of what makes you able to learn to teach and to enjoy teaching has come from your original nature and from the environmental forces that you encountered before you entered the teacher-training programme. But without training, regardless of your interests ability, and personality, you could not possibly perform at the level expected of the professional teacher in today's schools.

Since most prospective teachers lack experience in dealing with children, let us see how we can apply our knowledge of educational psychology to the actual business of classroom teaching. Let us attempt to identify some of the problems of directing classroom learning and see what application we can find for our knowledge of the learning process.

1. We know that in an hour's time a child may learn much or he may learn little. What makes a learning situation effective?

2. We know that the learnings that take place in the classroom are not ends in themselves. How can we guide learning toward educationally worthwhile goals?

3. We know that it is the child rather than the teacher who must do the learning. How can we so guide the learning situation that the child maintains an active attack on his learning problems?

4. We know that children in the same school grade differ widely in ability. How can we make adjustments for differences in learning ability?

5. We know that in spite of our best efforts, we cannot make every minute's work so fascinating for every child that learning will proceed automatically toward educational goals. How can we gain and preserve the leadership that we must have if we are to offer the necessary guidance of the classroom learnings?

6. We know that to learn the child must solve problems. How can we help him to develop work habits and problem-solving skills that will result in economy, persistence, and effectiveness in solving problems of increasing complexity?

7. We know that forgetting is ever an enemy of what has been learned. How can we provide for maximum retention?

8. We know that we must use minute-to-minute and day-to-day learning situations for the mastery of a large body of essential materials and skills. Can we find a general teaching procedure that will make maximum use of what is known concerning how children learn most effectively?

9. We know that not only must classroom learning be remembered but it must be made applicable to the problems that the child will meet in life. What criteria can we use for selecting the classroom learnings?

Let's take these professional problems one at a time and seek satisfactory solutions.

What is an effective learning situation? The answer to our first question is relatively simple. But to answer the eight other questions that we have listed, we must first identify the conditions of effective learning.

An effective learning situation is one in which the child strongly desires solutions for problems that block him from satisfying one or more of his motives. His need for security, self-esteem, the esteem of others, and new experiences are always present in the classroom. If he can see opportunities to satisfy these needs, if he must learn in order to do so, and if the learning is within his ability, the chances are great that he will learn effectively. But if the problem situation presents a threat to the child's security, or a loss in his self-esteem or esteem in the eyes of others, or if it fails to offer him new experiences, it will not lead to effective learning, no matter how many times the child is forced to read a certain passage, to repeat a certain answer, or to copy certain set of exercises.

Thus, in the effective learning situation the child is actively striving to solve problems. As teachers, we must achieve this condition and more. We must guide his activity toward educationally sound goals. How can we accomplish this?

From the standpoint of providing a felt need to learn, the most important characteristic of the classroom is that it is a social situation. There is a social interaction between the child and his teacher and between the child and his peers—he strongly desires the esteem of both. The classroom provides also a vast opportunity for new and interesting experiences. And, working with friends and a well-adjusted teacher on mutually interesting problems, the child should find security there. In addition, the classroom can satisfy certain of the child's habit motives. There is ample motivational force available for energising the learnings of the classroom. How can we direct this force? How can the classroom experiences be made rewarding to each child?

We know that for effective learning, the child must be trying to reach goals that are important to him. It is not enough that we see that the learnings he attains will be important to him in the future. They must be important now. How can we make goals that will be important, now?

The ability to write an effective business letter, the ability to talk convincingly to fellow adults, the ability to keep personal accounts accurately will be tremendously important to the child when he becomes an adult. But they will not be important to the child unless progress toward them results in recognition, self-esteem, new experiences, and security now.

The child can become extremely active in digging information from reference books, in writing a poem or a theme, in working an experiment in chemistry, or in preparing a talk. And he thus learns a great deal that will be useful to him as an adult. But he will be extremely active only if these activities satisfy present needs. He may need the reference material, for example, to defend a position that he has taken. He may need the poem or theme because it will give him the approval of peers, parents, or teachers. The experiment in chemistry may be a fascinating new experience. And he may have to give the talk in front of his fellow students. A boy raises a pig and keeps careful records of its costs not because of his future need for this knowledge but because of present rewards; a girl bakes a cake and makes an attractive dress not because she will some day be a homemaker but because she wants to wear the dress or receive praise for her skill in making it.

This, then, is the secret of directing effective learning toward educational goals. You are always aware of the long-range objectives toward which you guide the child—but you offer the child immediately attainable ones. Although you evaluate effective learning in terms of educational goals, you recognise that the child strives toward personal goals. And each child in your classroom will attack problems that temporarily block his attainment of personal needs.

An effective learning situation is not enough. You must guide the child's activity toward goals that are educationally worth while and you must help the child to maintain an active attack on the problems that stand between him and his goals.

Basic Problems

Why must you know how to guide the child to an active attack on his problems? Will he not strive actively to solve problems if his goals are important and attainable? Actually, the maintenance of the child's attack on problems is one of your most important professional tasks. You may know that the goals are extremely worthwhile but the child himself must be led to see how they can satisfy his needs. You may know that the goals that are being set are attainable, but without your guidance the child may not see that they are. And without guidance the child's attack may be sidetracked. Each child will require redirection from time to time if he is to persist in solving his problems.

Let's see how we can help the child to maintain an active attack on his problems without guiding and restricting his efforts to such an extent that his learning becomes ineffective.

To say that learning is an active process does not mean that you as the teacher should busy yourself in pouring out information every minute of the day. In fact, the more active you are in solving problems before they are felt by the child and in illustrating ideas before the child has had a chance to search for applications, the more passive the child is likely to be.

The amount of mental activity in which a pupil engages seems to be closely related to how often the teacher is content to remain silent. Teacher glibness, or words for words sake, almost certainly interferes with the learning process. Even the most able student needs time to ingest ideas and information. The illustra-tions and applications that occur to the child as a result of his own thinking are far more valuable than the flood of information emanating from an over-fluent instructor.

You know from your own experience that one student may get a great deal from listening to the lectures of an able teacher, whereas another may get little or nothing. The reason is that the first student is stimulated to think by what he hears. He goes beyond what is said, recalls examples, forms hypotheses, and sees relationships. But the second, fearful of missing a single fact, tries to remember every word. For the first one, every sentence creates a problem; the other merely tries to hang on from one sentence to the next—the only problem he meets is that of trying to remember everything he hears. The immature student is incapable of creating his own problems as he listens to the teacher's discussion. You must take the time and the trouble to suggest problems to him that will challenge his interest.

But how do you take the group of children that sit in your class (or run noisily about the room) on the opening day of the semester and lead them to identify attractive goals? How do you transfer the general activity into the activity that is essential to effective learning? How do you use the child's own needs to maintain an active attack on classroom problems?

For one thing, you will utilise the child's desire for your esteem. You will want to learn the names of the students in the classroom as soon as possible. You will want to find out about their abilities. Take time for a friendly word with each child and show an interest in him. Students are eager to serve and feel more like members of the team when they are asked to contribute their energies and talents. Encouraging each child to share in classroom responsibilities builds rapport and cooperation. Your interest and trust may help transform a potential problem child into a stable, confident citizen.

And you use the child's own needs to hold his attention to the task at hand. Every child wants to win the esteem of his peers. This force, properly channeled, can be of great value to you in creating an effective learning situation.

If most of the students find a task rewarding, and if they are anxious to carry it through to completion, group pressure alone is usually enough to hold down disrupting forces. Many leaders have succeeded by not pushing to the front and not attacking a problem until the interested group was aware of the problem's existence. Instead, they wait until the problem becomes so troublesome that the group actively demands a solution. By seeming to ignore the problem until others demanded that it be solved, and only then leading the group to the attack, they have been able to establish strong and effective leadership.

One of the important motives of the child is the desire for new and interesting experiences. Children resent boredom and do not learn well when they are bored. Although we find it difficult to make each day an exciting new adventure to each child, there are numerous ways in which we can prevent classroom learning from becoming monotonous. A change of pace or a change of activity helps prevent boredom. Particularly among younger children we must vary the mood and the activity frequently. We can use different problems during the same work period or we can try different approaches to the same problem. For example, one part of the period may be given over to individual work, another part to a discussion by the class as a whole, and another part to work in small informal committees. The use of a wide variety of materials—motion pictures, recordings, maps, and models—insures an effective change of pace. Your own appearance and actions can be an element in preventing boredom and promoting active learning—try to speak in an interesting rather than a monotonous voice, wear clothing with some colour, inject humour into the learning situations.

As you work with children you will find that you can suggest methods for attacking specific problems rather than giving them the solutions. You become sensitive to signs of inattention or of departure from the problem at hand. You give individual help where it is needed, but you do not stop an active attack even though you feel certain that it is not the most direct approach to a solution. You will find that some children require much more guidance than others. You will discover that for some children the larger problems must be broken into smaller problems.

We know that some children lack the ability to progress at the rate we expect of children of their age. But unless they can maintain their self-respect and feel pleased with their progress, they will not learn as rapidly as they can and they will seek satisfactions for their needs in other activities. How can you adjust the learning problems so that each child finds success in the classroom?

First, you must be sure that each child is allowed to complete one task before he begins another. This is particularly important to the child of lower ability, since unless he can complete a task he gains a feeling of failure rather than success from having attempted it. His ability does not allow him to keep several tasks in mind at the same time. You must be sure that each task you lead him to attempt is in keeping with his potentialities for successful completion. The learning that a child acquires from carrying out successfully a relatively small, but carefully chosen, portion of the course work is far more permanent than the learning achieved by muddling through the entire work of the course in a vague and haphazard fashion.

Children sometimes complete the work of a grade so unsatisfactorily that they are required to repeat it. Almost without exception, at the end of his second time around, the repeater has achieved little more mastery than he achieved the first time. If he does show any improvement, the chances are that it is the result of his year's growth in mental maturity rather than of any benefits derived from the previous inadequate exposure to the materials. How can this problem be met in the classroom? Is there any way of adjusting the content of the course to the student who is simply incapable of mastering the entire pro-gramme that has been prescribed?

Ideally, the teacher should be able to plan the class work so that some children can master the most necessary skills and the most important knowledge while more able children go on to more advanced activities in keeping with their abilities. At present, however, the organisation of our schools makes such adjustments difficult. But it is a worthy objective. An intelligent adjustment of course content results in far greater permanence of learning than does our present procedure of exposing all members of the class to the same amount of material. It is impossible, of course, for the teacher to do this job by himself. He needs sincere help from curriculum-makers and textbook writers.

However, there are ways in which the skillful teacher can adjust for individual differences in ability and at the same time keep the class together within the broad limits of the course. For example, as soon as you have become acquainted with the ability of each member of the class (through personal conferences, test data, and a study of the child's past record), you can adjust your assignments to fit the child's needs. In a social studies class, you might suggest that one sixth-grade child should investigate the types of animals found in Brazil by reading about them in a supplementary fourth-grade text, and suggest to another that he study the differences in government between Brazil and the United States by using supplementary references of eighth-or ninth-grade difficulty. When you use differential assignments of this sort, you will get the best results by encouraging each child to volunteer for the projects that are of special interest to him. Be careful to call upon each child to present his own findings and be sure that each child is rewarded in examinations for achieving at the level of which he is capable. By rewarding each child and by holding him responsible for his learning, you encourage him to form desirable work habits. But if you hold him responsible for concepts and materials that are beyond his ability to master, you will force him into confusion and discouragement.

The differential assignment gives the pupil of low ability a chance to make a real contribution to the class attack on a general problem. In your planning, do not be content simply to provide reading materials that are written at different levels of difficulty but that contain the same information. That is not enough. Instead, encourage the class as a whole to attack the same large problem and encourage each member of the class to contribute different facts and ideas to its solution.

Our knowledge of individual differences in abillity makes one fact clear: Good teaching does not decrease individual differences, either in background of knowledge, mental growth, or special skills. In any one year of instruction, the bright child, if he is really challenged, may grow as much as one and a half to two years in mental ability, reading ability, and general educational achievement. The dull child, even with maximum opportunity and the best of teaching, can scarcely be expected to grow even one year for each year of instruction. Your job as a teacher, then, is not to try to improve on the child's mental equipment, but rather to help him make the best possible use of what he has.

There are numerous ways for seeing that each child finds success in learning to the best of his ability. For example, the child must be successful on the examinations that he takes. One way for making this possible is to examine only on core skills and facts and to use other methods of appraisal and reward for the special contributions of the more able child.

You must use care in pitching your level of instruction so that all children will have an opportunity to learn. Materials presented to the entire class must be understandable by even the most retarded child. You must not allow yourself to be so carried away by the gleaming faces and understanding nods of the bright children that you leave the average or dull child completely confused. Yet if you direct all instruction at the retarded child you fail to offer the bright child the stimulation that he needs.

What is the solution? Obviously you must devote a large portion of instructional time to helping each child identify the problems that he can solve and to furnishing him with the guidance he needs. And the oral instructions or information that you direct to a group of children must be understandable by every child in the group. Material that you present orally as well as material that you assign in books must be chosen with due regard for the ability of the child to understand.

Teacher as an Ideal

As a classroom teacher, you must furnish leadership. The kind of leadership that you furnish will be a most important determinant of the effectiveness of the learning situation. You could decide to be autocratic—you could seek to decide the minute-by-minute activity of each pupil. You could tell your pupils how you want everything done and, if you had the strength and persistence, you might thus achieve what is sometimes called a well-disciplined classroom. But you would not have an effective learning situation. You would drive your pupils to conform to your wishes by threat of failure and fear of punishment. Your pupils would be working to escape goads rather than working toward goals. For effective learning, the child's attention must be focused on goals that he needs to attain.

There is a second possible type of leadership. You could decide to allow your pupils to take all responsibility, to make all decisions, to set all standards of behaviour, to determine what, when, and how to study. Your role could be no more important than that of any individual pupil—in fact, you could strive to be one of the pupils. This type of leadership is known as *laissez faire,* or "let-alone". If you were to behave in this way, you might have activity in your classroom but it would not lead to active learning, except occasionally and by chance. You would not be offering the guidance that is expected of the professional teacher.

Fortunately, there is a third type of leadership—democratic leadership—which has come to be accepted as the only type of leadership that the professional teacher may offer. It maintains an active attack on educationally worthwhile problems. You help the child to find appealing goals and to identify the problems that he must solve to attain them. Your leadership involves an element of salesmanship. You know that the child has certain needs. You offer him opportunities for satisfying these needs through learning in the classroom. Your skill in doing this will determine how actively the child will attack his problem and how effectively he will learn.

The leadership that you furnish should not stifle the development of pupil leadership or block pupil responsibility. But, particularly during the opening weeks of work with a group, you must be present promptly at the time class is to begin and you must be ready to assume leadership. If you fail in this responsibility, you will find that other leadership will emerge before you realise it, and the class may be held in undesirable directions. The easiest way to make your leadership acceptable to the pupils is to have a plan for beginning work and for setting the stage for an effective learning situation.

In leading your pupils to attack problems you do not direct the behaviour of your class so much as you furnish an example. Your own behaviour sets the pattern for student behaviour. The fact that you are a mature person to whom the community has delegated authority means that your influence— for good or bad— will be great. You can abuse your authority and abandon your leadership by exhibiting inconsistent or childish behaviour. You can strengthen your leadership by behaving with maturity and stability.

In short, your must show by your own attitude that you expect to set the pattern of behaviour in the classroom. If you expect the class to start promptly, you yourself must start promptly. Instead of shouting over the din of conflicting voices, you wait for order and quiet before you begin. A quiet voice promotes quietness, but a loud voice is a challenge to the pupils to outshout you. By making full use of class time through such techniques as having papers arranged by rows before distributing them and having individuals designated to get materials rather than allowing group congestion, you create an atmosphere in which getting down to business seems the natural way of behaving.

"Discipline" is not an imposed state. Rather, it develops from the desire of the individual child to conform to the behaviour of the group and from his discovery of socially acceptable ways for attaining self-esteem, the esteem of others, new experiences, and security.

If you are successful in setting standards of expected behaviour and in creating an effective learning situation for each child, you will automatically have a classroom with excellent "discipline." Instead of an unbroken, frightened silence, you will have a state of activity in which children feel free to attack felt problems. It will be a goal-directed rather than a goad-directed situation.

Ideally, as time goes on you will want to act more as a spectator than as an overt leader. But you can assume that role only after every child has met a problem that he is actively attempting to solve. Until this situation has developed, you must maintain direct contact with all the members of the group, or at least with those who are not yet able to identify goals beyond the problems at hand.

Thus you first help the class to get the general group goals identified. Each pupil sees for himself how achieving them will satisfy his needs. You start out from a situation that has familiar elements for every child. Perhaps you are to begin the social studies work with a study of the pioneer—his problems and how he met them. You start with something that is familiar to all members of the class. You may ask the students to consider the area around their own homes. What did it look like in pioneer times—no buildings, no streets or roads, no towns. How would a pioneer obtain food, clothing and shelter? During a short discussion it becomes apparent that different students can contribute to different phases of the problem. One may have a grandmother who was a pioneer, another knows of a log cabin still standing, another wants to know how a pioneer obtained soap, wove cloth, or made leather. Another is interes-ted in hunting and wants to know about the firearms of the pioneer. Still another may have an idea that plants furnished medicine, flavouring, and dye. Individual differences, leader-ship, committees, and individual projects begin to break out from this first group approach.

It will require weeks of effort to build an atmosphere of satisfaction and interest in the work; you can destroy this atmosphere in a few moments by delivering a reprimand intended for one or two persons to the whole group. If a few are tardy, noisy, careless, rude, or otherwise not reaching acceptable standards, this must not be made a cause for threatening the esteem, interest, and security of all. The skillful teacher pulls out the best for comment and sets up attractive goals to lead, but he seldom feels that it is desirable to drive.

Methods in Practice

Every teacher, no matter what his special interest, is responsible for helping pupils develop efficient study habits and techniques. Children must be taught how to read, for example, not only so that they can gain knowledge from reading but also so that they can integrate their new knowledge with what they already know. They must be encouraged to challenge and to evaluate what they read. We are interested here in how the development of these techniques leads to the creation of an effective learning situation.

When a child enters the classroom, we cannot assume that he knows how to study effectively. The study habits that he develops under your influence will be determined by the kind of assignment and examination you give, and by the way in which you guide class discussions. If you emphasise detailed, isolated facts, for example, the student will follow your lead and build his study habits around the same emphasis. If you emphasise broad relationships and underlying values, he will adjust his study habits accordingly.

In many courses, it is necessary for students to develop special study habits and skills. If students are to be expected to obtain information from charts and graphs, for example, you will want to be sure that each child knows how to read them with understanding. Or you may want to provide practice in using the library and special study aids, such as chapter questions, the index, and the glossary.

In a science class, a good procedure is to choose a portion of the new assignment and to ask the students to read a certain paragraph in it. Then you might ask one of the students a question to test his knowledge of the new material, or you might ask him to propose some questions that will test understanding of the paragraph. You may want to proceed well into the assignment, paragraph by paragraph, following the same procedure.

You will certainly want to explain the effectiveness of recall as a study procedure and provide frequent class exercises that require the use of recall in the supervised study of the course materials.

How much material a child reads before he stops to recall will depend upon the difficulty of the material and the number of ideas it contains. In mathematics, the study unit may be only a single sentence, in chemistry a paragraph, and in the social sciences two or three paragraphs. Encourage each child to spend a few minutes in recall at the end of each large study unit and to check on the completeness of his recall before he proceeds.

Since a well-formed habit furnishes its own source of motivation, the formation of good learning habits should be one of your prlmary aims. Training in the development of these habits should start with the earliest tasks and should continue for as long as the child remains in school. The child who frequently experiences the satisfaction that accompanies the successful completion of his tasks soon comes to value that feeling and is reluctant to leave a task unfinished.

Effective study techniques, then, are teachable, and they are an important part of the equipment of the efficient learner.

When we studied human learning, one of our major discoveries was that review has a tremendous effect on retention. Forgetting is cut to a minimum when review is correctly scheduled and carried out. Review is particularly powerful in aiding us to remember clearly for a long period of time. But we know that we cannot expect the child to review properly until he understands the value of review and has established efficient habits of reviewing. You will be responsible for using instructional procedures that promote and encourage review. There are many ways in which you can do this.

Recalling yesterday's material to set the stage for today's class, summarising the lesson and the unit, introducing new problems that require the use of previously learned materials and procedures, and the written examination are all effective review techniques. Their greatest value, however, is the long-range effect they have on the learner: When the child learns to expect reviews and is rewarded for reviewing, he develops the habit of reviewing.

When you begin your teaching, you may find that you are proceeding far too rapidly to new materials and skills without providing sufficient time for the development, elaboration, illustration, and review of each important concept along the way. Almost all new teachers have that experience. You may be tempted to cover the entire course in a week or two, and to be satisfied that your explanations and instructions are so clear that each child must understand the material. In your eagerness, you may forget that teaching is much more than just dispensing information and answers, and that you cannot transfer understandings directly from your mind to the mind of the child. You cannot guide him directly to goals. He himself must meet problems and find applications. The child needs time to accept and to review the information and understandings that you yourself have taken years to acquire.

You will need to be especially careful to avoid these faults if you were a brilliant student yourself. If you found the curriculum of the elementary and secondary schools easy to master, you may become impatient with students who are less capable than you were. This is a regrettable tendency, because your high intelligence and broad scholastic background should help rather than hinder you in guiding the average and below-average child to solve his learning problems.

The Review of Yesterday's Learnings. To be certain that the children have the material they learned yesterday under control and ready to take its place with what they are to learn today, you will need to devote some time to review at the beginning of each class meeting. Your technique in conducting this review will determine whether or not each child is to participate actively in it. A particularly poor technique, one that you will want to avoid, is to call on a good student to summarise yesterday's work. Certainly this saves time, but it accomplishes even less than if you were to give the summary yourself. As soon as you have announced which child is to recite, the review ceases to be a problem for the other children. Once they discover that only the most capable students are always called on, they simply retire from the review session. As a result, only the students who have already proved their ability actually profit from the reviews.

A far sounder procedure is to direct your questions to the class in general and to allow time enough for each member to formulate his reply. In this way, everyone reviews before anyone recites. You may want to give a weaker student the opportunity to make the first contribution, and then encourage the stronger students to furnish additional points. By emphasising and confirming what each pupil gets right in his contribution, you reward him for his effort. You can usuallly assume that any errors will be corrected by the pupils who contribute later. This general procedure for conducting review encourages each child to form the habit of reviewing. He learns to recall yesterday's material as he enters the classroom and as he prepares the day's new assignment.

This emphasis on class review does not mean that formal drill in response to questions about facts, dates, and names has again become an approved educational practice. Emphasis on review is simply a modern application of the discovery that learnings are soon lost unless we place them in new frameworks, apply them to new problems, recall them, and make them ready to serve as a basis for new learnings.

As you gain experience, you will come to recognise how important it is to devote a large portion of your instructional time to nailing down, reviewing, and integrating the principles, understandings, and skills that are of crucial importance. Even when you present new materials, you will find review valuable. The old rule of presenting the new in terms of the old has not become outmoded in teaching practice. If facts or principles are worth learning, they are certainly worth reviewing.

The Summary as a Review. You must be sure, then, that new knowledge is built upon and becomes integrated with what is already known. You will want to emphasise the relationship between new material and present knowledge. To insure that this relationship is meaningful, try to encourage the pupils to supply appropriate applications and illustrations, instead of handing them out yourself. Near the end of the class period, take time to summarise today's learnings. Tomorrow's assignment should come logically from the problems identified in today's summary. The summary and its culmination in the assignment are extremely important parts of effective teaching technique. The summary lesson at the end of each unit provides a further opportunity for reviewing the progress that has been made and for identifying new problems. It gives the children a chance to make a logical transition to the new unit by tying together the material that they have learned and the problems that they are yet to solve.

The Examination as a Review. The examination itself has an important function in review. The child is motivated to review before the examination. He reviews while he is taking the examination, and he reviews when the examination is later discussed in class. We shall talk more about the use of the examination as a learning device and as a method of appraising the child's progress. Here we are interested in how the examination implements review.

When we know that we must actually demonstrate our grasp of materials, we are motivated to learn them. It might seem that merely knowing that material will be useful at some later time should provide sufficient incentive for learning it. Sometimes that is enough, but not always. The effectiveness of incentives depends in part on how soon they can be realised. Knowing that we will be rewarded tomorrow for having new material under control is a greater incentive than simply knowing that the material may be useful some time in the future. For this reason, short, frequent examinations have a greater motivational effect than do longer but less frequent examinations.

Some General Principles of Review. A few new facts and principles, well understood, are of more permanent value than many facts and principles inadequately understood. The amount of new material that a child can learn each day increases as he grows in mental age and as his background of information develops. Thus, in the lower grades children must spend far less time learning new materials and far more time reviewing and integrating what they have already learned than must children in the upper grades.

As a professional teacher, you will realise that working out the correct solution is less important to a child than is the experience that he gains in facing the problem. And so it is with review itself. As each student reviews, his new knowledge is revitalised and integrated with his past learnings. The act of review is much more than simply getting back to the level of learning that had been achieved before forgetting took place. It leads to new understandings and to new relationships. It reveals to the student exciting generalisations that are infinitely more permanent and useful to him than are isolated facts and ideas.

Art of Organisation

We have tried to identify the factors that are important in creating an effective learning situation that moves toward educational goals. Let us now examine the important professional problem of directing the minute-to-minute effective learning situations toward broad week-to-week and year-to-year objectives. What approach have teachers found most effective in planning for a day-to-day progress toward the broad course objectives?

Many years ago, Johann Friederich Herbart (1776-1841) listed five formal steps that he considered basic to good teaching procedure. These steps, little modified except for changes in name and a reduction in formality, have persisted to the present time as the psychological basis for directing effective learning. They are: preparation, presentation, association, systematisation, and application. Let us see how these steps are related to what we know about the learning process.

Preparation. Preparation (or exploration and assignment, as it is called by some writers) consists principally of arousing in the child an eagerness to learn. The child's awareness of a problem, and his belief that he can satisfy certain needs by solving it, are the primary requirements of an effective learning situation. His need may be simply a desire for new experiences (sometimes called curiosity), or he may want to win the esteem of his fellow students or of his teacher. As you introduce each new unit and make each day's assignment, you can suggest to the child how the coming activities will help him to satisfy his needs. Making assignments is not a matter of doling out jobs. Rather, it is an opportunity to set up attractive goals and to suggest ways in which they can be reached. Children learn very little unless they feel the need to solve a problem. Assigning a certain number of pages to be read fails to pose any real problem, except that of finding the necessary time. And it fails to satisfy and need, except the need to avoid censure for failure to carry it out.

Properly used, the assignment gives us a golden opportunity to bring into play the psychological motives of each child. It leads directly to the development of a need and an eagerness to learn. It brings problems into focus and it suggests to the child ways in which he can satisfy his needs. It gives direction to his work. It is here that we can provide for individual differences in ability and guide each child toward the path that he is best able to travel. It is here that the child develops his mental set to learn and to remember.

One of the results of a carefully planned assignment is that the child voluntarily assumes responsibility for his learning. If his interest is great enough, you will need to do little more than guide him from time to time when his efforts lead him into a particularly difficult phase of the assignment.

How much time should be spent in making the assignment depends on several factors: the type of subject matter, whether you are introducing a new unit or just giving day-to-day direction, and the maturity of the pupils. Few teachers can be accused of spending too much time in making assignments. The tendency is to spend far too little time.

Ideally, the next day's assignment should grow out of the summary of the day's accomplishment. It follows the summary and usually precedes the period of supervised study. Since it does come near the end of the class period, many teachers fall into the habit of treating it casually, forgetting that preparation is the first and most important step in learning. We must be constantly on guard not to become so engrossed in the work at hand that we fail to build a need for the work to be done before the class meets again. At the beginning of a new unit of work, for example, an entire class period can profitably be devoted to making the assignment. With experience, you will learn how much time is needed for making the daily assignments. In any event, making assignments must not be a dictatorial act. The more successful you are in building a need for learning, the more democratic the learning process becomes.

Presentation. There is a wide variety of methods for presenting the materials that the pupils need in overcoming the problems and in reaching the goals identified during the assignment. You will make a detailed study of these methods in other professional courses. Here we can say simply that the specific methods used will depend somewhat on the subject and on the age and abilities of the pupils.

In literature and the social studies, for example, much of the presentation of the material that the child needs for solving his problems is individualised. The child reads materials that are appropriate to his abilities. In the natural sciences, presentation often takes place in the laboratory. In mathematics, you yourself may present the necessary background material, or you may encourage the pupils to "discover" it by themselves under your guidance. No matter what technique you use, presentation must never degenerate into a mechanical handing out of information. Although you are anxious to guide the child to effective means of solving his problems and reaching his goal, so far as possible the actual exploration should be conducted by the child himself.

The actual solutions that the child discovers as he searches for materials that will solve, his problems may be far less important than the skills that he gains in learning how to solve problems. You will find that questions such as "Where can we find out about this?" or "How can we divide this job up so that some of us can do one part of it and some can do another?" are far more effective than are direct suggestions on where the solutions can be found or an apportioning of individual parts of the job by you.

With many types of problems you may want to suggest that the class should form committees to take over specific parts of the project. It may be that the materials or ideas for meeting certain types of problems should come from resources outside the classroom. This may be accomplished by letting the children write letters, visit city officials, make trips to libraries or museums, or arrange for field trips for the purpose of collecting information or observing conditions. Whatever method is used (laboratory, class discussion, reading, visual aids, field trips, or committees) the direction and choice often can come from the students, under your guidance. Allowing each child to contribute to the solution of the group's problems can lead automatically to an adjustment for individual differences in ability, background, and interest and to a tremendous energising of the activity.

Association. This step has been called assimilation by some modern writers and comparison and abstraction by others. To a large extent, it consists of seeing that the mastery of the new materials grows out of the previous mastery of similar materials and problems. The new learning must take place as a building on and an integrating with the old.

In studying government, the child learns first about his own city or country government, and then proceeds to state and national government. In studying geography, he begins with the rivers, climate, and raw materials of the region with which he is familiar, and then goes on to the features of broader regions with which he is less familiar. He moves from the known to the unknown. He approaches the problems faced by other groups of people or by other nations, either during his own time or at other times, through his knowledge of current problems. History, geography, and sociology must have their roots in the daily lives of the pupils. Facts about the culture of other peoples (the food they eat, the clothing they wear, and the houses they build) take on meaning when they are studied in relation to the problems posed by climate, soil, raw materials, plant and animal life, and transportation routes. Since these factors influence our own living habits, they provide a meaningful approach to the habits of others. By understanding that cultural patterns are the expression of human needs, the child is able to comprehend the behaviour of whole groups and nations of people in terms of his own felt needs and problems.

A failure to provide for significant association in the learning experience encourages children to be satisfied with pat verbalisms at the expense of true understanding. Facts are necessary, of course, since they must precede application. But unless the child is able to utilise facts in actual situations, they are of little value to him. If the child's school experience is to be valuable to him in later life, he must develop the ability to apply the facts he learns in school to other situations. By providing for meaningful association at every phase of the learning process, you can guarantee that the facts he learns will take on meaning in ever-widening contexts.

Systematisation. This step, which has been called organisation by some modern writers and generalisation by others, is closely interwoven with presentation and association. Since children are limited in experience and background knowledge, especially in the early grades, it is your responsibility to suggest to them how the new facts they encounter fit into orderly patterns of knowledge. Fortunately, the tendency to generalise is inherent in all human beings; it is one mark of intelligent behaviour. If the infant lacked this tendency, he would never learn to avoid touching all hot stoves after he had touched one. As he matures, he must learn to extend his powers of generalising to less vivid experiences, to abstract facts and concepts. He must gradually become aware that all knowledge is part of an organised system.

Through learning to generalise his knowledge, the child learns to take the well-learned elements of one situation and recognise where they belong when he encounters them in a new situation. Generalisation is a key to the transfer of training from one problem situation to the solution of another.

At an elementary level, the child discovers that methods for determining the square inches in the rectangles that are pictured in his arithmetic book can be applied also to computing the square feet in the playground or the size of a surface that is to be painted. At a higher level, he recognises that the Golden Rule can be applied as a guide in his relations with others.

Application. In this step, the pupil uses the knowledge that he has gained from a particular study unit in some concrete situation. He uses his organised knowledge of punctuation, for example, in writing themes. But if you want to make sure that he can generalise his new knowledge, you will see that he continues to apply it in all the writing he does after he has learned the specific elements of punctuation. The more often we apply the materials we have learned, the deeper our general understanding of them becomes and the longer we retain them.

Application satisfies the motivation that the pupil experienced during the assignment period. It gives him a feeling of security and self-esteem. The pleasant feeling that accompanies successful application serves to fix the new learning securely in his mind, ready to be used again when it is needed.

Now we come to our final problem: We know that classroom learning must prepare the child for life's needs. Though technically the curriculum-maker specifies what should be learned by the children in your classes, you yourself determine what is learned by each child. How can you appraise the relative values of the possible learnings of the classroom? How can you guarantee that what should be learned, is learned?

Incidental vs. Planned Learning. The child learns much in the classroom that has not been listed in our lesson plans or included in our written course of study. He may notice the colour of the room, and the presence or even the purpose of items of instructional equipment left in the room by another class. He may learn how to live with his classmates with the least amount of unpleasantness, and he may learn to make allowances for the day-to-day variations in the teacher's mood. However, most of these so-called incidental learnings occur only if some problem arises in his mind about the colour of the room, the use of a piece of equipment, or getting along with his class-mates or with his teacher. He acquires little that is not needed for the solution of actual problems. For example, you may have lived in your present neighbourhood for some time and yet cannot recall the location of the nearest fire alarm box, whether or not there is a telephone pole near a certain corner, or the number of steps on your front porch.

Certainly frequency of an experience does not guarantee that a child will learn. Unless weaknesses in his writing become a problem for him, a child can write a hundred letters or themes and show no improvement. Even if you help him to develop good work habits they soon deteriorate unless his good habits make the work easier or in some other way are rewarding to him. If poor habits meet his needs as well as good ones and if there is no demand that he attain a certain degree of efficiency, poor habits remain. In short, mere presence of opportunity to learn does not guarantee learning.

We recognise, then, that no important fact or principle may be entrusted to incidental learning alone and that all the really important skills, ideals, and attitudes must be taught by every teacher regardless of his subject-matter specialty. But the child can gain much from so-called incidental learnings if you take full advantage of your opportunities. Although certain specific learnings are a part of a social studies class, for example, at the same time you can teach, incidentally, oral and written English, spelling, and effective habits of learning. And in the English class as you teach oral and written expression you can help the child to develop emotionally and socially. But you must be conscious of these incidental goals. You cannot expect the learnings to occur automatically.

For this reason, whether you teach in the elementary or in the secondary school, you must be aware of what each subject that the child studies can contribute to his total curriculum. In addition to knowing the specific goals of your subject, you must know the general goals of education and the specific goals that each other teacher strives to reach. The personal and educational development of boys and girls—not the mere teaching of English, sciences, mathematics, art, or music—is your major professional responsibility.

Social Utility. You will be responsible for the teaching of a broad area of subject matter and skills. Some of the pupils in your class will have the ability to achieve nearly all the learnings that are set as objectives for your class. But there are others who can achieve but a small portion. We know that a few learnings well mastered are much more valuable than an inadequate exposure to many learnings. What criteria can you use for selecting that portion of the curriculum that is most important to the child? Let's examine the criteria that are used by the curriculum-maker when he builds the total course of study for a grade or subject-matter area.

The most common criterion of the curriculum-builder is that of social utility. He seeks to determine whether a certain bit of information, a concept, or a skill has sufficient value that it should be learned by every child, by most children, by only the most able children, or by no child. The curriculum-maker recognises that the accumulated knowledge of our society is so vast that each individual masters but a comparatively small portion of it. We must select those items of knowledge most necessary to the life of the child in a social world.

Each child must be given the best possible preparation for meeting the problems of later life. He must prepare for a vocation, for citizenship, and for satisfying leisure-time activity.

If you teach in the high school, you should be enthusiastic about what your specialty contributes to the total educational growth of each child. If you are a social-studies teacher you will see that the problems of the world and the necessity for training in good citizenship make preparation in the social studies extremely important. If you teach science, you will have spent many years in getting acquainted with the wonders and values of that field and you will be convinced of the value of your contribution. If you teach English, you will know that excellence in written and oral English has wide practical and cultural value and that far too little time is available for its development. Whatever you teach – physical education and health, art, music, mathematics, and languages, or any other portion of the curriculum – you will see that children need the knowledge and skills that you can offer them. But you must not allow this enthusiasm to prevent you from coordinating your effort with the efforts of those who teach different subjects.

There is little doubt that each child could be a better citizen if he could possess the knowledge that is held by the professor of social science or at least by the college major in that field. There is little doubt that science is important. Its importance has been demonstrated both in the winning of wars and the development of a peacetime world. Ability in oral and written expression and an appreciation of good literature contribute much to the success and happiness of the individual. There is no doubt that without health all other learning avails us but little and that art and music are strong contributors to the peace and happiness of the individual. The only legitimate question that can be raised in any issue of this kind concerns the best use that we can make of our limited time for education and the limited abilities of even the superior students.

Particularly if you teach in the elementary grades where you have control of the child's time for most of the day, you must not allow yourself to concentrate on any one subject-matter field to the neglect of other fields simply because of your own personal interests. Too often a teacher who has a particularly strong interest in natural science, social science, art, languages, or music devotes a large portion of the available time to one of these areas while reading, arithmetic, spelling, writing, and other necessary skills receive too little emphasis. When this happens the child fails to get the preparation for life that he needs. We see examples of this in the secondary school also. Suppose that you are convinced that a knowledge of early American history is extremely important and interesting yet you are assigned to teach a class in local government. And suppose that you disregard the name and purpose of the course and emphasise American history, with the result that the children never gain an adequate knowledge of local government. What happens when, at a later period, a portion of their curriculum is devoted to a study of American history? As you can see, material they already know will be repeated and your students will have missed completely the knowledge of local government that they should have obtained.

Thus, since there is a limited period of time and even the better students can learn but a few new things each day, the decision on what to teach cannot be made on the basis of which elements of knowledge have or may have value. The decision must be made on the basis of which combination has most value in meeting the social, economic, and personal needs of the child.

Although the creation of an effective learning situation is a basic professional task of the teacher, your responsibility cannot stop there. Just any learning will not do. Learning must have a purpose. It must be organised toward the child's present and future life needs. Learning problems must be chosen in accordance with each child's abilities and life goals. We must apply our knowledge of the principles of learning and motivation as we guide the learning of each child in the classroom.

5

Techniques of Teaching

Motivation as a term is both a fascinating and frustrating subject in the field of educational psychology. It is fascinating because all of us are engaged in something or the other most of the time. A child is playing, a girl is singing, a medical student is preparing to be a doctor, a social worker is helping his fellow men, a philosopher is discussing and thinking and a politician is planning for elections. The reason for such acts is motivation. Motivation makes a fascinating game in which all individuals are engaged, though sometimes it is right and sometimes it is wrong.

Motivation is also frustrating because we at times wonder about our own motives. How many times have we all had the sad experience of having to say to ourselves, "Why did I do that?" "It's not like me; I don't do things like that". We may have been unaccountably rude to the bus driver on the way to town; we may have spent some of our savings foolishly; or on a hard day, the cat got in our way and we kicked it. We realize that we must have been motivated to act as we did but what were our motives and why?

In vocabulary of psychology, we come across hundreds of words which refer to motivation: "wants", "striving", "desire", "need", "motive", "goal", "aspiration", "drive", "wish", "aim", "ambition", "hunger", "thirst", "love", "revenge", etc. If we try to define we can define them differently, but their meanings overlap so much that it is difficult to maintain uniformity. It is a process by which an individual is "inspired, goaded or coaxed to do something". It is one of the most important conditions which aid learning. The psycho-physiological construct implies the individual to achieve his predetermined goal(s). Bhatia confirms: "To motivate is to induce movement". Motivation, then, must be considered as the process by which a child may be prepared to respond to situations which are directed towards the achievement of objectives. Motivation is a broad-based term and encompasses many aspects of behaviour. It might be designated as "the tendency for the direction and selectivity of behaviour to be controlled by the conditions to consequences and the tendency of this behaviour to persist until a goal is achieved". Motivation is purposive; without the presence of goals this process may not start at all.

Controlling the Classroom

Every human behaviour is motivated. Without motive a living being cannot move even a step ahead. In other words, behaviour of men is controlled by some motives. The teacher, in order to make his teachings effective should have a good knowledge of motivation and its effect on learning. Science of motivation teaches a teacher how to motivate a student to learn. It also helps him to study individual difference among students. Learning is a behaviour which is aroused by a wish of fulfilling a necessity. In the same way learning is also a goal-oriented activity. Several factors contributing for its success are - environment, mental set-up of the learner and skill of the teacher. Teaching is fulfilled in a disciplined environment, backed by a strong motivation of the students. It is difficult to teach without any knowledge about motivation. It arouses interest of learners and makes them attentive and interested.

Art of Motivation

The word motivation has been derived from the Latin word 'mover' meaning to put into action or to move. So it is the process of arousing movement in the organism. The process that puts the organism into physiological or psychological action, and by which man is able to fulfill his needs and desires is called motivation. According to psychologist Woodsworth, "motivation is the activity in progress."

Motivation supplies the human being with energy to act. Discussing from this point of view we know that learning is impossible without motivation. Motivation is an internal process. We can understand the nature of motivation by observing the behaviour of an organism. According to McDonald, motivation is change of a power structure in a human being which is related to stimulus and reaching a goal. From this definition we come to know about three dimensions of motivation.

Motivation takes its origin from the change in energy level.

Motivation is an inspiration that affects the personality. By it, psychic tension is aroused.

Motivation is backed by a desire to reach a goal.

Other psychologists have also tried to define motivation in their own way. They are mentioned below:

Atkinson defined motivation as, "the arousal of tendency to act to produce one or more effects". D.O. Hebb holds that the term motivation refers:

(i) to existence of an organised phase sequence.

(ii) to its direction and content.

(iii) to its persistence in given direction or stability of content.

Maslow has advanced the theory of hierarchy of needs ranging from basic physiological needs to self-actualization. According to him, "motivation is constant, never ending, fluctuating and complex and that it is an almost universal characteristic of particularly every organismic state of affairs".

According to H.W. Bernard "motivation refers to all those phenomena which are involved in the stimulation of action towards particular objectives where previously there was little or no movement towards these goals".

Motivation refers to a definite set of mind of the child which inspires him to reach his goal. So it is the duty of the teacher to motivate the student to develop in the learning process, that would enable him to reach a higher goal in his future life.

Motivation begins with drives and ends with adjustments. The *Oxford Dictionary* defined a motive as "that which moves or includes a person to act in a certain way, a desire, fear or other emotion or a consideration of a reason which influences or tends to influence a person's volition, also often applied to a contemplated result of object, the desire of which tends to influence volition." In ordinary sense motivation is an internal energy which enfuels us to carry out an intention. Our intentions may be varied and one's intention may differ from another. Hence motives have been used in different senses. It has broadly been classified into two categories. They are:-

1. Primary Physiological Motives: They are hunger, thirst, pain, sex, impulse, etc.

2. Secondary Psychological Motives: This includes wishes for social status, approbation, authority over others, etc.

But this two way classification is not final and universal. Psychologists have put forth their own classifications. Again this classification is not clear cut. For example, though sexual drives are included in the first category, it depends much on social status and social consciousness of the individual. Some other psychologists have classified motive into three categories such as: (i) Physiological motives, (ii) Social motives, (iii) Personal motives. Shatter has divided it into four classes. They are motives of security, motives to reply, motives of agreement and motives of new experience. In another classification motives have been divided into self-respect, security, social value, self-importance, social identification and socialisation etc.

Needs, drive and incentives are the building blocks of the structure of motivation. It is a complex phenomenon which is influenced by multiple variables operating within the organism and in the environment. A number of psychological and physiological factors are involved in motivation. Emotion also affects motivation. Emotional states act as drives and they can reinforce motive in progress. Likewise, habits, mind-set, values and attitudes of the individual also influence motivational process. We will discuss what role the three important factors (needs, drives and incentives) play in motivating an individual to act.

(a) Needs: Men have countless needs and most of them have to be met with in order to make the existence of a human being possible on the earth. Some needs such as love, pity, anger, affection, etc, are emotional. In the same way, social needs are there and they include social status, fame, respect, etc. Man adopts various methods to fulfill his various social needs. For example, a hungry man strives for food, and adopts various methods to get food for himself. Here changes occur in his behaviour. Psychologist Maslow has categorised the needs into six groups.

1. Physical Needs: They are bare necessities of life like food, water, air, rest, house, work, etc.
2. Security and needs of self-defence: Endeavours to do away with misery, helplessness, incapabilities etc.
3. Emotional and mental requirements: Love, affection, pity, sympathy etc.
4. Social needs: To establish one's ownself in society.
5. Aesthetic needs
6. Needs of self-realisation.

(b) Drives: Man lives in an uncertain stage, if his needs are not fulfilled. He tries to get rid of such a situation. He tries one method or the other. The stage of uncertainty supplies him with energy, drive and skill to get over his difficulties. Drives help man to be active.

(c) Incentive: Every organism is influenced by his environment. Many factors of environment that attract him and others leave a distaste in him. These factors also control his behaviour. They fulfill various physical needs and brings internal satisfaction to a human being. While teaching new lessons the teacher should take into cognizance the necessities of the students and should take the help of incentives, because in order to be effective the teaching process should be interesting. So this method should be applied in classroom teachings. The factors of environment which enables the learner to learn better are called incentives.

Techniques in Vogue

Learning is not possible without motivation. For better learning, the teacher should arouse interest in the students. Motives make a work to be started. When the student completes a task, he becomes satisfied. Then he argues and at times receives advice from others. It is because success in one learning experience motivates him to take into hand another task. He wants to master it and wants to become an expert. He is motivated to learn values. Hence some steps should be adopted in the classroom teaching to motivate the students. They are discussed below.

1. Reward and Punishment: Reward is the best incentive to make the student an expert. It arouses interest in him and motivates him to master the skill. But educationists differ on this point. Some of them opine that reward deviates students from their goal. They forget it and act in their own way. Reward is an outer factor, and self-actualization is not possible by it.

   Some educationists profess punishments to be the better method to correct the wrong behaviour of students. Correcting a wrong behaviour leads to learning of correct behaviour. But mere physical punishment is harmful and hence should be avoided. The teacher should be aware of that. The student should know the cause of his punishment. Only by this can he try to correct his wrong behaviour.

   Reward is a tool of motivation, not its aim. But in schools, teachers often use it as the goal and that is why aims of education are not met with any success. Reward leaves a negative effect on the child. Overuse of the method of reward makes the child think that he is coming to school only to get reward and not to learn.

2. Praise and Insult: Praise is a commonly used motivation in classroom teaching. Praise works better than insult or blame. All types and all grades of students gain from it. But the teacher should be cautious about it. In case of small children, criticism and insult works better.

Praise is required more for average students than for a genius. Again it works better in case of girls than in case of boys. Psychologists view that workability of praise or insult depends upon how the teacher manipulates these. But it is the duty of parents and teachers alike to motivate the child to learn by praising and appreciating his right moves and achievements. Blame or insult is generally negative in character. It hampers learning of all types of students. The extroverts often succumb to insult and show better results by its application. But it should never be applied to introvert students. Here loss is more than gain. To apply this principle, the teacher should come personally in contact with the student, and then find out the way to steer his behaviour by applying praise or insult.

3. Competition: Competitive attitude is advantageous both inside the classroom and outside it. It is a powerful source of motivation. It makes the child not only to reach his destination sooner, but also to show a better performance beyond expectation. Competition is of two types; individual or personal competition and group competition. The first yields better result than the second. But over-competition gives rise to pride and egoism. Emotions like jealousy, hatred, aggressiveness take their origin from it. There is no doubt that competition accelerates learning process but over-competition makes the student deviate from social norms. From this point of view group competition is encouraged in school curriculum. Above all, the teacher should be careful in handling this method to motivate students.

4. Knowledge of Progress: It is an important source, of motivation. When the student knows about his success and progress he is motivated to learn more and better, because his interest is heightened. It also helps him in correcting his mistakes. So progress of the child should be intimated to him from time to time.

5. Knowledge of Achievement: The student should set his own goal in learning. Again they should know the nature

and aim of the subject they are taught. In modern educational system, aim of education is fixed by the education committee and students toil for it. Their achievements are judged by teachers and the committee. But this achievement should be informed to the students. They should know the outcome of their labour. It supplies them with inspiration and motivates them for further learning. So in every school progress report of examinations are supplied to the students. In these reports the ultimate limit of their progress should be mentioned. Again, for periodical evaluation of students, a standard should be adopted in schools. Questions for such evaluations should be objective and purposeful. After evaluation the student should know his result.

6. Novelty: Analysis and change in age old curriculum is necessary to bring novelty to it. Children love to see new things. So instead of changing the subject matter in toto, something new can be added to it. It arouses their interest. Mixture of something new with old materials brings satisfaction to life process of human. beings. This truth should not be forgotten by the teacher. Not only the books should be novel in appearance, but also the method of teaching should be changing in nature. The child becomes interested and his attention is centered when he finds a new thing in his subject He is motivated to learn the whole of the subject for the sake of that small new portion.

7. Audio-visual Apparatus: Teaching, solely by lecture method is not so much effective as teaching by audio-visual aids. Teaching must be interesting all the time So in modern teaching system, the scientific tools are consid ed a great help to motivate students.

8. Interest: It is the most interesting factor of motivation. Children are curious by nature and want to know everything they come across. Their interest sometimes bores and irritates the elders. But the teacher should have patience and describe the things they want to know. Teaching and learning should not be exclusively book-

oriented. Writing, singing, and acting should accompany reading books and listening to lectures of the teacher. This is known as multidimensional activities of the teacher.

9. Self-importance: Every individual is aware of nis self-respect and so he does not allow his personality to be run down before others. If anything hampers his respect his mental stability becomes imbalanced. Feeling of self-importance is a social requirement. The teacher should take necessary steps to secure this in the student. If the student is aware of his own self he is motivated to learn better in order to maintain the standard of his personality.

An analysis of the above methods shows that motivation plays an important role in learning. But it depends a lot on the teacher who studies the environment, energy, calibre and choice of the students. There are some suggestions put forth by psychologists in order to motivate the students.

1. The students should be aware of what he is learning and what is the practical applicability of the learning material.
2. New method of teaching should be based on old system of education. It should not deviate from the old norms of education.
3. The learning material should be arranged in order and organised in a definite way. It should be in the ascending order of difficulty.
4. The student should not be under pressure and he should not be compelled to master a particular lesson.
5. Reward should not be given in terms of any object. It should be symbolic and signify his development.
6. A student should not be punished for his wrong response. The teacher can explain him his error and show him the right way. Punishments should be given only at the time of changing a particular behaviour.
7. The teacher should intimate the student about all his achievements.

8. Competition should be conducted groupwise. It should not touch personal life.

Above all, the role of the teacher is the most important. He is the friend, philosopher and guide to the student. So he should try his best to motivate students which will ensure their journey to the goal of their life.

A course in educational psychology can be justified as part of the teacher-preparation sequence only as it leads to an improvement in the effectiveness with which the teacher carries out the work of promoting the growth and development of the child. Throughout the chapters of this text, various psychological principles have been considered against the background of the work of the classroom. This chapter will attempt to pinpoint some of the more important applications and implications of these principles particularly as they relate to the organisation of educational experiences by means of which the maximum self-realisation of the whole child is to be promoted. The student must not expect prescriptions and rules of thumb: this book promised none, will give none! Further– more, it must be understood that the present chapter makes no claim to a complete coverage of the implications of psychology for educational practice. The discussion will be restricted to a few of the highlights and the student is urged to review the material covered in the various chapters not as something to learn for a final examination but rather as a foundation upon which educational practice must be based..

Education has undergone drastic changes since the turn of the century. Great progress in both educational thought and educational practice has resulted from such influences as (a) the contribution of educational psychology, especially in the area of a greater understanding of the nature of the learner and of the learning process, and (b) sociological changes leading to a new concept of the role of the school in modern democratic society. The net results, although not amenable to a succinct synthesis, are probably best reflected in the reorientation of educational practice toward the all-around growth of the child as opposed to an emphasis on any given aspect at the expense of the others as was characteristic of the school of yesteryear. What is more, modern schools—and modern teachers—here and there throughout the country not only exemplify the latest philosophical and psychological thinking put into practice, but also earn public recognition and respect through the caliber of the services they provide and of the product they turn out.

Yet along side this modernism that characterises certain schools and certain teachers, there exist throughout our country, schools and teachers whose Rip Van Winkle organisation and procedures are not only woefully ineffective but—worse—are definitely detrimental to the all-around growth of the unfortunate children who are subjected to their influence.

Ironically, much of the harm done to children comes at the hands of teachers and administrators whose sincerity cannot be doubted—who are fully convinced that they are acting in the child's best interest—but whose lack of under-standing of the basic principles of psychology and of education makes them, nonetheless—and no less—an undeniable hazard to the maximum self-realisation of countless children. Thus, daily, well-meaning teachers force children to participate in exercises in which they have no interest, push children to do things which are completely beyond their abilities, who berate, scold, nag, and fail them because students cannot meet their unrealistic standards, and who punish them when, in final desperation at this constant frustration of their needs, children misbehave. All this, because of a firm belief that hard work is good for anyone and that "if they tried hard enough, they could do it." Anyway, the content of the curriculum has to be covered—regardless of the cost! These teachers are apparently unfamiliar with such fundamental psychological concepts as the difficulties imposed by intellectual and experiential limitations, the complications caused by emotional blocking, and the negative attitudes that result from coercion, to name but a few.

In the same way, many teachers (perhaps not entirely well-meaning) are apparently under the impression that, unless children are driven with a whip like tigers in a circus act, the quality of their performance will be impaired, and that children will neither work nor behave unless kept under the constant threat of failure and punishment. So they would never think of giving a compliment for work well done, for fear the child will immediately rest on his laurels; but, on the other hand, they never miss an opportunity to criticise (presumably, as a way of building moral fiber and a striving for perfection). And the sad part is that these teachers feel they are doing their duty. That they might accomplish more by trying to understand the child and his problems and by encouraging him to do his best than by trying to crush him and to downgrade his self-concept, it seems, hasn't dawned on them!

Paralleling these inexcusable violations of the principles of educational psychology—or perhaps, more correctly, because of this failure on the part of certain teachers, who are supposedly psychologically trained persons, to comply with the principles of educational psychology in dealing with the child—our schools have not been overly successful in promo-ting his growth. As we have seen in the chapters on adjustment and mental health as well as in the discussion of social and emotional maturity and the concept of enlightened self-interest, the products being turned out of our educational institutions considered as a whole fall considerably short of perfection. However, since the school cannot be expected to shoulder the whole blame for failure in these areas, we may more appropriately evaluate the extent of its relative success in promoting academic growth since this is one area where what-ever credit or blame is due can, to a greater extent, be attributed to the efforts of the school.

Empirical evidence points rather conclusively to the fact that, no matter from what point of view we look at the work being done in the classroom, we invariably find little cause for rejoicing. This, of course, does not pertain to all teachers, or even to all schools, for some are doing an outstanding job: it does, however, apply to the majority and this is the standard by which parents and the general public measure our worth. Many critics have lambasted our educational institutions for their ineptitude and, whereas these criticisms are not always completely warranted, they are, nevertheless, not entirely without foundation. In fact, even such objective observers as Mursell and Burton mince no words in pointing out that our efforts have been anything but successful. Thus, Mursell not only gives examples of teaching in direct violation of the principles of educational psychology but goes on to say that these examples are, unfortunately, typical of many of our present educational practices.

Among the many examples of inefficiency and malpractice in the classroom which can be noted by any impartial observer who looks into the problem, one might mention the following:

(a) Much of the activities of the classroom consist of verbal discussions and descriptions with a heavy reliance on abstract and technical language. The logical outcome in too many cases is verbalism piled on verbalism, frustration, gradual disinterest, apathy, and misbehaviour. Thus, the child's knowledge of grammar does not lead to an improvement in his oral and written work, the teaching of science is often formalised and systematised into intellectual units which have no relation to his daily experience and interest, mathe-matics is rarely brought down to the level at which he can understand it let alone use it in living, and social studies are often taught in the abstract so that it is completely foreign to the problems he faces in everyday life.

(b) The unsuitable curriculum which dominates some of our schools interferes with promotion of the maximum self-realisation of the child both directly through the nature of the learning experiences it contains and indirectly through the shackling of the teacher and the consequent encouragement of ineffective teaching methods. The curriculum in the great majority of our schools is a subject curriculum; in many cases, according to Burton, it is a textbook curriculum "tragically unrelated to life needs" not only for children but also for adults, "for immediate and remote needs of anyone, anywhere, at any time." Under such conditions there can be no good teaching. Page assignments to a single text followed by a verbal quiz and drill aimed at the memorisation of facts— with no other aim than covering the text—is used by the "great majority" of secondary school teachers even though, again to quote Burton, "It would be difficult to devise an

> educational practice so grossly ineffective, so certainly calculated to interfere with learning..." Many of our schools still rely on such potentially damaging measures as coercion, competition, and punishment as a means of pushing meaningless material on defenseless children. As a result, the things that stand out in too many of our schools are lack of motivation, satisfaction with mediocrity and getting by, a great interest in "cinch" courses, and "goofing-off."

Schools exist for the purpose of providing meaningful experiences through which the growth of the child can be promoted most effectively. No one denies the fact that the child can—and does—learn many useful and important things out of school. However, such out-of-school experiences tend to be haphazard, uncoordinated, and not sufficiently organised and concentrated for society to be able to depend upon them for educating the child. School cannot be like life: it is precisely because of the failure of ordinary life experiences to provide a suitable education that schools have been established. Schools exist for the purpose of selecting those experiences that are worthwhile and meaningful to the child, of bringing them into vital relationship with him so that he can integrate them in a functional way, and guiding him in his reactions to these experiences so that they will be effective from an educational point of view.

Curriculum in Use

The sequence of experiences through which the school attempts to promote the growth of the child is known as the curriculum. Ideally, the curriculum should incorporate the best experiences one could devise to further his growth and development and its importance in the promotion of this growth can, therefore, not be minimised. In fact, a poor curriculum (in the sense of emphasising the unimportant at the expense of the essentials, of emphasising the unattainable and the useless, of being unrealistic) would automatically negate the very purpose for which the school exists.

Most, if not all, experiences are educative in the broad sense of the word. However, some experiences, even though educative, are detrimental from the standpoint of long-term growth of the learner. Also to be considered is the fact that a great many experiences which are educative in the beneficial sense can be found and that, if time were unlimited, the child could become educated by simply being exposed to them all— or at least to a large proportion of them. But time is not unlimited and the school, if it is to fulfill its responsibility to society, must choose among the many experiences to which the child could be subjected those that are likely to result in the maximum growth at the minimum expense in terms of his time and effort. Just what these experiences are is, of course, a matter of considerable disagreement.

The experiences incorporated into the curriculum are simply the vehicle through which desirable learning takes place and it is the learning that counts rather than the experience through which it is achieved. Yet, for all the talk about teaching the child (and not subject-matter), it is still a psychological fact that children learn only through the medium of subject-matter, *i. e.,* through the experiences to which they have reacted, for learning takes place as a result of the learner's responses and the latter occur only as a result of stimulation. Thus, subject matter is incidental to learning and the study of history or algebra is worthwhile to the child only to the extent to which it enables him to do something which is purposeful to him. The question is not one of teaching the child algebra or any other subject but rather of choosing the sequence of experiences that will promote in the most effective way the learning he needs for self-realisation. In this area, the science of psychology can make a definite contribution.

What to include in the curriculum is first of all a problem of educational philosophy as we have pointed out. Educational psychology also has a definite role to play in determining this curriculum: whether or not Latin or physical education should be emphasised in our schools, for example, centers around the extent to which the disciplinary and direct values of each in promoting child growth are greater than those of other experien-ces competing for inclusion in the curriculum. Likewise, whether the curriculum should be oriented toward the more formal aspects or those more closely related to the childs' experience cannot be considered apart from the effectiveness with which such learnings can take place.

Generally speaking, the long term goals of education, *e. g.*, ability to think clearly, a scientific attitude, tolerance, and social competence are a matter of educational philosophy. On the other hand, the more immediate goals and the means whereby both short-and long-range goals are attained are more properly the province of educational psychology. Thus, whether the teacher conducts a unit on sanitation, transportation, or city government as a means of promoting learning in the area of number work, reading comprehension, or civic responsibility is probably best decided on the basis of psychological rather than philosophical considerations simply because the extent to which an experience is truly educative depends upon such psychological factors as the child's interest, goals, and needs. Likewise, if one has to choose between two equally important goals to be achieved through the curriculum, preference might be given to the one which, according to the principles of educational psychology is relatively more attainable or functional—or both.

The school must constantly re-evaluate not only its methods but also its curriculum in the light of changing social and philosophical thought and especially in the light of new discoveries in the area of educational psychology. On the other hand, it must not initiate changes simply for the sake of change. Teachers are not believers in doing things by halves: when convinced that a suggested procedure is better than a present one, they are likely to make a complete shift without realising that perhaps the solution lies in a middle-of-the-road position— and educational procedures have a long history of pendulum like shifts over the years—from a completely phonetic approach to a total disregard for phonics, from rigid drill procedures to an easy going curriculum dictated by the whims and fancies of immature children, from a rigid teacher-controlled classroom atmosphere to a pupil-dominated state of classroom disorganisation.

Some of these changes have come in response to the demands of the public that certain courses be offered in the school (*e.g.*, sex education) or that a greater or lesser emphasis be placed on a certain phase of the curriculum because of its alleged importance or unimportance. Thus, statistics on the physical inadequacies of the American youth inducted into service during World War II led to an increased emphasis on physical education in schools only to have it cede to science and mathematics as a result of the clamor of scientists that accompanied the Russian Sputnik. Generally, Americans consider themselves practical and, in contrast to the European idea of the finishing school and the gentleman scholar, tend to emphasise the practical and even the vocational as opposed to the cultural and the theoretical. Likewise, there tends to be a more or less persistent demand for the specific and the tangible as opposed to the general—a trend which has met with considerable favour among harried teachers eager to meet the demands of still another emphasis in American education, namely, adequate objective performance on various tests of academic achievement.

Some of the demands made upon the school have come from professional educators and psychologists and have been based on sound research evidence. Thus, a greater emphasis on the "life adjustment" curriculum more closely related to the everyday life of citizens in a democracy—as opposed to the more abstract and classical curriculum has roots in the thinking of such educational and psychological leaders as Dewey, Thorndike, and others. On the other hand, pressures have also been applied by various groups for a return to a curriculum or to methods which do not make psychological or pedagogical sense. And, unfortunately, rather than attempt to educate the public, schools have at times given way to these demands despite the fact that, in the final analysis, the only important consideration is the welfare of the child. The effect of public pressures is evident in many classroom procedures and methods: thus, fear of public censure has made schools cautious in their adoption of newer techniques of classroom management, of teaching, reading, of dealing with the whole child, and of differentiated treatment of children with different abilities and background. Indeed, the fact that we still grade children and report their progress on the old-fashioned report card, that we regulate our assignment of homework to the wishes of parents whom we have never bothered to educate is hardly indicative of professional status on the part of the teacher who ought to know what is in the child's best interest and who ought to be willing to exercise leadership in school matters rather than relinquish it to the school board, the PTA, or the general public. This is not to imply that all public pressures have been misdirected and that the school should not be sensitive to the needs of society as reflected in public opinion. It is simply that teachers need to be reasonably convinced of the desirability of the changes advocated before making them.

The curriculum represents the content by means of which the school stimulates the child's growth. It is, however, necessary for the curriculum to which the child is subjected to be broken down into units for, obviously, it cannot be assimilated as a whole. This breakdown can be done in various combinations of two major ways:

(a) the subject-matter organisation in which learning is arranged around some central topic logically organised and generally selected in advance by the curriculum-maker to fit the school on a local or even a statewide basis;

(b) the experience organisation centering on problems related to the desire of students in a class to satisfy some need or achieve some purpose.

These two approaches are not entirely independent and separate: certainly all curriculum units incorporate both subject-matter and experience. Likewise, both can result—and have resulted—in desirable outcomes. Since these approaches in their extremes represent extremes in philosophical and psychological orientation, a study of their major contrasts is of interest and value here.

Whereas the differences in the two approaches involve many facets that defy easy synthesis, the major difference lies in their orientation. The subject-matter approach is teacher-centered; it is predicated on the assumption that it is the function of adults to (a) select and organise the content, (b) present the material, (c) direct the learning, (d) measure the results, and (e) diagnose difficulties and provide remedial work where indicated. There is an implict assumption that unless teachers organise, teach, prod and test, the child will learn little or nothing. By contrast, the experience school is pupil-centered and the work of the teacher lies in (a) setting the stage and utilising the student's purposes in selecting the experiences by means of which they are to learn, (b) giving moral support and whatever help students need to achieve their purposes, and (c) cooperating in the evaluation and in the planning of the next step.

A great deal of discussion of the relative advantages and disadvantages of these two approaches can be located in textbooks and professional journals under such headings as traditional and progressive, conservative and modern, teacher-centered and pupil-centered, and even autocratic and democratic, all used more or less synonymously. In addition, the progressive method has, at various times, been called the project or the activity method or the experience curriculum. Unfortunately, much of the writing on the subject has simply reflected the opinions of writers with a bias in one direction or the other; it is not uncommon, for instance, to find the discussion casts one method in its best possible light while, at the same time, emphasising the shortcomings of the other. Therefore, as we turn to a discussion of the two approaches, the student is cautioned against letting his prejudices on the subject obscure the real issues and to distinguish between what is an inherent strength or weakness in a method and what is more correctly an abuse—or perhaps an abuse to which the method is prone.

Assessment Process

The primary weakness of the teacher-centered approach stems directly from the fact that it is oriented toward adult goals and relies on adult direction, a situation which can easily run counter to the principle that an experience is educative to the extent to which it is brought into vital relationship with the needs, goals, and purposes of the learner. It is based upon the philosophical view of education as a preparation for life, a position which Snygg and Combs (354) show to be psychologically unsound since the child cannot solve problems he does not have—and cannot have. Because he would have to be an adult to have the self-concept of an adult, the only possible outcome of a curriculum based on such a premise is a childish response to an adult problem. As they very aptly point out

> ... the process of equipping children with a repertoire of specific facts, skills, and techniques which will enable them to meet specific situations in adult life proves as impractical in theory as many generations of frustrated teachers have found it to be in practice.

With the advance of educational psychology and the clarification of the nature of the learner and of the learning process—out of which the pupil-centered approach evolved— it has become increasingly evident that more effective learning is likely to result out of letting classroom experiences grow out of the child's purposes and goals than having them preselected and preplanned in detail by the curriculum-maker. Of course, with a certain degree of psychological insight, the curriculum-maker can make a reasonably valid attempt at relating the curriculum to the purpose and development of the average child; he would certainly agree, for example, that the introduction into the curriculum of the Magna Carta, the Bill of Rights, and other historical events of man's struggle for independence should coincide with the adolescent's need to gain emotional independence from adults. However, it takes considerable ingenuity for the curriculum-maker to devise a curriculum that will fit all children of a given grade, regardless of ability, interest, and experiential background. It also takes considerable ingenuity for the teacher to promote the readiness and the motivation for whatever topic comes next in the curriculum sequence. In other words, the traditional preplanned curriculum does not lend itself well to taking advantage of the spontaneous interests and purposes of the class and of the opportunities for effective learning that sometimes present themselves.

An obvious question arising out of the discussion of the preceding paragraph concerns the continuity of the experience from which the child is to learn. In the teacher-centered school this continuity is provided automatically by the expert curriculum-maker who plans the whole sequence. The experience school, on the other hand, guided as it is by the interests and purposes of the child, has no such inbuilt guide toward its ultimate goals and, in extreme instances, can degenerate into the aimless wanderings for which the project method was often ridiculed with the much-repeated "Teacher, I wish we didn't have to do what we want to do, today." Obviously, when the planning of the curriculum is put into the hands of children, their education is likely to be fragmentary and incomplete. But proponents of the pupil-centered method do not advocate that the curriculum be left to the whims of children. They are as fully convinced as anyone else of the absolute necessity of having the general curriculum sequence—and particularly the overall goals—planned in advance by experts. The freedom they allow children under the direction of the teacher is in the choice of particular experiences by means of which the objectives of the curriculum are to be attained. (Parenthetically, it should be noted that this puts the teacher in a key position, a professional person in a position to do a professional job. And it allows no room for incompetence.)

It is, of cours true that the experiences planned by children often lack the tidy organisation which an adult can give them and, at times, the teacher may feel a concern for the muddle in which children can get and a compulsion to step in and direct the learning along the lines common to the traditional method. However, the emphasis upon logical organisation, often accepted as the greatest strength of the teacher-centered method, needs to be questioned. It rests upon the assumption— obviously false—that the material can be absorbed ready made from a structural standpoint in much the same way as impressions of wet ink are absorbed by a blotter. Organisation, continuity, and meaning lie in the learner, not in the material, and it is the learner who must organise his experiences. They cannot be organised for him and, although the arrangement of the material by adults may facilitate the process of reconstruction by means of which he can obtain meaning out of his experiences, the process is certainly not automatic. In fact, the beautiful (adult) organisation of the material may have no meaning for the child with his particular background of ability and experience, as many teachers have realised as they despairingly read on the examination the child's garbled renditions of the explanations so clearly stated in the book or given in class.

Of primary importance in connection with any learning situation is the matter of the motivation of students and this is one area which has a definite bearing on the relative effectiveness of the two methods. To the extent that the traditional curriculum is selected by adults and oriented toward the attainment of adult goals, it has to rely on the ability of the teacher to sell these goals to children. This, certain teachers are able to do effectively in at least a good percentage of the time for a good percentage of the children, especially since certain topics and subjects have a certain inherent appeal to the children for whom they are intended. Teacher approval is an important aspect of the total situation and many good teachers are able to have children gradually develop interest in the subject-matter as well as a positive self-concept as it relates to academic work.

The situation is not always so ideal, however. Since the goals are adult goals, often related only remotely to the goals of a good fraction of the members of the class, it is not surprising that, for many children, their attainment or unattainment is a matter of relative indifference. As a consequence, motivation has to be extrinsic, and an excessive emphasis on competition, grades, and other external incentives is more or less a natural adjunct of the traditional school, as a number of pupils, denied the satisfaction which stems from striving for meaningful goals, work to avoid punishment or for a grade as something to salvage out of an otherwise distasteful activity. Very often students have as their primary goal the circumventing of the goal set by the teacher. The latter, on the other hand, uses whatever means his ingenuity enables him to devise. Some teachers are relatively restricted in imagination and can think of nothing beyond sarcasm, scolding, failure and punishment, and various forms of threat in order to force the class toward the prescribed goals— presumably on the assumption that (a) learning is learning, regardless of the means used to promote it, and (b) if children are made to comply long enough, they will continue to comply through the operation of habit motives. Very effective learning actually occurs in many cases. However, for many other children, whatever learning does take place is often relatively meager and superficial, but there is certainly nothing superficial about the negative attitudes that are promoted.

The pupil-centered classroom, on the contrary, by using the student's purposes and background as the starting point and by placing on his shoulders a greater share of the responsi-bility for his education, is more likely to stimulate ego-involvement and whole hearted acceptance of the goals toward which he is to strive. Since it is his problem in the sense that he had a hand in choosing it and planning its execution, he is not only more likely to work effectively in carrying it out but also to derive a greater degree of satisfaction at its solution. (Note, for example, the difference between the learning of the student preparing a speech to hand in to his teacher as an assignment and that of the student preparing a speech in connection with his campaign for election to office in the student government.) As a result, the need for external incentives with which to goad him is correspondingly reduced and the likelihood of a virtuous circle of success, interest, and self-actualisation is correspon-dingly increased.

The fact that apathy, misbehaviour, and ineffectiveness in learning are more or less direct resultants of the unsuitability of its goals and the unrealistic demands it makes upon children was not fully appreciated by the traditional school. Rather, as pointed out by Beaumont and Macomber, it considered motivation and misbehaviour as appendages extraneous to the business of the school to be dealt with through external incentives and, where necessary, through punitive disciplinary measures. Many teachers today are equally shortsighted and much of the difficulty still to be found in our schools with respect to motivation and discipline is the direct outcome of their failure to relate their procedures and their curriculum to the needs and purposes of children. This is well stated by Snygg and Combs in the following quotation:

> It is quite likely that much of the conflict between pupils and teachers which still occurs in school is due to the fact that the schools are run by teachers who are chiefly concerned with preparing the student for his function in adult life and are filled with students who want to satisfy their needs here and now.

Thus, whereas the student-centered classroom, by adapting the work to the group and to the individual child and, thereby, providing him with the opportunity for continuous satisfaction for his needs, undercuts the child's need to misbehave, the traditional school often has to resort to repression. However, repressive discipline does not make the curriculum any more suitable: it merely increases the tensions associated with the frustration of the child and, whereas it makes for order—and a certain amount of learning—it often has a detrimental effect on his overall growth.

The practical significance, to those who would guide the growth of children, of the point discussed here cannot be overestimated. No matter from which aspect of his self-realisation it is viewed—academic growth, personal and social adjustment, attitude and character formation—it is evident that the individual, whether a child in school or an adult at work, must find satisfaction for his needs out of meeting the demands of the job or the classroom rather than have to rely on extrinsic incentives such as grades or salary or the satisfaction of such side activities as the after-school athletic programme, the after-work bowling league, or the coffee-break friendships. As it pertains to the school child, this means that the organisation of the classroom and its curriculum must have inbuilt satisfactions, *i. e.*, it must make it possible for the child to derive his major satisfactions, not out of getting a grade or misbehaving, but rather out of solving meaningful and challenging problems, and out of contributing to the attainment of group goals. The fact that the student-centered approach tends to have greater possibilities from this standpoint constitutes one of the strongest arguments in its favour.

The advantages noted so far of relating the curriculum to the goals and purposes of the learner are of obvious importance but we still have to consider what is to the average layman the most crucial question, namely, the extent to which experiences so organised lead to effective and desirable learning outcomes. Critics of the progressive school, on the thesis that work is work and play is play (Tom Sawyer to the contrary notwithstanding) have, at times interpreted the fact that children have a good time or enjoy school, that they do "what they want to do" as evidence supporting their contention that little learning is taking place. They fear that giving children a say in the choice of activities will result in their selecting what is easy and pleasurable (another instance of soft pedagogy) and that, as children flit from one pleasant activity to another, little will be learned. They fear, for example, that children in the progressive schools will be weak in the fundamentals which are more difficult to integrate into an experience unit.

Two factors prevent the learning in the pupil-centered classroom from being oriented toward the easy and the pleasurable but useless. One of these is the fact, previously stated, that the general curriculum and the over-all goals of pupil-centered schools are set by adults and not by children so that, except in cases of teacher incompetence in the use of the method, the danger is relatively small. The second consideration is even more fundamental: children want to grow, to be challenged, to explore new areas. To fear that children will seek easy task, is to fail to grasp the central theme of the concept of the phenomenal self, advanced by Snygg and Combs:

> Such criticism would fail to take into account the fact that in shifting the major purpose of education from the acquisition of subject matter to the development of an adequate phenomenal self, we have shifted to an activity for which the child does not need to be motivated. Building a satisfactory phenomenal self is the primary motive of his every act. His basic need is for the preservation and enhancement of his phenomenal self.

It is only when the child is under threat (due to unrealistic demands, failure, and punishment) that the student plays it safe: normally, the fact that they do not lead to self-enhancement will prevent him from seeking easy tasks. Furthermore, new and more mature interests come easy to the child whose curiosity and initiative have not been blunted so that he will want to forge ahead toward new conquests.

Also related to the question of the effectiveness of the progressive school in promoting desirable learning outcomes is the criticism often heard of the time allegedly wasted by students as they select and plan an activity (by comparison with the traditional approach in which the teacher comes fully prepared with the work of the day). There is, of course, in any procedure calling for group planning, a danger of having endless and pointless discussion. There is the further danger that the final plans and products will be not nearly as perfect as they would have been had the teacher taken a more active part. All of this may be frustrating to the perfectionistic teacher—and even to the brighter members of the class. The highest degree of efficiency and perfection would probably be attained when the teacher did it all by himself or appointed the best students to carry out the project in the name of the class but this would hardly result in much learning on the part of children. The important thing is not the product but the learning that takes place in the process. Group selection and planning of classroom activities are essential aspects of the pupil-centered approach and they are at the very foundation of its success. Far from being wasted, the time taken results in the selection of an activity which is realistically related to the needs, goals, capacities, and interests of the group, in the ego-involvement of the various members in the cooperative attainment of group goals, and in the clarification of the part each is to play. The outcome is not only a more effective contribution on the part of each individual child but a greater degree of satisfaction and self-fulfillment. Cooperative selection and planning of units spell the difference between the child going aimlessly and apathetically toward a goal known only to the teacher and one working on an activity which he sees as real and potentially satisfying. As pointed out by Wingo

> ... the most fruitful kind of learning experience is one in which a person or group evolves a plan for dealing with a meaningful situation, puts the plan into action, and then evaluates the outcome of the plan in terms of its original purpose.

The fear that student participation in the selection and planning of classroom activities will lead to their becoming "happy morons" whose learning is meager and fragmentary has not been borne out by research. Comprehensive studies such as the Eight-Year Study (2) and many others have invariably shown students of progressive schools to be at least up to par on the fundamentals and considerably superior in ability to reason critically, to apply what they know, and to integrate their experiences. They also tend to be superior in cooperation, self-confidence, sociability, effectiveness of expression, breadth of interest, and creativity.

It is particularly worthwhile to note that the superiority of the pupil-centered approach is largely from the standpoint of the functionality of the learnings it promotes. The teacher-centered method is reasonably effective in promoting the learning of isolated facts and skills (provided it can deal with the motivational problem) but psychology is not interested in knowledge per se unless it is reflected in behaviour. When all is said and done, the activities of the school, its curriculum, and its methods must be evaluated in terms of the difference it makes in the life of the learner: the employer, for example, is more interested in whether the graduate can do the job than he is in the number of facts he can reproduce for an examination. This is actually a fundamental distinction: whereas the traditional school with its subject-matter orientation stresses the acquisition of knowledge as an end in itself, the modern school is interested in knowledge only as it becomes an integral and functional part of the learner's life. Or, stated differently, whereas at times the old school seems oriented toward making the pupil a "cyclopedia of useless information", the aim of the modern school is not merely to "engender information and skill but to guide his purposes, attitudes, and interests..."

Since the activities of the pupil-centered classroom stem from the existing motives of the child and are, therefore, more in line with his background of ability and interest, they are more likely to be functional in guiding his further purposes. Thus, a child working on a unit on city government which involves him in interviews with the city commissioners is more likely to appreciate the working and importance of city govern-ment—and also more likely to develop civic attitudes, effective-ness of expression, and social graces—as a result of having lived the experience rather than having merely studied about it in his civics book. Such an approach is also more likely to be effective in fostering self-reliance, pupil initiative, habits of independent study, or problem-solving techniques. In other words, an experience unit is more likely to originate from the whole child and to be reflected in changes in the whole child, *e. g.*, understandings, applications, appreciations which go beyond the confines of subject-matter.

Contributing to a considerable extent to the ineffectiveness of the conventional school from the standpoint of the functionality of the learnings, it promotes the fact that, with its compartmentalisation of subject-matter, it often cuts across real experiences and reduces education to the memorisation of isolated facts along a narrow and artificial path. This is not a necessary accompaniment of the traditional method but definitely a weakness to which it is prone. Because it is defined in terms of subject matter, it encourages the development and use of a text designed to incorporate said subject-matter as decided upon by the curriculum-maker. In the absence of a more meaningful guide to the learning of the child who, in many cases, has no great interest in it anyway — in a series of easy steps — the subject-matter approach often becomes a textbook approach and, in its extreme form, degenerates into a chapter-at-a-time or page-at-a-time routine devoid of any purpose beyond that of covering the book before the end of the year. On the contrary, the ultra-flexibility of the pupil-centered approach, if nothing else, at least discourages the exclusive use of a 'pres-cribed' text and encourages the development of resourcefulness and proficiency in locating and integrating information from multiple sources.

Also vitally involved in the relative success of the teacher-centered and the pupil-centered methods is the extent of their adaptability to individual differences among children. Generally speaking, the former, with its preplanned curriculum, does not permit easy adaptation of the work of the school to individual differences in ability, interest, and experiential background. This is especially so when it gets tied down to a textbook which is then followed slavishly on a page-by-page basis despite the fact that, being pitched at a certain level, it frustrates both the duller and the brighter child. For successful operation, without undue departure from its basic procedures and its preplanned curriculum, it has to place considerable emphasis on development of the required pupil readiness. However, pupil failure and retention are often too useful a crutch for teachers who are accustomed to fight unmotivated students, and wholesale retardation is rather typical of the old school's attempt at dealing with individual differences. Equally, if not more objectionable from the standpoint of effective education, is its emphasis on drill oriented toward the attainment of limited objectives. By the very nature of its curriculum and the apparent assumption that the same lesson is equally educative for all, the traditional subject-matter approach tends to make unrealistic demands upon many children. Probably its most effective measure from the standpoint of actual reduction in the range of individual differences – and one of the most vicious – consists in encouraging the dropping out of frustrated and bored students. In more recent years, "social promotions" have replaced retention and state laws have curtailed the incidence of drop-out, but these have hardly made the tradi-tional curriculum and methods any more adaptive to differences among children.

The pupil-centered method, by contrast, is more flexible: not only is the class likely to select units that are more realistically in line with its interests and resources; but it can also make adjustment for individual differences in the allocations of responsibility for the various aspects of the project among members of the group. This enables each child to derive the benefit and the satisfaction of making a contribution in keeping with his talents and interests.

Of major significance from a modern psychological point of view is the much more effective use made by the student' centered approach of the fact that the classroom involves a social situation and, as such, constitutes the teacher's best ally in promoting the all-round growth of the child. Whereas the traditional school with its emphasis on competition and individual assignments discourages the development of group spirit and group cohesiveness and often promotes a pupil-versus-pupil (and pupils-versus-teacher) situation, the pupil-centered approach encourages the development of a social situation in which each member contributes to the cooperative attainment of group goals and in which the teacher is a resource person helping children toward self-realisation. As a result, not only does it tend to make possible greater academic gains through the inter-stimulation of members and a greater degree of ego-involvement of the individual child but, through its group organisation, it provides practice in the democratic resolution of group problems through group discussion and group planning.

On the other hand, one must not make the volume of discussion going on in a classroom the criterion of its quality. Certainly, discussion is often futile and, at times, most undemo-cratic. Not only can it become essentially a pooling of ignorance, but it can degenerate into an endless verbiage on the part of a few empty-heads, endless arguments over inconsequentials, and domination by a few demagogues within the group. The teacher needs to be particularly skillful in moving discussion along and keeping it on the right track and in preventing a few individuals from monopolising the conversation or from making a mockery of democratic processes. It would seem logical to assume, for example, that if someone has to dominate the group, it might as well be the teacher who is at least better informed and better trained.

The child-centered approach is also generally more effective in promoting wholesome attitudes. The fact that it gets children involved in cooperative activities in which each member contributes to the attainment of group goals is conducive not only to the development of cooperation, consideration for others, social and civic responsibility, enlightened self-interest—all of which are of prime importance in a democratic society—but it is also conducive to the actualisation of these attitudes through active participation in worthwhile and meaningful activities. This is one area in which the traditional school is often lacking: on the assumption that knowledge is sufficient for the development of desirable attitudes and behaviour, it is, in many cases, concerned almost exclusively with the imparting of knowledge. If the child develops negative attitudes toward the school, toward learning, toward persons in authority, that is too bad—as long as he learns. This is, of course, not to imply that it invariably produces negative attitudes; for the nature of the attitudes developed would vary with the nature of the atmosphere of the class, the relative success of the individual, and other factors. It would be ridiculous to suggest that these are always, or even generally, unsatisfactory. On the other hand, it is probably true that the progressive method is more oriented toward the importance of attitudes in the determination of the individual's behaviour and, because of its emphasis on group participation toward the attainment of meaningful goals, it tends to be more effective in promoting positive attitudes.

The previous discussion has pointed to the relative superiority from the standpoint of psychological theory of the pupil-centered over the teacher-centered approach. The evidence also points to its superiority from an empirical point of view, although considerable variation may be expected from situation to situation. The former lends itself more readily to the promotion of the major objectives for which the modern school exists but, as may be expected, the extent to which its potential advantages are realised depend in no small measure upon the capability and the ingenuity of the teacher and other aspects of the local situation. Thus, as we have stated, a project on city government which calls for interviewing city officials might be expected to produce a better understanding and appreciation of city government than the study of it in a book but this would not necessarily be so. It is entirely possible that the child might get little beyond the name of one or two of the commisioners and a few minor details while missing out completely on seeing the complete picture in perspective. It seems reasonably clear that a combination of the traditional and progressive approaches, depending on the suitability of one or the other for a particular unit of the curriculum would result in more effective learning than would complete adherence to one alone. Certainly not all tasks are amenable to the group project approach, for example.

Likewise, one or the other of the two methods may tend to be more suitable for certain students. Thus, the traditional method by making fewer demands on the child in terms of self-direction, ingenuity, initiative, and originality may provide a more reassuring atmosphere for the emotionally insecure child—and teacher. Also, it is likely that the logical organisation of the subject-matter approach is more effective for the bright or mature student or for the college situation and that the activity method is better suited to the elementary school. Thus, Burton expresses the view that:

> The education of little children, or beginners... is believed to proceed better when experience units are used by competent teachers.
>
> The education of students who have more adequate reading ability and who have achieved sufficient maturity to be able to learn through verbal abstraction... is believed to proceed better when the assign-study-recite-test procedure as currently improved is used by competent teachers.

Generally the elementary school is more oriented toward the use of the activity method than is the high school. This may stem in part from the fact that teachers-in-training choosing the elementary level are perhaps more oriented toward children whereas those going to the secondary level are more oriented toward subject-matter. It may also be, of course, that arithmetic is more adaptable for inclusion in a project than is solid geometry, for example. Yet the Eight-Year Study was conducted—with considerable success—at the high school level, and therefore the question may be raised as to whether some of the ineffectiveness of our high schools may not be related to their use of antiquated techniques. On the other hand, the grade school must be cautioned against exclusive reliance upon projects and activities: the young child needs contact with concrete experiences but experiences are useful and usable only when synthesised into generalisations—and the subject-matter approach may well be an effective way of integrating these experiences, once he has had them.

The pupil-centered approach is not without its critics. Some of the criticisms to which it has been subjected are ill-founded and based on a lack of understanding of what the school is trying to do, the psychological principles underlying its techniques and procedures, and the role of the school in modern society. This may perhaps be blamed on a failure of the school to communicate with the public. Many critics have used the schools as a scapegoat in connection with their frustrations over the prevalence of juvenile delinquency, over international tension and the cold war, and hurt pride that "practical and scientific America" should have 'allowed' Russia to launch the first rocket to the moon.

Criticisms can also be expected in as much as some people are against any change and are likely to resent any departure from the "good old days" when they went to school. And, of course, the fact that those who did graduate from the old school (with the drop-outs and the repeated grades eliminated from the discussion) did know how to spell, read, and compute, and that, as a group, they are now successful in the community, only adds strength to their conviction that the progressive school is "off the track". (On the other hand, some people will accept anything simply because it is new—in the case of education, perhaps unconsciously feeling that any change from the old school which they attended would have to be an improvement.) Other criticisms, however, represent valid objections to what may be considered misuse or abuse of the method—or perhaps objections to the price the progressive method may have to pay in order to reap greater benefits in other directions. Educational psychology, of course, does not have all the answers and certain techniques which it apparently endorses may actually be in considerable error.

As we have also seen, the teacher-directed approach is not without certain merits, particularly as it applies to the promotion of academic growth and if this were the only consideration, it could probably be modified rather than abandoned. Its greatest weakness lies in the area of promoting the all-round growth of the child where, to be effective, it would generally have to undergo considerable modification from its present organisation. This is not to say that the traditional method is incapable of dealing with the whole child. Whereas it is often associated with the teaching of facts and skills by methods that are frequently dull and boring, reinforced by coercion, there is no denying that many teachers who have used the method with ingenuity and insight into its possibilities have not only made the subject-matter approach exceedingly interesting and challenging but have also turned out graduates educated in the best sense of the word.

There is reason to suspect that the superiority of the progressive method stems from the type of teacher it attracts almost as much as it does from any superiority inherent in the method. Many of the teachers in traditional schools, upon which criticism of the method has been based, are perhaps not as well qualified and as familiar with the principles of educational psychology as those who, by training and experience, want to experiment with a new method and to apply psychology to the classroom, and who are also more apt to be understanding and flexible in dealing with children. Also involved may be an important personality difference: the teacher who is secure and who displays competence, initiative, and resourcefulness tends to be more willing to experiment—realising that the progressive class, being more loosely organised, might result in bedlam if things go wrong. The insecure teacher, on the contrary, is likely to stick to the safer subject-matter approach. It should also be noted that whereas a dull, unintelligent, and incompetent teacher may be able to go through the motions of using the traditional method, on an autocratic, page-assignment basis, such a teacher could not handle the experience method. In fact, a definite weakness of the progressive method lies in the demands which it makes upon the ingenuity and competence of the teacher. In the hands of the wrong teacher—or even the inexperienced teacher—it can lead to disastrous results. Both methods lead to good results in the hands of the competent teacher—the pupil-centered approach merely allows more freedom for the competent teacher to display his competence.

Programmed Action

The classroom depends for its effectiveness upon its compliance with the principles of psychology. The list of these principles is, of course, too long to be reviewed here. Therefore, this section will attempt simply to give a very brief overview of the major ideas of this text, an understanding of which is essential to the teacher interested in effective classroom procedures.

The author, being unaware of any particular virtue in ignorance or incompetence, does not wish to minimise in any way the importance of the knowledge of subject matter, of methods, and other aspects of teaching: a teacher lacking in these areas is simply unqualified. Nevertheless, this text has consistently emphasised the view that an understanding of the why of the child's behaviour is the key to guidance of his growth and development. It is the author's contention that the greatest source of failure in the classroom stems more from the teacher's inability to deal effectively with the motivational and personal aspects of teaching than from any other cause (as indeed it does in any situation involving people as they interact with each other). It is not uncommon for a supervisor to find that a beautiful lesson plan has been worked out by a teacher who has a good grasp of the subject, who has also brought in a nice balance of audio-visual aids and other illustrative mate-rials, and who is fully prepared to teach—the only thing that is missing is an appropriate answer to the question: "Specifically what would make the children in the class interested in the material to be presented?" Many an otherwise good lesson has floundered on that question. Accordingly, the following points may bear reconsidering:

(a) The key idea which any prospective teacher must never lose sight of is that behaviour is purposive: it always occurs in connection with the satisfaction of the individual's needs;

(b) However, as a result of his previous experiences, the individual learns to satisfy his needs in a specific way, i.e., not only to seek the satisfaction of his needs but to do so through the attainment of specific goals. Thus, motives rather than needs determine the individual's behaviour: not only will the individual satisfy his needs but he will satisfy them in ways consistent with his past experiences, his habits, his values, his self-concept.

(c) In the face of the multitude of unsatisfied motives with which the individual is invariably confronted (some of which are reinforcing, others conflicting, each with a certain vector strength in a given situation), behaviour is the net resultant of relevant motives. Thus, behaviour is oriented toward the satisfaction of dominant motives. Conversely, the individual can be relied upon to take whatever steps within his power he needs to take, in order to attain the purposes which are important to him. He can do no more and no one can expect him to do more!

(d) Since behaviour results from unsatisfied motives, a certain degree of tension is conducive to learning. On the other hand, excessive tension is likely to result in anxiety and ineffective, if not deviant, behaviour. Probably no other developmental concept has greater implication for effective living than that of the development on the child's part of security, *i. e.*, relative freedom from anxiety.

(e) Every experience the individual undergoes is potentially satisfying or frustrating depending on the degree of readiness he brings to bear upon the situation. Every aspect of his development has a bearing on the attainment of his goals and he cannot be considered except in his totality.

(f) Maturity implies behaviour that is effective in the attainment of goals and constructive from the standpoint of the welfare of others. Any educational system must not only orient the child toward the concept of enlightened self-interest but must also provide him with practice in social living, i.e., practice in making decisions involving the welfare of the group of which he is a member.

(g) Not only does the social group provide the maximum opportunity for satisfaction of the individual's needs but, indeed, only through the group can the individual attain maximum self-realisation.

(h) The school, as an agent of society, has no greater mission from the standpoint of the welfare of both society and the individual than the development on the part of the latter of sound character based upon a foundation of positive attitudes and ideals of integrity, morality, and consideration for others.

The same concepts apply to the classroom: the key to effective educational experience lies in the motives of the child. The child will exert himself with whatever capacity he can muster when he is working toward goals that are real and meaningful in terms of his needs, motives, and purposes, on one hand, and his background of ability and experience, on the other. His need for self-enhancement will not permit him of do otherwise. Such experiences, in turn, will make for (a) maximum learning, retention, and functionality from the standpoint of successful living; (b) success and maximum tension-reduction and self-fulfilment; and (c) desirable attitudess and values. On the contrary, to the extent to which the child is forced to participate in experiences which are not related to the attainment of his goals and purposes, aversive effects-apathy, superficial learning, frustration, negative attitudes, misbehaviour, maladjustment—are bound to follow.

The implementation of this principle into actual classroom practice is obviously too comprehensive a matter for complete coverage here. The discussion will, therefore, be restricted to a listing of the following as minimal essentials of such a programme:

(a) An understanding of children:

1. In general: the teacher needs to understand children in terms of the psychological principles that govern their growth and development, of the particular characteristics and problems of children, of the role of readiness and maturation.

2. Individually: the teacher cannot provide meaningful experiences for a child whose ability, interests, background, values, goals, or purposes he does not know.

(b) A suitable curriculum:

1. There is need for a good selection of educational experiences designed to promote desirable behaviour changes in individual children in the most efficient way. These experiences must not be standard for all children in a given grade or class but must, on the contrary, be tailor-made with respect to content and method of presentation to fit the particular child.

(c) A social situation conducive to the maximum self-realisation of the child:

1. The children of the class must be integrated into a cohesive group characterised by unconditional acceptance of individual members, effective communication among

members and between members and teacher, commonness of purpose, and enthusiasm in the attainment of worthwhile goals.

2. The teacher, as a group leader, must be one who can communicate with and inspire children.

(d) Effective guidance of the process by means of which the child is to achieve his potentialities:

1. Guidance is needed if experiences are to be satisfying to the child and effective in promoting his growth. At the same time, the teacher must realise the necessity of having the learner actively involved in the learning process and must provide for ego-involvement through the operation of realistic and clear-cut goals.

2. Effective learning centers around such concepts as problem solving and meaningfulness and implies experiences that are real in terms of the child's purposes, interests, abilities, and background. It must, in turn, be reflected in functional behaviour and in more mature interests, goals, and purposes.

3. The school programme should capitalise on the child's natural desire to grow and be synchronised with his natural pattern of development so as to promote his maximum self-realisation.

4. Meaningful group participation in the pursuit of realistic and worthwhile goals is one of the best means of (a) promoting the development of personal and social adjustment and of sound attitudes and character, and (b) of having them reflect in positive behaviour.

(e) A competent, sensitive, and dedicated teacher:

1. The teacher is certainly the most important cog in the educative machine and, although we cannot list all the characteristics and traits which would be desirable for a teacher to have, we may at least mention the following: (a) a thorough grasp of subject-matter; (b) ingenuity and

competence in setting the stage for the maximum growth of the child, in guiding the learning process, in welding students into a cohesive group working toward common goals; (c) sensitivity to the needs and problems of children, a firm conviction in the inherent dignity of the individual, and a dedica-tion to the cause of promoting his maximum growth; and (d) an awareness of his responsibility as a leader of youth, of the importance of personal integrity, and a sincere interest in the welfare of children.

2. Ability to relate to children and inspire them toward the moral values and democratic ideals of bur society.

The education of the child is obviously a complicated task which does not allow for quick solution or easy prescription. Society has a general idea of the type of person a graduate of its schools should be; it can even list tentatively the require-ments and perhaps describe the process for educating such a person as we have attempted to do, in part, in this text. And on the surface, it would seem that these are not only necessary but reasonably sufficient conditions for the promotion of an educated person. Education, however, may be likened to housebuilding—whether we get an effective and livable house out of the required quantity of cement, lumber, and other materials depends to a large extent on the professional caliber of the architect and the builder, so also does the quality of the final product turned out of our schools depend to a large extent on the professional competence of the curriculum maker who devises the programme and of the teacher who puts his plans into action. An error on the part of either can negate the best efforts of all concerned.

There is not complete agreement as to what to include in the curriculum and—within limits—perhaps it is not necessary that there should be, since it is the growth that results from a given experience rather than the experience itself that counts. But there should be reasonable agreement as to what constitutes an effective—and an ineffective—teaching method. The technological progress which has put America in a position of world leadership has not been achieved through procedures that were "good enough". It is time we begin to expect from our schools the same degree of efficiency that characterises other areas of scientific endeavour. We need to re-evaluate our schools and their procedures, not for the purpose of labeling them 'traditional' or 'progressive' but rather for the purpose of identi-fying those that bring about results and those that do not; not with a view toward immediate implementation of a panicsponsored crash programme, such as the Sputnik-inspired increased emphasis on science and on stiffer grading, but rather with a view toward bringing educational practice in line with sound philosophical and psychological considerations. When this is done, we shall no longer have to apologise for our failures, and our students will be as adequate as per their potentialities.

6

Teaching Mechanism

Many a significant change have taken place in the school during the last decades, but probably none is of greater significance than the increased concern over the personal and social adjustment of the child. From a rigid emphasis on academic learning very often at considerable cost in terms of his adjustment, schools have come to recognise not only the importance programmes designed to promote the more personal and social aspects of his growth, but also of making the regular classroom programme much more guidance and adjustment-oriented. The primary responsibility for the child's adjustment lies with his parents who set the basic pattern of adjustment through the security they provide him, particularly in his early years. The teacher's influence is only slightly less important, for it is he who, in the main, holds the key to whether the experiences the child undergoes in school throughout his formative period will lead to satisfaction and self-fulfillment—or to frustration and self-defeat.

Throughout life, the individual has to adjust to the demands of his external environment as well as to those of his physiological and psychological make-up. Thus, the individual is continually eating, drinking, seeking affection or approval, trying to gain status. The adjustments he makes in response to these demands are not always the most desirable or wise from the standpoint of his long-term welfare but they are, nevertheless, adjustments in the sense that they are attempts to satisfy some of his needs. Only in death does the individual cease to adjust.

Adjustments may be defined as the process by means of which the individual attempts to maintain a level of physiological and psychological equilibrium; or more simply, adjustment refers to behaviour directed toward tension reduction. Implied in this definition is a state of harmonious relationship existing between the individual and his environment so that adjustment is a matter of the interaction between the capacities of the individual and the demands of his environment. Thus, adjustment is specific to a given individual under specific conditions and the term adjusted is meaningful only in terms of 'adjusted to what?' It follows that adjustment is related to such factors as the particular culture in which one lives, the sex of the individual, his socioeconomic status, and other factors peculiar to him and to the environment to which he must adjust. Thus, a boy from a lower socioeconomic group who refuses to fight may be considered maladjusted by the standards of his social milieu whereas the boy of a higher socioeconomic group who does fight may also be considered maladjusted by the standards of his social group.

Adjustment is only relative and temporary. It is impossible for the individual to become adjusted for no matter how contented he may be over the fine meal he has just had, he can be out of harmony with his environment in a matter of hours if his next meal is not forthcoming. Furthermore, he almost invariably has problems in connection with his personal life or his business that disturb his adjustment. Thus, when we say we are trying to promote adjustment on the part of the child, we really mean that we are trying to develop his capacity for adjusting on the assumption that, if he can learn to face in an adequate fashion the problems with which he is confronted today, he may be expected to be adequate in meeting the problems of tomorrow.

The question may be raised as to the desirability of promoting adjustment on the part of the individual. Since adjustment implies the question 'adjusted to what?', one might wonder if it is in their and society's best interest to have people adjust to conditions of poverty, slums, and other negative features of their environment. A different aspect of the same question concerns the extent to which progress on both the social and the personal level is being brought about by persons who are maladjusted. Generally, the producer, the achiever, the reformer are maladjusted in the sense that they are not in harmony with the conditions they find. The drifter and the loafer, on the other hand, tend to be perfectly contented with conditions as they are—no matter how bad. We do not want the child in school to be too content with his present state of ignorance: we want him to be under a certain amount of tension so that he will be jarred out of his complacency and made sufficiently anxious so that he will learn. As we have seen, motivation with regard to any form of learning—whether academic or in the area of personal and social adjustment—is simply a matter of raising the anxiety level of the individual as a means of spurring him to learn more appropriate behaviour. Thus, the child who boasts must be made sufficiently anxious by the inadequacy of his present behaviour that he will seek a more adequate adjustment.

Adjustment is, of course, directly connected with the concept of needs—or more specifically, adjustment refers to the adequacy of the behaviour patterns by means of which the individual habitually satisfies his needs. Thus, in as much as everyone has, at all times, multiple needs to satisfy, everyone is perpetually faced with adjustment problems and everyone is, therefore, potentially capable of being adjusted or maladjusted depending on the adequacy of his need-satisfying behaviour. A person is considered maladjusted, for instance, if he consistently satisfies his needs of the present while increasing the severity of the problems of satisfying his future or his more basic needs, e. g., the child who satisfies his needs through daydreaming rather than developing the skills which would permit him to convert his fantasies into actualities. Likewise, adjustment implies that the individual must satisfy his needs within the framework of the rules, regulations, and mores of the social group in which he finds himself. For, unless he can satisfy his needs in ways consistent with the standards of society, he is likely to find that his behaviour involves him in conflict with the social order and leads to further problems of adjustment.

The adequacy of the adjustment which the individual makes depends in considerable measure upon the severity of the adjustment problems with which he is faced. If the situations to which he must adjust (in relation to his potentialities) are such that he can satisfy his needs without undue difficulty, he is less likely to resort to asocial or a typical behaviour and he is, therefore, more likely to be adjusted. Severe and continued frustration of his needs, on the other hand, is likely to lead to maladjustment as the individual in desperation grasps at any straw that will cause even a momentary reduction in the tension associated with the frustration of his needs.

The severity of the adjustment problem with which the individual has to cope would depend on such factors as (a) the nature of the need being denied; (b) the extent to which it is being denied; (c) the extent to which other needs are also being denied; (d) the possibility of substitute goals and partial satisfactions; and (e) his basic security and the degree of his awareness of the frustration of his needs. As long as his frustration concerns only a few of his needs, or even a larger number but to a minor degree, the individual can generally get along much just as a car can run even though not all cylinders are supplying maximum power. However, when the problem becomes unusually severe, he is likely to become desperate and deviant behaviour is likely to result.

Art of Adjustment

All the laws and principles of learning apply to the concept of adjustment—whether the behaviour involved is desirable or undesirable—in exactly the same way as they do to the learning of academic material. Thus, not only does the individual learn his adjustments but his learning follows the same sequence of steps as we discussed in the chapter on learning, namely:

(a) The individual is motivated by virtue of a need being temporarily unsatisfied.

(b) He looks to some goal as a potential satisfier.

(c) Progress toward this goal is blocked by a barrier. (Note: This barrier may be physical, personal, social, societal, or cultural, or it may involve a conflict between incompatible goals.)

(d) Emotional tension develops and varied response ensues as the individual attempts to reach the goal and reduce the tension.

(e) The goal—original or substitute—is usually reached and equilibrium is restored.

(f) Those reactions which are instrumental in reaching the goal and reducing the tension are learned whereas those not effective in this connection are dropped.

The very fact that learning takes place only when the individual's present pattern of response is no longer adequate in meeting the demands of the situation implies that a certain degree of inadequacy and incompetence is characteristic of any learning situation. However, since an adjustment problem relates to the individual in a much more personal way than does the learning of, say academic material, it is more likely to involve feelings of inferiority and insecurity and these are quite obvious in the insecure person's tendency to derogate others, his poor reaction to competition, his oversensitivity to criticism, and his overresponse to flattery. Thus, if the individual's present behaviour patterns are adequate for him to cope with the situation readily, he has no adjustment problem. If, however, the situation in which he finds himself is one in which he lacks the ability to attain his goals, he is faced with an adjustment problem, and the more severe the problem, the greater his insecurity and the more likely is the development of a typical and ineffective behaviour.

Behaviour patterns are learned as a result of the individual's attempt to reduce tension associated with the frustration of his needs. Once learned, they maintain themselves by providing some satisfaction and they develop into habit motives which give stability and permanence to his behaviour, hence, Shaffer and Shoben's definition of personality as the individual's persistent tendencies to make certain kinds and qualities of adjustment. The fact that behaviour is learned in the process of satisfying one's needs may seem hard to believe in view of the short-sightedness of many individual's behaviour on certain occasions and that of a few individuals on most occasions. Yet this is the case and, even though the learning of undesirable behaviour generally tends to be less conscious and less deliberate than the learning of desirable behaviour, it is nevertheless learning in the accepted sense of the term; it is the modification of behaviour as a result of experience and is explained on the basis of the same principles as any other form of learning. All behaviour – however stupid or shortsighted – has a purpose as the individual interprets the situation: very often his overconcern with the immediate situation causes him to select immediate goals that are not in line with his long-range welfare. The unlearning of undesirable behaviour, on the other hand, calls for considerable effort since, once established, any form of behaviour becomes such an integral part of the total personality that it is quite resistant to change. It is especially resistant to change in the case of the insecure person who cannot afford to take a chance experimenting with other modes of adjustment.

Generally, if he keeps trying long enough, the motivated individual is able to overcome or circumvent the obstacle to his goal or reach a substitute goal which is reasonably satisfying. If his behaviour is completely ineffective with respect to the attainment of his goal, he will, of course, be forced to continue trying other modes of reaction until some degree of satisfaction is achieved through substitute behaviour. There are times, however, when the individual's behaviour is only partially ineffective, leading to goals which are partially satisfying. Unfortunately, since it provides some satisfaction, such behaviour will tend to be learned in accordance with the laws of learning even though it is not in the individual's best interest from the standpoint of his long-term adjustment. It is also characteristic of this type of behaviour that it has to be repeated continually in a desperate attempt on the part of the individual to drain off the tension as fast as it accumulates. This is rather evident in the case of people who boast or show off despite the poor reception their behaviour gets from others.

It may also be that the individual reaches a goal which, though satisfying in terms of his motivation, may involve him in difficulty with the rules of society. If he is not sold on the rules involved, his only concern is in not getting caught and, if he is able to avoid detection, he is 'ahead of the game.' On the other hand, society makes a deliberate attempt to have its rules and regulations internalised by the individual and, to the extent that it is successful in so doing, the individual will not be able to violate the constraints of society without automatically upsetting some other need or destroying some value of importance to his continued adjustment. Thus, sexual immorality may or may not result in guilt feelings depending on the extent to which it has become accepted as wrong by the particular individual. Likewise, the delinquent may not see where he is wrong and may feel discriminated against when society punishes him. In other words, social problems are not necessarily personal or clinical problems. When a problem is both social and personal, adjustment is more difficult since the person must first resolve the personal before he can deal effectively with the social aspects.

There may also be times when the individual cannot attain his goal without some form of outside help. This may entail nothing more than a need for coaching in a special skill such as dancing, or it may call for psychological counseling which, when provided, will allow the individual to achieve reasonably complete adjustment. On the other hand, the obstacle may be of such magnitude and resistance, by reference to the individual's potentialities, that he may never attain his goals. In such cases, he is likely to become desperate and to aggravate rather than solve his problem. His only salvation may lie in his being removed from the situation or in his being provided with considerable support. If this is not possible, his only escape may be in breakdown, with possible eventual recovery with psychiatric help and improvement in the conditions that caused the difficulty.

Thus, maladjustment arises out of attempted solutions at tension reduction which give only partial or temporary relief, or out of attempts which, although acceptable at one time, become so entrenched as habits that the individual is not able to outgrow them. It generally occurs in situations which are so resistant that the individual exhausts all the more desirable alternatives, or in situations which are so complicated that he cannot get insight into the relative dangers of the attempted solutions.

Adjustment differs from maladjustment in degree rather than in kind. Normal adjustment simply entails behaviour that is within the range of tolerated differences, where the limits of such a range are uncertain and highly flexible. More specifically, the adjusted person shows a relatively high degree of integration and consistency in his behaviour, displays behaviour that is essentially effective in attaining his goals, faces problems realistically, and devotes his energies to the realisation of his purposes. In addition, he has found satisfactory solutions for the major problems which he faces and has effective ways of releasing tensions so that he is relatively free from conflict and tension. In effect, he displays the emotional and social maturity which we have discussed in Chapters 5 and 6. On the other hand, when the individual is caught between a resistant obstacle and a persistent motivation, frustration and tension will mount to the point of causing excessive interference, and even disorganisation of behaviour. It may be, for instance, that internal conflicts will cause the person to be at cross purposes with himself with resulting indecision and inability to coordinate his efforts in the attainment of his goals. If this pattern tends to be typical of his behaviour, he may be said to be maladjusted, although there is no dividing line at which a person ceases to be adjusted and becomes maladjusted.

Maladjustment may be revealed through any number of symptoms, many of which—at least in their milder forms—are also characteristic of normal adjustment. Among the more common, we might mention the following: explosive behaviour, general restlessness (including nail biting and other nervous habits), preoccupation (daydreaming, absent-mindedness, worry), withdrawal (excessive reading for vicarious excitements, shyness and general avoidance of social situations), and minor physical dysfunctions. Another set of symptoms such as crying, temper tantrums, fixations or delays in normal growth, dependence on others, lack of motivation, inability to make decisions or to assume responsibility, attempts to win sympathy, and selfishness are often signs of immaturity rather than maladjustment, i.e., reflect failure to learn more mature ways of behaving rather than the learning of undesirable behaviour patterns. On the other hand, they can also be indicative of maladjustment, at least in the sense of a lack of harmony existing between the individual and his environment. Furthermore, regardless of differences in the background of immaturity and maladjustment, both are difficult to deal with: to the extent to which they have resulted in some satisfaction to the individual and are incorporated into his self-image and changing calls for major reorganisation of the total personality. Furthermore, an improvement in behaviour cannot take place in a vacuum and immature or maladjusted persons are likely to encounter difficulty in finding people endowed with sufficient patience to put up with them, let alone provide them with the permissive and supportive environment they need in order to improve.

The Structure

As we have seen in the earlier part of the chapter, the individual learns certain behaviour patterns by means of which he attempts to satisfy his needs. Thus, the boy who is frustrated as a result of inability to find satisfaction for needs of social recognition or self-esteem by being on the honour roll, compensates by making the football team or rationalises that only sissies are interested in academic work, or even perhaps develops neurotic symptoms such as headaches that prevent him from studying so that his inability to make the honour roll is quite understandable. These habits, known as adjustment mechanisms are neither disorders nor symptoms of maladjustment: they are simply the adjustment the individual makes when confronted with certain needs, on one hand, and certain situational realities, on the other.

Adjustment mechanisms can be arranged according to any number of systems depending on the basis of classification used. None of them is too satisfactory; behaviour is the resultant of multiple causations and is invariably so complicated that it tends not to fall into neat categories. Thus, a given mechanism may resemble the other mechanisms in its category from one standpoint but also resemble mechanisms in adjacent categories in other respects. Furthermore, a certain adjustment situation may give rise to any number of different adjustment mechanisms so that being able to identify the mechanism displayed by a given individual at a given time, either by itself or in terms of the category to which it belongs, is of limited value in dealing with the underlying problem. Yet despite these arguments and the obvious necessity of considering any classification as merely suggestive, classifying adjustment mechanisms is probably justified on the grounds that it brings out the common features among them and tends to make for a greater understanding of their nature.

Probably the simplest classification system is one in which adjustments are divided into those that are direct, i.e., reactions by means of which the individual attempts to overcome the obstacle and reach the original or a substitute goal, and those that are indirect, i.e., reactions in which the individual withdraws, rationalises, or generally gives up trying to reach the goal he has set. A more comprehensive classification system is that of Shaffer and Shoben in which adjustment mechanisms are divided into five categories: (a) adjustment by defense; (b) adjustment by withdrawal; (c) adjustments involving fears and repression; (d) adjustment by ailment; and (e) various nonadjustive reactions. In general, the discussion in this chapter will follow this outline in a somewhat abbreviated form and the reader is referred to their excellent text and other sources for additional information.

The mechanisms to be discussed in this section are those in which the individual is still attempting, by minimising his failure or attaining success by other means, to defend himself against feelings of inferiority occasioned by his failure to attain his goal. As we have seen, all adjustment mechanisms relate to feelings of inferiority but, whereas these feelings may lead to withdrawal or even ailment, the mechanisms in this category represent attempts on the part of the individual to maintain self respect through a defense against such feelings. Included in this category are a variety of reactions ranging all the way from attention-getting devices to the more serious attempts to project the blame onto others, with compensation and rationalisation being the most common.

Compensation represents an attempt on the part of the individual to overcome feelings of inferiority arising out of personal limitations in a given area by striving for success in the same or a different area. Thus, Demosthenes is said to have overcome a speech impediment by practicing speaking with pebbles in his mouth. Likewise, a boy may compensate for relative weakness in academic work by becoming an athlete or he may compensate in a peculiar area, e. g., collecting snakes or college banners, where, because the competition is less keen, he is more likely to attain relative success.

A common form of compensation concerns compensation through others. Parents, for instance, who perhaps feel inadequate as a result of their lack of education will go out of their way to have their son or daughter go to college and even to graduate studies. This type of compensation implies identification of the person with the individual through whom he compensates in order to get vicarious satisfaction of his needs througn the achievement of the latter. Thus, a father will identify himseh with his son with the result that the son's academic achievement becomes that of the father. Compensation through others is involved in the popularity of sports and of movies in which the spectator identifies himself with the players and obtains vicarious satisfaction through their achievement. Two observations in connection with such compensation are in order: (a) With the present emphasis on professional-type sports, high schools and coneges are reducing drastically the number of their students who can derive satisfaction for their needs through actual participation rather than through identification with the team; (b) Parents who compensate through their children can occasionally make it rough on the children: the parent who harbors a deep sense of inadequacy and frustration as a result of his inability to get past the fourth grade may do his son considerable damage by insisting upon unrealistic standards of academic achievement. In the same way, the alumnus who could not toss the pigskin ten yards when he was in college may well demand the head of the coach whose won-lost record is somewhat short of perfection.

Compensation is also involved in such common attention-getting devices as boasting, lying, and exhibitionism as well as in more complicated reactions such as compensation against evil in the abstract in which the individual crusades with unusual zeal against such 'evils' as tobacco, alcohol, or sex as a means of defending himself against feelings of undesirable compensation, particularly when it applies to the area of sex. Thus, teaching and nursing might be considered forms of sublimation of the sex drive.

Rationalisation consists of giving plausible but untrue reasons for one's behaviour as a defense against having to admit that, by objective standards, the behaviour is silly, irresponsible, or otherwise unacceptable. Rationalisation is an unconscious mechanism: when false reasons are given knowingly, they are lies, not rationalisations. Rationalisation is a face-saving device which goes back to Adam's "The woman whom thou gavest to be with me, she gave me of the tree, and I did eat." It may take on any number of forms, including 'sour grapes' or 'sweet lemons', or the blaming of incidental causes, e. g., kicking the stool for its having been in the way.

A more serious form of rationalisation is involved in the mechanism of projection, wherein the individual perceives in others the traits or motives in which he feels his own inferiority. Thus, the child accuses the teacher of having hostile feelings toward him while, in reality, it is he who is hostile toward the teacher. Prejudices and logic-tight compartments, in which obviously false beliefs are held despite logical evidence to the contrary, also have elements of rationalisation and projection along with various degrees of delusion.

In mechanisms involving withdrawal, the individual is no longer seeking to achieve satisfaction for his needs through the attainment of his goal but rather runs away from the frustrating situation. Those mechanisms are generally undesirable since they do not solve the problem and yet remove the individual from the pressure that would force him to do something more constructive than simply withdraw. Teachers should be particularly aware of the relationship between simple withdrawal and more serious forms of maladjustment such as schizophrenia and should be alert to danger signs. They should be aware of the fact that the child who never misbehaves, who is often the model child may be in grave danger of later difficulty and is, therefore, a more serious case of maladjustment than is the troublemaker who is fighting to satisfy his needs.

Probably the simplest and the most common forms of withdrawal concern bashfulness, timidity, negativism, and general seclusiveness in which the individual, perhaps as a result of having been the victim of frustration and failure along with repressive discipline refuses to take part in situations which may mean further failure. Another well-known form of withdrawal is fantasy, or daydreaming, in which the individual becomes the conquering hero for whom success and revenge are unlimited or the suffering hero whose misfortunes cause even his enemies great sorrow. Fantasy is not harmful in itself; it may even give the individual ideas that he can then proceed to put into practice. However, it possesses the danger of being used in lieu of more constructive behaviour, for as long as the individual finds no satisfaction for his needs, he will be forced to continue seeking some adjustment but, when he gets partial satisfaction from his fantasies, he is more likely to rely on them more and more and, as a result, become progressively less capable of doing something more constructive about his problems. On the other hand, not all retiring children are in immediate need of a psychiatrist: some people enjoy peace and quiet and teachers should refrain from using social participation as the sole criterion of adjustment.

A less obvious form of withdrawal consists of plunging into a number of occupational or social activities or becoming drowsy, or turning to alcohol, narcotics, or even sweets as a way of running away from one's problems. Occasionally, a person with severe problems which he can neither resolve nor escape from will turn with a vengeance to his work or will get ; involved in numerous activities in an attempt to forget. Sometimes, such a person will have a nervous breakdown and people are likely to pity him and commend him for having worked so hard that he became ill when, in reality, the hard work was the result of the same difficulty that eventuated in the breakdown but not its cause.

Procrastination is another common variety of running away from difficult situations which is indulged in by very normal people. Also common is retrogression in which the individual goes back to a more immature mode of behaviour, i. g., adults resort to crying as a way of solving problems and the preschool child who has become quite grown-up may revert to infantile behaviour when a new baby is born in the family.

Everyone has at least minor fears. In fact, fear (insecurity) is a basic component of all adjustment mechanisms: in compensation, fear is dispelled by overassertion of adjustment, while in withdrawal, the individual avoids fear-producing situations. On the other hand, persistent and excessive fears, particularly of an abnormal nature, i.e., phobias, are indicative of maladjustment. A person might have an intense fear of dogs as a result of having been bitten by a dog but it is something else for an individual to have frantic fears of high places, of low places, of crowded places, of wide open places—none of which is a normal stimulus for fear.

Generally, such abnormal fear can best be explained in terms of the individual's having had an unpleasant experience in connection with which he or she feels some degree of guilt. Because of these guilt feelings, there is a tendency for the individual not to face the situation but rather to repress the incident into the unconscious as a means of avoiding anxiety. But a repressed incident is not a dead incident and it comes up to consciousness again in a disguised form. So the girl who has been sexually assaulted in a situation in which she feels she was not completely blameless finds her fear of the original situation transfer from one object or situation to another till, for no apparent reason, she now fears being in a large room or has an intense fear of being left alone even for a few minutes— stimuli which are symbolic of being without protection. Repression serves the purpose of protecting the self but it is one of the most dangerous mechanisms because the underlying dynamics cause unexplained behaviour. As long as problems are kept in the open, they can be understood and dealt with but, once repression has taken place, the individual can be helped only by a competent clinician.

Also involving the repression of guilt feelings is the mechanism known as reaction formation, in which a person goes out of his way to be nice and considerate of another person as a way of reacting against the opposite feelings which the individual harbors with some guilt. Thus, the mother whose career ended with the birth of her child may react to a desire that the child be dead by granting his every wish and working well beyond the call of duty in seeing that no harm befalls him. Such behaviour may become quite compulsive for, as in the case of the obsession-compulsion of Lady Macbeth, the behaviour is related only indirectly to the goal and the compulsive reaction has to be repeated in a desperate effort to relieve the tension which seems to accumulate as fast as it can be dissipated by such relatively ineffective means.

When the individual is caught in a conflict, he may unconsciously resort to ailment as a way out of his predicament. These ailments do not have an organic basis—at least they do not have an organic basis that we know of—but rather are of psychogenic origin. They are generally known as psychoneuroses (or simply neuroses) under which can be grouped two broad areas of physical dysfunction: (a) various forms of hysteria such as localised pains, paralyses, and anesthesias; and (b) motor psychoneuroses (or functional hysteria) such as occupational cramps, stammering, and stuttering. A number of servicemen, for instance, suffered from shell-shock during the First World War and war fatigue during World War II, both terms referring generally to some form of hysteria. Thus, to use a fictitious example, a soldier is in the front lines. He is very scared and wishes he could be somewhere else, but among the values he has incorporated into his self-concept are bravery and loyalty which prevent him from leaving and 'letting his buddies down.' If he is wounded, perhaps in a minor way—immediately he is taken away from the danger zone and his conflict is resolved: he is no longer afraid nor does he have to feel guilty about not being in the front lines since it is accepted that wounded men should be out of combat. In due time the wound heals but a certain pain or stiffness remains in the wounded area so that he cannot rejoin his unit in the battle lines. He has—unconsciously—made an adjustment of a neurotic nature as a means of avoiding conflict.

Many psychologists feel that the majority of speech disorders such as stuttering and stammering are cases of functional hysteria. Likewise, a good fraction of the cases of arthritis, hay fever, asthma, migraine, headaches, backaches, and other ills affecting the average person are considered to be of psychogenic origin, and medical doctors estimate that over half of their clientele is made up of people whose ailments are psychogenically induced.

The cure in cases of hysteria is generally slow. First, the person must be motivated toward a cure: the soldier will not improve as long as he knows that the day he is discharged from the hospital he will be back in the firing zone. Then he must be given the means of saving face, for he cannot get out of the hospital cured the day armistice is signed. Since it is relatively difficult to change the basic personality of the individual which led to the hysteria, it is quite a problem to change the basic motivation and it is typical of patients suffering from hysteria to be indifferent to their troubles. In fact, since the hysterical symptoms serve to reduce the conflict, it is quite likely that, unconsciously, they actually enjoy their ailments and have no inclination to get rid of them.

It is generally agreed that persons with hysterical symptoms tend to be socially immature and highly suggestive so that when they are ready to be cured they may respond to treatment by a specialist who can convince them that a cure is possible. An interesting case of such a cure is that known as stocking anesthesia in which a patient whose leg is completely insensitive to any feeling will, at the suggestion of the therapist, recover feeling in the leg as a stocking (which has been put on the leg for suggestion value) is gradually rolled down an inch or two each day. Also, generally useful in the treatment of neurotic patients, is the common practice among medical doctors of giving them painful injections and foul-tasting medicine as a means of making their symptoms unsatisfying, but such treatment may serve to convince the patient of the reality and severity of his illness. Furthermore, cures of this type merely remove the symptoms and, unless something is done about the underlying conflict, curing one symptom will only lead to the occurrence of other symptoms and even of more serious difficulties.

The other Aspect

As stated before, when behaviour is only indirectly related to the goal and, therefore, yields only partial satisfaction, the individual finds it necessary to repeat it in a desperate attempt to drain off tension as it accumulates. In such cases the individual is likely to be in a constant state of tension as evidenced by digestive upsets, insomnia, diffuse motor activity, and anxiety. To the extent that the person fears taking the risk involved in attempting to reach the goal, he is incapable of taking positive action: the worrier, for instance, does not take positive steps to solve his problem; he simply continues to worry—often not even knowing what he is worried about.

Among the more common forms of nonadjustive reactions might be mentioned: (a) neurasthenia, which is a form of persistent anxiety state characterised by nervous exhaustion as in the case of the chronic invalid, and (b) hypochondria, a general preoccupation about health and an exaggeration of minor disorders. In these cases, as in the case of hysteria, there is generally to be found in the background of the individual a favourable experience with illness. Thus, the woman who feels lonely and neglected, as a result of her children and husband having developed interests outside the home, may find that illness on her part keeps everybody home in the evening for a change. She may unconsciously feel that being sick is an effective way of satisfying her needs. As with hysteria, the cure is difficult to achieve: the person must first become convinced that giving up the partial satisfactions connected with being sick will be more than compensated for by the satisfaction of being well. It is, of course, much better to avoid the development of such symptoms. A good rule to follow with regard to hysteria and neurasthenia, for instance, is never to make illness a pleasant experience. Thus, the child who has a headache at nine-o'clock should be put to bed for the rest of the day—minus comics and TV. If he is realty sick, the rest will do him good, while if the headache is of a psychogenic origin, putting him to bed will discourage the formation of hysterical symptoms. It is, of course, necessary to deal with causal factors. Perhaps some of the pressure at school should be lightened or the child should be made to realise that it is not necessary for him to be sick for people to take notice of the fact that he exists.

All people have needs: therefore, all have to make use of adjustment mechanisms. In fact, adjusted as well as maladjusted persons make some use of most of these mechanisms. Adjustment and maladjustment are a matter of degree and, even adjusted people daydream, rationalise and develop forms of hysteria such as migraine headaches. On the other hand, many of these mechanisms can be considered potentially dangerous—although each would have to be evaluated in terms of the particular individual involved and the particular situation in which he finds himself. Speaking in general terms, adjustment mechanisms are considered undesirable in the following cases: (a) when they displace some more constructive mode of adjustment; (b) when they are relatively ineffective in satisfying needs; (c) when they introduce greater problems than the need they satisfy; and (d) when they create adjustment problems in other people as in the case of fighting. Perhaps a more adequate—although less explicit—guide for the evaluation of adjustment mechanisms can be found in Shaffer's statement that only those adjustments that fail to satisfy individual and social needs are maladjustments.

Understanding with Students

Every experience which the child undergoes affects his adjustment one way or another. It is, therefore, essential that the teacher understand each child as an individual if he is to provide educative experiences that will be conducive to his maximum growth. Actually, the average teacher can be only partially effective in this respect: not only does he not have the time and opportunity to make a through study of each child while at the same time attempting to have the class as a whole attain certain academic standards, but he is also relatively untrained in the area of the psychodynamics of behaviour. To make matters worse, behaviour, being the product of multiple causation over a period of years, is relatively complicated. In the field of medicine, the trouble can be identified by the symptoms and, once this is done, a rather complete understanding of the disease including its etiology and its treatment is attained. In the area of maladjustment, on the other hand, symptoms rather rarely identify the trouble since learning plays an important part in determining the behaviour by means of which the individual attempts to satisfy his needs. Hence, each case tends to be unique so that labeling a child an extrovert really does not tell us how his behaviour can be improved or how he can be handled best. Likewise, let us hope that the adjectives good and bad will soon drop out of the vocabulary used by teachers to label children and that they will be replaced by the concept of understanding and helping them.

Nevertheless, in the final analysis, it will be the teacher, not the psychiatrist or the clinician, who will do most for the vast majority of children in the development of effective behaviour. Qualified or not, the teacher must make understanding of children and their behaviour one of his primary responsibilities—for understanding children is an integral aspect of teaching them, not something one undertakes when things get out of hand. And whereas love is not enough, it is essential, and, when coupled with sensitivity and a good grasp of the basic principles of psychology, it will go a long way. In fact, it will go the whole way with most of the children in the classroom, for children don't have personalities made of glass: they have a wonderful resiliency to stress and strain and all they want—and all they need—is perhaps a little help here and there, but mostly, just a chance to grow.

Unfortunately, the easy way (the lazy way) is not to bother, simply to present academic material, make assignments, and ignore the fact that children are people with individual characteristics and problems. To understand children calls for time and effort, and the more understanding a teacher is, the more they will come to him rather than to other teachers who won't help them. But it is time and effort well spent for it pays dividends in pupil adjustment and in teacher satisfaction. A little help given at the right time will often put the child back on his feet and it is surprising to see the number of children, perhaps drifting in the wrong direction, who have found themselves as a result of a little understanding on the part of a sympathetic teacher. In fact, it is debatable whether any saving is effected by ignoring students except in the case where, in final desperation, they drop out of school. When they remain in school, whatever saving is involved, if any, is very shortsighted even from a purely selfish point of view, for neglected students soon fall behind, become discipline problems, and generally multiply a hundred-fold the teacher's problems. It just makes good sense to set up a definite appraisal programme designed for such purposes as knowing the child as an individual, providing the faculty and the guidance staff with information upon which to base counseling, increasing the child's self-understanding, and providing the basis for effective parent-teacher cooperation.

If we are to understand the child, we must know something of the experiences to which he has been subjected to and the forces which have played upon him. Thus, the child who has been

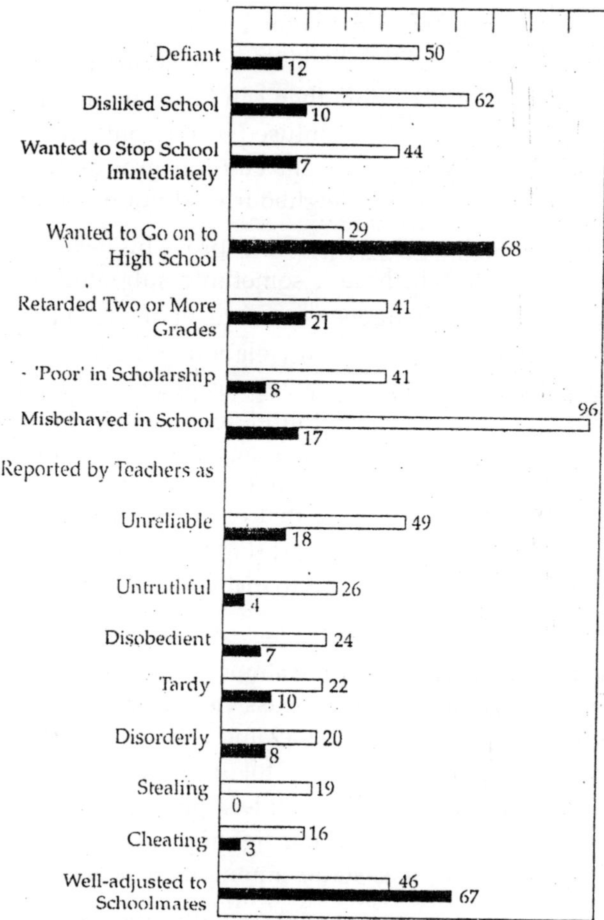

Fig. *Reactions of delinquents and nondelinquents toward the school situation.*

mishandled throughout his childhood may well have deep-seated problems that will defy superficial treatment. This would often be true of delinquent children, for instance, who rarely get the understanding and the help they need in order to be able to change their pattern of behaviour. Of course, each child is unique and no group diagnosis can be made as to the causes or the treatment of delinquency. Many delinquents, for instance, simply have not internalised the constraints of society, a situation likely to occur when adults make unreasonable or inconsistent demands on the child or when they allow him to grow like Topsy without any demands being made upon him. He needs discipline but only when it is consistent and based on love and security does it lead to character formation, i.e., only then can he grow in self-direction. Thus, the delinquent is often confused by the conflicting demands made upon him by the different cultural groups to which he belongs, e.g., to fight in his neighbourhood but not at school.

Furthermore, he is not helped to improve his behaviour by the harsh treatment to which he is sometimes subjected when he is caught. Actually, delinquency is more than the matter of the commission of an act which is in violation of the law: it generally involves the whole child, his values, his goals, and his purposes and delinquents have been found to be more independent, extrovertive, vivacious, impulsive, aggressive and adventurous than nondeliquents, but also to exhibit less self-control. Adjustment to the school by comparison to that of nondelinquents is also of interest here. As shown in the chart (Fig.), delinquent children are more likely than nondelinquents to dislike school, to misbehave in the classroom and to be truants.

Likewise, teachers, belonging almost exclusively to the middle class and subscribing to middle-class values, may have difficulty in understanding lower class values and behaviour. Children from the lower socioeconomic group, for example, tend to express aggression more directly and consider fighting as the thing to do when someone crosses them: not fighting would cause them to lose self-esteem as well as status among their peers.

They tend to be somewhat more authoritarian and punitive than children from a higher group. Above all, as a result of the experiences they have undergone, they subscribe to a set of values, particularly as it relates to education and school, which is so different from that prevailing in the predominating middle and upper social groups that for them to adjust to the demands of the school is often a matter of considerable difficulty. And their problems are not made any easier by the fact that the curricular offerings of the school and the demands made upon them are often unrealistic from the standpoint of their background, their goals, and their purposes.

Delinquency and aggression, while understandable from a clinical point of view, pose quite a problem to the classroom teacher. Whereas in clinical work the expression of hostility is often the key to psychotherapy and whereas such clinicians as Homey are of the opinion that unexpressed hostility is the chief cause of anxiety and neurosis, there are limits to the extent to which the teacher can allow feelings of aggression and hostility to be expressed in the classroom so that, no matter how desirable such expression may be from a mental health and personality development standpoint, it has to be curbed. To the extent that a permissive atmosphere exists in the school, the child can express hostility without guilt feelings but, in view of the social situation involved, care must be taken to channel hostility into constructive ends rather than let it interfere with the growth of other children or with the morale of the group. In the meantime, when delinquency or aggression does occur, the teacher needs to remember that it is a symptom of something relatively basic rather than merely an undesirable act. Perhaps the child is acting in accordance with his system of values as derived from his socieconomic and cultural group and may need re-education and a redetermination of his goals and values. He may not even know his behaviour is unacceptable. Perhaps he is trying to tell all concerned that the demands and the standards imposed upon him are unrealistic and that the curriculum is unsuited to his needs. In the same way, the child who is absent frequently because of headaches and other minor ills resulting from his unconscious attempt to avoid a difficult situation, may need understanding and a lightening of the demands made upon him so that he can learn to see the school as a pleasant place in which to be.

In order to be effective, a pupil appraisal programme must be systematic and based on sound theoretical considerations. The problem involved is that of accumulating whatever data are pertinent to the uniqueness of the individual, including his own reactions to these data and to himself as a person. It is necessary to consider all the children—not only the troublemakers as is so often done now—and to make as complete an appraisal of each individual child as possible. Since behaviour involves the whole child, problems in one area are likely to lead to problems in other areas so that an understanding of the child calls for seeing the total child in his total environment. It is also necessary to see him in perspective by considering his present status in terms of his previous experiences, his unresolved difficulties, his present values as well as his present and future goals.

This calls for taking a number of appraisals at different times and in different settings so that we can arrive at an understanding of his typical behaviour patterns rather than be misled by unusual incidents. Furthermore, if we are to understand the child, it is necessary to tap all relevant sources of information, among the more important of which might be mentioned the following:

The Child: Obviously, no other source can give us as good an understanding of the child as the child himself. There is, therefore, need for the teacher to get acquainted with him—in connection with the formal situation prevailing in the classroom and especially under conditions of free atmosphere such as might be found in the homeroom or on the playground. Of course, he does not understand himself too clearly so there is no point in expecting him to give a psychiatrist's explanation of his underlying motives and unresolved conflicts, but his behaviour will provide the competent teacher with the means whereby he can be understood. Informal contacts and interviews conducted in an atmosphere of permissiveness and acceptance can be most valuable: allowing the child whose behaviour has been undesirable to give his side of the story, for example, can give the teacher valuable insights into what makes him tick. Useful information can also be obtained from such instruments as the Money Problem Check List and the various personality and interest inventories available commercially, although these should not be necessary in a grade school where teachers have the same children all day for a whole year.

The Home: The child cannot be understood apart from his home. Therefore, the teacher needs to know the general status of the home, and especially the attitudes which parents and siblings and even the community hold toward the school, toward the teacher, and toward education. He needs to know the parent's views toward such things as discipline, their system of values, their goals, and their general expectations from the child. But most of all he needs to know something about the emotional climate of the home for very often the child's problems at school are very closely related to his problems at home, and, if he is having troubles there, he has all the more need for understanding at school, lest he is sour on all adults.

It is also important that the teacher appraise the socioeconomic and cultural status of the home for, when the home and the school subscribe to different cultural and economic values, the child may be involved in conflict to the extent that accepting the school may appear to him as the equivalent of being disloyal to his home and to his peers. In fact, the teacher needs to remember that no matter how bad the home situation, the child has certain loyalties which he cannot violate without conflict and that he, therefore, needs to be careful in his attempt to reach him and guide his growth toward higher cultural standards.

The Child's Former Teachers: The teachers who have had the child in class should have in their possession considerable data accumulated through observation and other means. In most schools, for instance, teachers are encouraged to write anecdotal records on the children in their classes and, when they are conscientious in the matter, anecdotal information of considerable value in understanding individual children can generally be found in their folders. Unfortunately, anecdotal records tend to be time-consuming and busy teachers often report only the unusual and the negative rather than the more typical aspects of the child's behaviour. Where this is the case, their use should be discouraged, for, unless they are a fair sample of his behaviour and are objective and accurate, they can do him more harm than good. Even at best, care must be taken that they do not prejudice future teachers against certain children and Rogers questions the keeping of records from this standpoint. The same comment can be made with respect to gossip and general impressions often exchanged among teachers.

Tests and Other Formal Instruments: Much of the information we need about the child as, for instance, his intellectual capacity, his special abilities and talents, his academic status, and perhaps his interests and personal adjustment cannot be obtained with sufficient precision by the usual observational and anecdotal techniques just discussed and recourse must be made to more formal and technical instruments. Of course, these instruments have to be used cautiously and with due awareness of their limitations but they provide objective evidence that is certainly indispensable to the classroom teacher, particularly as it is used to confirm data from other sources. There is need for a formal testing programme consisting of standardised tests that will give a broader basis for evaluating progress to supplement the data obtained through the informal, and even the incidental, appraisal made by the teacher, as well as those obtained through rating scales, questionnaires, and inventories.

Of primary interest from the standpoint of the school are the child's motivation, his values, goals, aspirations, and interests as well as his attitudes—for these are the prime determinants of what he will do. Most of these things are, unfortunately, rather difficult to appraise except by means of subjective judgment. Interests, of a vocational nature, for instance, can be measured through a number of standardised interest inventories but other interests have to be appraised through observation of his leisure time activities, or through the analysis of the themes he is asked to write on such topics as 'My Hobbies.'

Probably no more important aspect of this area can be found than the child's attitudes toward the school itself. The attitude of the individual child can usually be determined by observation and interview but when it comes to group attitudes, a more valid appraisal of the morale of the student body and pupil reaction to the various aspects of the school programme can probably be obtained by means of an unsigned questionnaire such as that suggested by Hand, a few sample questions from which are reproduced below.

I In general, how well do you like your school? (Check one).

(1) I like it very much.
(2) I like it.
(3) About half and half.
(4) I dislike it.
(5) I dislike it very much.

II How proud of your school are you? (Check one).

(1) I am very proud of my school.
(2) I am proud of my school.
(3) I am not proud of my school.
(4) I am ashamed of my school.

III If you are proud of your school tell your main reason why.

IV If you are not proud of your school, tell the main reason why. In general, are you satisfied or dissatisfied with the way you are treated by teachers and other school officials? (Check one).

(1) Very well satisfied.
(2) Satisfied.
(3) Half and half.
(4) Dissatisfied.
(5) Very much dissatisfied.

V Do the pupils in your school treat one another fairly and kindly? (Check one).

(1) Yes, practically all of them do.
(2) Yes, most of them do.
(3) Yes, about half of them do.
(4) No, most of them do not.

VI All in all, how well satisfied are you with your school? (Check one).

(1) I am very well satisfied with my school.
(2) I am pretty well satisfied.

(3) About half and half.
(4) 1 am dissatisfied (not satisfied).
(5) I am very much dissatisfied (not satisfied) with my school.

The personality of the child, his emotional balance, and his habitual traits are of immediate concern to the teacher for the bearing which they have on the other aspects of his behaviour and growth. Much of the information which the teacher needs in this area can be obtained by observation, particularly in the grade school. Of course, the teacher needs to be alert to the limitations of observation but, very often, observation is the only means available for obtaining data regarding the child's personality, and all that can be done is to strive to make observation as valid and reliable as possible. Whenever feasible, one's observations should be supplemented by other techniques or confirmed by the observations of others: research in the area of intragroup relations, for instance, has shown the relative inadequacy of teacher observation as a means of appraising the social composition of the classroom.

Additional information can be obtained from having children write themes on such topics as 'My Biggest Problem.' A number of standardised inventories are also available such as the California Test of Personality, the Bell Adjustment Inventory; and others; but most of the more common inventories are rather easy to fake and it is essential that the student be convinced that the only reason for his filling out the inventory is to enable the teacher or counselor to be of greater help to him and that, therefore, it is in his best interest to give candid answers. Even then some faking will take place and the results should be interpreted rather cautiously. At the more advanced level, such tests as the Minnesota Multiphasic Personality Inventory and the projective techniques are relatively more adequate for appraising the personality of the individual but, on the other hand, they require special competence in interpreting the results.

These data should be incorporated into a cumulative folder made available to all teachers who have contact with the child. This folder must be complete, accurate, and concise; otherwise, it will not be worth the teacher's time to consult it. Clerical assistance should be provided for such purposes as putting these data on a profile which will tell at a glance many of the things which an interested person wants to know. Such clerical tasks can be time-consuming and take the teacher away from other things for which he is paid and for which he is better qualified. Unless such help is provided, many teachers will not cooperate or will do only a perfunctory job. A good cumulative record system should provide the teacher with the basic information he needs in dealing with the vast majority of his students. On the other hand, special cases will occur in which he will want to consult with the principal, the counselor, the doctor, or the social worker in order to get new insights into the problem of a given student. At times, it may even be necessary to carry out a case study in which the teacher, the doctor or nurse, the psychologist, the social worker, and perhaps others will each contribute what he knows about a given child. Unfortunately, such detailed studies are extremely time-consuming and can be carried out for a few advanced cases only—often too far advanced for any major improvement to be effected.

7

Practical Learning

In education one of the most pressing problems is to help students develop effective methods for learning. The school demands that the child spend many hours, many days, and many years in learning the subject matter, skills, and attitudes essential for effective living in a civilised community and for active citizenship in a democracy. Then the child goes on to spend many more years learning to be a teacher, a doctor, a lawyer, or a minister. In short, nearly everyone devotes a substantial portion of his life to being a professional learner. Yet, strangely enough, few are ever taught efficient learning procedures.

Is it because nothing is known about the learning process? Not at all. We know a great deal about it. We know that efficient methods of learning can cut in half the time required by inefficient methods. And we know that the speed with which material is forgotten can be greatly reduced.

As a professional teacher, you will use your knowledge of the learning process every day—for arranging your lessons and units, for deciding what materials and activities to include in them, for determining what materials you will assign for study and how you will assign them, for deciding how and when you will help the child to review and to summarise what he has learned, and for preparing and scheduling examinations. And, though in the primary grades the child's minute-to-minute learning activities are carefully planned by his teacher, finally he must become able to learn independently. Thus you must teach each child how to learn most efficiently. You must teach him the best methods for learning how to spell words, how to develop speed and accuracy in multiplication and addition, how to learn his lines for a play, how to organise and learn the essential dates, names, and events in history, how to improve his skill in typewriting, baseball, or dancing, and how to improve his ability to read.

As you can see, you have two important professional uses for your knowledge of the learning process: (1) you will plan your classroom activities so that maximum learning takes place, and (2) you will teach the child how to learn effectively when he himself must plan his approach to the learning task.

You obtain personal as well as professional dividends from a study of effective methods for learning. You, as well as your students, will continue to learn throughout life. When you apply the principles of learning to your own study, you are likely to increase your professional competence. For example, would you expect someone to teach you to swim, to type, or to dance if he himself had never become able to swim, type, or dance? Ordinarily not. You would demand that he know more than the rules and theory of the skill. And so with a knowledge of effective methods for learning. You can best teach the child how to learn effectively and you can best use your knowledge of the learning process in building effective classroom situations if you first learn how to apply this knowledge to the learning that you must do yourself.

Fortunately, the best methods for learning are easy to master, and the time that they save us is ample payment for the few hours that we expend to become familiar with them. As with all new knowledge, though, mere mastery of efficient learning methods is not enough. We must put the effective methods into practice every day over a period of time before they will have any real effect in overcoming the inefficient learning habits that most of us have fallen into. Inefficient habits are stubborn creatures; they hate to be displaced. Luckily, the children in your classroom will not have had so many years in which to build up stubborn, inefficient habits. They will have less resistance to adopting efficient habits and will be more likely to embrace the methods that give the greatest rewards for time spent on study.

So far, we have been talking as though everyone meant just the same thing by the word "learning." True, we all have a fairly clear idea of what the term means, but, as we have discovered before, a precise definition helps us to direct our thinking more accurately. A definition is especially necessary here, since the word learning is so often used to include the effects of maturation as well as the effects of the more conscious, controllable act of learning itself. Thus, we speak of the child's "learning" to walk, but we should recognise that walking is dependent upon maturation as well as upon learning.

What we mean by "learning." Learning is the acquisition of new behaviour patterns, or the strengthening or weakening of old behaviour patterns, as the result of practice.

As we can see, learning includes a wide variety of changes in behaviour. The changes may be readily detected in the overt behaviour of the individual or they may be changes in his stock of ideas. Even a primitive, uncivilised person learns nearly all those actions that enable him to obtain food, clothing, and shelter and to communicate with his fellows. And civilised man learns in addition all those actions that make him different from a primitive man. Our methods for getting along with others, our ability to read, to write, and to use mathematical symbols, our skill in games, our health habits, our attitudes, and our control of our emotions—all are learned.

In our definition, we need to require that the changes in behaviour occur as a result of practice so that we can eliminate those changes that result from physical growth and maturation. However, we recognise that much of what we learn is learnable only after we have reached an adequate level of physical and mental maturity. And though mental or physical action—practice—is a necessary condition for learning, practice alone does not cause learning. Practice may or may not produce changes in behaviour patterns. What, then, are the important determinants of the amount of learning that will take place? Let's examine the learning process.

The learning process. Motives or drives are fundamental to the learning process. If we are to learn, we must first have some goal and then encounter some block that prevents us from attaining that goal. If we encounter no block—no difficulty of any kind—the chances are that we have already learned the behaviour necessary to reach the goal or that we will not learn it until our goal becomes more attractive and more demanding. The block or problem, then, rather than the number of repetitions of the experience, is the essential element in the learning situation. When we consider how little we learn from certain of our experiences, this becomes obvious. We may enter a building many times and be able to recall little concerning the doorway, steps, wall, or floor.

The child or even the adolescent may eat with his fingers and chew with his mouth open. So long as this behaviour is adequate to meet his needs, years of practice result in no improvement in his table manners. But if he becomes aware that his behaviour blocks his attainment of esteem in the eyes of his peers, and if he sees that he can regain their esteem by changing his habits, he strives hard to change and he learns rapidly.

When a child is frustrated in his attempts to reach an attractive goal, he changes. His muscular tension increases; he is less comfortable and less relaxed than he was before the block arose. He seeks a solution. Either he must destroy the block, climb over it, go around it—or find a new goal. He may simply try out one route around the block to his goal and, if that fails, try another. Or he may make intelligent use of his past experiences. If, as a direct, or accidental, result of his trial-and-error behaviour, he overcomes the block and reaches the goal, his search is ended and his muscular tension is reduced. He learns in two ways from this experience: (1) he learns how to solve his present problem, and (2) he learns a *procedure* for attacking future problems. What is there in this experience that is important to his future learning procedure? Simply this: The last attempt the child makes—the attempt immediately preceding success and the lessening of tension—is the one that he is most likely to repeat the next time tension arises, especially if either the goal or the block is similar to those he encountered in this problem.

For example, consider the baby who receives attention or food only when he cries. He soon learns to cry regularly in response to any problem that he encounters. Or suppose that a boy has a strong desire to get on the school football team. He is motivated by his need for the esteem of fellow students and also by the interesting experiences that he may enjoy. But he is blocked by his inadequate size and lack of skill in dodging, tackling, and handling the football. His past experiences and general intelligence will determine the extent to which his attempts to solve his problem are planned or random. His personality and the length of time that elapses before he sees a solution will determine the extent of his general tension. But there will be some tension and it will increase if his search for a solution fails. He has several possibilities for reducing his tension. He may choose a substitute goal, convince himself that it is worthy, and gain esteem and new experiences from it. Or he may make a direct attack on the problem. He decides that he can gain weight during the summer by eating heavily and that he can become stronger by doing heavy lifting. He gets a football, rigs up a tackling dummy, and practices the fundamental skills that are required. Then, when the football season begins, he attempts to make up for his inexperience by trying particularly hard.

If his efforts are successful, when he is faced with a similar problem in the future he is likely to adopt the same general type of attack that was successful in solving this problem. Why did he try so hard and why did he learn so many things? Because the goal appealed powerfully to many of his motives and because he met many problems as he sought to reach it.

In short, the learning process involves a motive or drive, an attractive goal, and a block to the attainment of the goal. All three aspects of the learning process are essential.

This general pattern of learning dominates the whole of human behaviour—from birth to death. It affects the personalities and adjustments of children and adults alike. It dictates how successful children will be in learning the simplest facts and the most complex skills, in school or out of school. Acts that lead to a satisfaction of needs tend to be repeated and acts that do not lead to satisfaction tend to be discarded. Although the pattern itself seems simple enough, we discover that we are dealing with what is really an extremely complex process when we try to understand and guide human behaviour, with its infinite variety of experien-ces, attitudes, abilities, and goals.

Solving problems by manipulating ideas. When we were discussing the learning process, we used the expression "trial and error", and mentioned that learning often involves physical movement and several failures (errors) before the learner finally reaches his goal. Not all learning, however, involves such plodding, painstaking behaviour. Human beings are able to profit from past experiences. We can retain our experiences in the form of ideas. Then, when we meet familiar situations in the future, we can reach down into our store of experience and come up with appropriate ideas. And we can manipulate our ideas and in so doing find suitable solutions to a relatively new problem. Thus, learning may take place through the manipulation of ideas. The familiar pattern of motive-goal-block is still present, but we work through the process with little or no overt physical activity.

A boy may encounter the problem of obtaining an apple from a tree. He may reach for the apple, throw stones at it, climb the tree, or get a pole long enough to knock the apple from the tree. Or he may rapidly manipulate ideas involving all these possibilities without appearing to move. He may recall that he can't reach objects six feet above his head, that his thrown stone will be deflected by the lower branches of the tree, that climbing trees is hard on clothes and brings disappro-val, and that his brother once retrieved his fish line from a tree by using a fishing pole. In fact, his past experiences and general ability to see relationships may allow him to see the correct solution without trying inadequate solutions.

Our first or our thousandth manipulation of ideas or attempts to motor solutions may be successful. And, through the manipulation, our ideas take new forms—we learn. Likewise, ideas manipulation and motor attempts may be, and quite likely will be, going on at the same time. Then the learning comes from a combination of the ideational and the motor attempts.

Science as a Tool

Laboratory experiments have produced valuable data on learning and forgetting. Though most of the laboratory experiments have used relatively meaningless (nonsense) materials, the findings help us understand what takes place in the learning and forgetting of the meaningful materials of the classroom and of life. Actually, the basic difference between the meaningless materials of the laboratory and the meaningful materials of the classroom is that in the classroom we deal with situations that are similar to those we have encountered previously. That is what makes them meaningful. If we were not already familiar with it, the combination c-a-t used in the classroom and the nonsense syllable j-i-x used in the laboratory would be equally meaningless. And if we had not already had considerable experience with finding our way on country roads or city streets, the problem of learning our way about a new city would be as meaningless as the laboratory problem of learning our way through a maze.

For these reasons, a knowledge of some of the findings of the psychological laboratory can form a useful basis for a discussion of the learning of meaningful materials.

Learning curves. Learning curves usually are drawn on a graph, with the base line divided into units of time or the number of trials required for learning. The vertical scale is divided into appropriate units of accomplishment—puzzles solved, material retained, and so on. The curve drawn against these two scales gives us a handy way of comparing, for example, accomplishment at the end of various time periods.

Learning curves that report the learning activity of one person over a relatively short time are likely to be very rough, since drastic changes may be caused by accidental distractions or temporary loss of motivation. If we want to get a stable, meaningful picture, we have to take the learning achievement of many persons (or of one person on many different tests), find the average achievement at the end of each trial or time period, and then make a graph based on these averages.

Age and learning ability. Is there a best age for learning? For a long time it was believed that certain ages were best for learning poetry but that other ages were better for learning, say, arithmetic or geography. Many studies have been made of learning ability and its relation to the age of the learner.

It appears that the ability to learn new and unfamiliar materials increases until about age 16 and then remains very nearly the same until the late 20's. Then there is a slight drop with each year, until at about age 70 the drop becomes rather sharp. The sharp drop occurs when senility, sometimes called second childhood, is reached. We must be cautious in interpreting this graph, however. Remember that it represents the average for a great many persons. The learning ability of some individuals, especially those who are engaged in activities that require the learning of new materials, may continue to increase far beyond the age of 16 and may not decline until much later in life than is shown to be the lot of the average person. The beginning of senility in individual cases may come at a much earlier or much later age than that indicated on the graph. In learning outside the laboratory we seldom encounter completely new materials. Consider the learning tasks that you are called upon to face. You can understand scientific concepts and you can solve problems of dealing with adults—you can learn—at a level far beyond what you could at age 16. Why is this true? Obviously it is because of what you have learned since you were 16. The situations you now meet contain far fewer new elements than they would have had if you had been forced to meet them at age 16. We have here a basic principle of education. The average child, at a rather early age, ceases to increase in sheer mental power. But if we can help him to gain an ever-increasing background of skills, knowledge, and social experiences, we prepare him to handle problems of ever-increasing complexity.

How is this curve of learning ability useful to us in the classroom? It shows us how the ability to learn new materials tends to rise from infancy to maturity. It tells us that the average 14-year-old child can learn new materials of any kind faster than the average 10-year-old can.

But obviously we cannot wait until the time of maximum learning ability before we introduce the child to the school curriculum. There is too much for him to learn, and much of the learning demanded of the 16-year-old depends directly on what he has learned years before. Certain types of learning, such as writing, playing a piano, singing, swimming, and dancing, involve motor skills as well as mental development. If the child fails to begin to learn such skills at an early age, special muscle groups may not be developed and coordinated by the time that he reaches his maximum learning ability. In addition, if he is to attain great skill in such activities, he must continue to practice for a long time after the basic learning has been achieved.

And there are other factors to consider. The young child who is interested in playing an instrument or skating will devote more time to learning these skills than will the average older person. By distributing his practice time over a number of years, he will attain greater mastery than if he had begun only after he had reached maturity. In the classroom, then, we must work with children who have not yet achieved their maximum ability to learn new materials. Yet their success after they have reached that maximum depends largely on how rich their previous learning has been.

Perfect Process

Although Motivation and learning ability are important determinants of learning efficiency, other factors also have a strong influence. Fortunately, nearly all these are factors over which we can exercise some control in the classroom.

The value of recall. Effortful recall is a powerful deter-minant of learning and retention; it pays tremendous dividends per unit of time consumed. One of the important values of a good examination is that it requires recall or an attempt to recall. Similarly, classroom discussion requires the student to recall previously learned information and to apply it to new problems. Recitation is an important method for inducing recall. The teacher uses the recitation to clarify and strengthen learning and the skillful student uses it in his independent study. Recall also takes place when the learner rehearses mentally the physical movements demanded by a game or skill. And review, though it often includes new learning, owes much of its effectiveness to the recall of information that already has been learned.

Ordinarily, recall results in a highly motivated form of additional practice with a special problem introduced—that of attempting to reconstruct a situation from our ideas alone. The educational psychologist sometimes refers to recall as "study with the book closed."

An experiment performed many years ago indicates that when the learner alternates between reading and recitation he is far more successful than when he uses all his available time for reading alone. Other investigators have reported similar findings.

Table

The Effectiveness of Time Spent in Reading Vs. Various Proportions of Time Spent in Recall During the Study of Biographical Sketches as Measured Immediately After Learning

Percentage of Time Spent in		*Scores*				
Recall	*Reading*	*Grade 8*	*Grade 6*	*Grade 5*	*Grade 4*	*Grade 3*
0	100	88	89	80	86	75
20	80	95	98	95	100	89
40	60	105	106	104	97	97
60	40	105	104	109	111	122
80	20	107	105	105	104	113
90	10	100	98	107	102	104

To make it easy for us to compare the learning that took place under each of the five methods, the experimenter computed the average score made by the pupils in each grade under all five methods and called that 100. Thus a score of 88 (average score for grade eight using no recall) is seen to be only 88 per cent as effective as the average under all methods and 88/107 as good (about 82 per cent) as the score when the pupils used 80 per cent of their time for recall.

We can see from Table that in each grade, when the children spent from 40 to 90 per cent of their study time in attempting to recall the material, they made far better scores on a test given immediately following the learning than they did when they spent all their time reading the material. The material studied by each grade was of the same general type— highly factual biographical sketches. However, the students in the upper grades had longer and more difficult sketches than did the students in the lower grades. We can see that a test following learning shows that recall was very effective indeed.

Table

The Effectiveness of Time Spent in Reading Vs. Various Proportions of Time Spent in Recall During the Study of Biographical Sketches as Measured About Four Hours After Learning

Percentage of Time Spent in		*Scores*				
Recall	*Reading*	*Grade 8*	*Grade 6*	*Grade 5*	*Grade 4*	*Grade 3*
0	100	80	74	71	79	62
20	80	96	79	81	95	76
40	60	127	113	104	100	107
60	40	131	123	122	116	123
80	20	129	119	107	107	117
90	10	121	102	115	102	114

What about the retention of such material when a test is given at a later time? Table reports the scores made by these same students on a second test given from three to four hours after the test reported in Table.

Table indicates that recitation did much more than increase the speed of learning. Materials thus learned were much better remembered than were materials learned through reading alone. The recitation, then, reduced the time needed for learning and increased the persistence of learning. Why? There are several reasons.

First, the conscious use of recall during the process of study demands that the act of reading be effortful. It prevents the reader from letting his eyes dance lightly along from word to word while he focuses his thoughts on last night's party or tomorrow's football game. It holds his attention to the business at hand. It obliges him to set specific goals and to make an immediate evaluation of his progress toward them.

Second, recall that is followed by a re-reading gives the learner a chance to check immediately on the accuracy of his learning. Correct information is confirmed and incorrect information is rejected.

Third, recall requires greater muscular activity than does reading alone. As the learner tries to repeat the material, often in his own words, he tends to use at least his throat muscles in the process.

Fourth, when the learner recalls material by himself he builds up confidence in his ability to recall it at a later time. There is less chance that panic will rob him of his learning when he tries to draw on it for an examination or a real-life situation.

Here is a particularly good example of how we can use our knowledge of the learning process both to teach children how to learn and to build effective learning situations. For example, the child should be shown (probably as early as the second or third grade) that the most effective way to study spelling is to read each word carefully with close attention to how it is spelled and then to get someone else to pronounce the words while he writes them. Or, if he cannot get someone else to do this, he can cover a word with a card and write it after a quick glance at the word. Later on, the children are taught to make liberal use of recall for learning poems or lines in a play. And in the process of work-type reading, the child is taught to read a paragraph and then to test himself over the content. The teacher, of course, can provide for recall in many ways—examinations, summaries by the child, and class discussion, to mention a few.

The advantages of distributed practice. In any learning situation, the amount of study time available is limited. What is the best way to use it? If Mary has five hours a week to spend on learning a given assignment, should she spend it all at once or space it into five equal parts of one hour each, or work out some other arrangement?

This is a hard question to answer. No one solution is satisfactory for all types of learning tasks. There is evidence, however, that for most learning activities a certain amount of practice spread over a period of time is much more effective than the same amount of practice crammed into a short period of time. In learning motor skills, such as typewriting, skating/or dancing, far better results are obtained through spending a few hours each week for a number of years than by spending five times as many hours per week in one-fifth the same number of years. And the effectiveness of the more gradual learning seems to persist for a longer time after the practice has ended. However, if sufficient motivation is present, and if the child does not become tired of the task, he will obviously achieve more learning in 30 minutes than in 15.

Certainly if the learner's goal is to achieve permanent mastery of meaningful materials, he will secure better results through distributed practice than through massed practice. However, forgetting takes place rapidly after any type of learning. So if the learner's goal is merely to pass a test at some definite future date, he will obtain the best results by using the total available time shortly before the test. That is one reason why "cramming" before an examination is so popular. Cramming is the result of a short-term philosophy of learning that some students have developed and that poor teaching procedures have encoura-ged. So far as results measured on the test are concerned, massed practice is definitely the most economical technique. The results of the practice are fresh in the student's mind, and the student is highly motivated by the knowledge that this is the last chance he has to learn before the hour of reckoning.

In terms of permanent values, however, cramming is disastrous. The student whose aim is only to reach an immediate goal is already disposed to forget what he has learned as soon as it seems safe. As a result, he finds that the courses and examinations he encounters in the future are based on material that is less and less meaningful to him, since he fails to retain what he has learned in the past.

In planning the effective learning situation, the teacher must make numerous decisions concerning the most valuable use of classroom time. Sometimes, as in the case where a school play is to be given or a poem is to be learned, interest would be lost if the learning were spread over too long a time. But for most classroom learnings, we can distribute practice advantageously. By using frequent short examinations rather than infrequent longer ones, we can guarantee that practice will be spread over a longer period of time. And we distribute practice as well as encourage recall when we see that the child uses previous learning to attack new problems. For example, in the primary grades we teach the child to use initial sounds and endings of words as a cue to pronouncing new words. Rather than spending a long period of time in learning all these sounds, the effective teacher distributes their learning over many weeks, introducing one initial sound every day or two and seeing that the child develops his understanding of them by letting him give the initial sound and the ending of words that he does not recognise. The teacher will find that distributed practice is particularly effective when a rather large unit of material, such as the atomic weights of the various elements studied in a chemistry class or the vocabulary of a foreign language, is to be learned.

The influence of mental set. An active intent to learn is much more likely to result in success than is mere passive attention. We may ride the same bus to and from school for many weeks, watching the houses along the way or even sitting beside the driver. Yet, if we were called upon to take the wheel and to follow the usual route, we would encounter difficulty. Had we been at the wheel during the first trip and forced to find our way, and had we known that we would be called upon to repeat the trip at a later time, we would have learned the route much more quickly. Similarly, if we read one book with the knowledge that we will be tested on it the next day and also a year later, and if we read another with the understanding that we will be tested on it the next day only, our memory of the material from the first book will persist for a longer time.

There is another way in which mental set affects the student's learning. Students approach their study in different ways. One decides to study a lesson for two hours; merely putting in the time becomes his primary objective. His attention focuses more on the clock than on his lesson. Another has specific purposes to accomplish during his study. He is searching for questions that may be asked on the material or he is attempting to condense the material into his own words. The mental set of the latter certainly is far more conducive to effective learning.

How we forget. If there was no such thing as forgetting, the task of the learner and of the teacher would be simple indeed. But the problem of forgetting dominates the whole process of learning. Some forgetting even takes place during the actual learning of material. The learning curves that we talked about before are influenced by the process of forgetting. If they were not, it would be as easy to learn five new words the second five minutes of learning time as it was the first five minutes. But we find that not only must we learn new things but we must also remember, re-learn, or keep from forgetting the old. Names we know today are gone next year, and the facts we knew last night have vanished before today's examination. Early studies of forgetting served toillustrate the size of the problem.

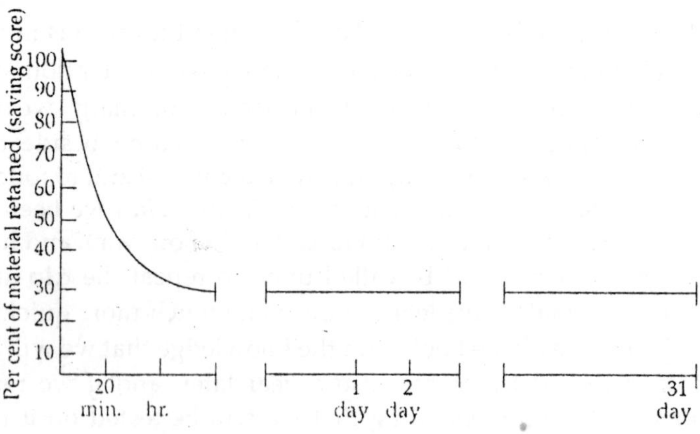

Fig. *The Ebbinghaus curve of forgetting.*

Ebbinghaus derived his curve from experiments in which he was both the observer and the learner. To simplify his task, he invented what is known as the nonsense syllable, which insists of a vowel between two consonants, such as x-o-y, j-b, or c-i-z. He arranged these syllables into lists of various lengths. He studied a list, recorded the date, hour, minute, and the number of readings that were necessary before he was able to repeat all the syllables (through spelling them out), and then laid the list aside. He followed the same procedure in learning list after list. From time to time, he tested his memory of the lists he had previously learned. Since he never learned a list beyond the level necessary to repeat it once, and since in the meantime he had learned other lists, ordinarily he could not remember any of the syllables in an earlier list until after he had re-read it at least once or twice. It began to appear that he remembered nothing! However, when he tried to relearn a list, he found that he was able to master it much more easily than he could master a list he had never learned before. This was an indication that he had not completely forgotten it.

In order to determine how much was left of his original learning, Ebbinghaus used what is called a saving score. If he required 25 readings to learn a list, and 15 to relearn it, he assumed that, he had saved the results of 10 readings, or 40 per cent of his original learning effort. In making a graph of his memory of this list, he would say that he had made a saving score of 40.

Ebbinghautrus study was published in 1885, long before most areas of psychology had developed highly scientific methods. It is a classic example of careful and thorough experimentation. Even with other types of material, either meaningful or nonsense, the general shape of the Ebbinghaus curve is still found to apply.

We should not conclude from the Ebbinghaus curve that during the 20 minutes after learning we forget 40 per cent of meaningful material, or that we forget 80 per cent by the end of a month. The important fact is that we do forget at a relatively rapid rate immediately following learning and at a much slower rate as time goes on. If we can determine the amount we have forgotten at some specific time after learning, we can estimate how much we would have forgotten during some longer or shorter period of time. For example, if approximately 60 per cent (20 minutes for Ebbinghaus' materials and methods) of meaningful material is remembered at the end of a month, we might predict that without review 42 per cent (60 minutes by the Ebbinghaus curve) will be recalled at the end of three months.

Many factors contribute to the high percentage of forgetting observed by Ebbinghaus. These factors will be discussed in greater detail under their individual headings later in the present chapter.

Why we forget. For many years, it was customary for psychologists to say that forgetting was caused by disuse. But scientific attention to the problem, especially during recent years, indicates that disuse is far from being the cause or even a cause of forgetting.

As time passes, wood is eaten by termites, houses are consumed by fire, people grow old, and men forget. However, none of these changes are caused by the lapse of time. Granted, if termites are present they consume more wood in two years than in one. But the termites rather than time consume the wood. To attribute any of these changes to the lapse of time is to fail to recognise the true cause-and-effect relationship.

Almost all psychologists now agree that interference is the cause of nearly all our ordinary, day-to-day forgetting. Both past learnings and future learnings interfere with the memory of what we learn today. The interference is much greater between some types of material and for some methods of learning than it is for others. What conditions determine the degree to which one learned act interferes with another?

Similarity of materials. When we were talking about Ebbinghaus, we mentioned that one reason he forgot a large proportion of the nonsense syllables he had learned was that between the time of original learning and the time of recall he studied many new lists of nonsense syllables. Materials that we learn just after or just before we learn similar materials are particularly likely to be forgotten. Suppose that on Wednesday the children in your classroom learn the poem "America." Ordinarily, you could expect them to remember most of the poem on Friday. However, if on Thursday they learn "The Star-Spangled Banner", they will remember "America" less accurately than if they had not studied the second poem. Moreover, they will remember less of the second poem than if they had not learned the first on Wednesday. Had one of the poems been humorous rather than serious, or had one been sung and the other spoken, the degree of similarity, and, consequently, the amount of interference between the two would have been reduced.

Degree of learning. Another important factor that influences forgetting is the degree to which material has been learned. If one poem is learned thoroughly over a period of a few days, it is not likely to be forgotten when a second poem is learned. Here is a strong argument for thoroughness in learning. Thoroughly learned materials are less easily interfered with and consequently are remembered better than are partially learned materials. In addition, well-learned materials do less damage to other learning, past or future, than do poorly learned materials. And we can see why this would be true. As we become acquainted with them, two brothers, two buildings, or two poems become less similar. We become increasingly aware of the differences between them.

The value of review. Careful review is a valuable aid to memory, particularly when it is begun soon after the initial learning. Figure illustrates how the shape of the curve of forgetting is changed by review. Curve I (which you will recognise as the Ebbinghaus curve) shows the rapid decrease in the percentage retained during the period immediately following initial learning. Curve II shows how the curve is altered when the material is reviewed to the point where it is as well remembered as when it was first learned. Curve III represents the still slower drop that takes place after a second review.

The first review should take place soon after learning, in order to avoid the great loss that takes place during the initial period of rapid forgetting. To be most effective, a review must be more than a second exposure to familiar material. It should provide for recall or an attempt to recall followed by an opportunity to confirm or reject what is recalled. But it goes beyond this. Although no new materials are presented, during a review the child learns many

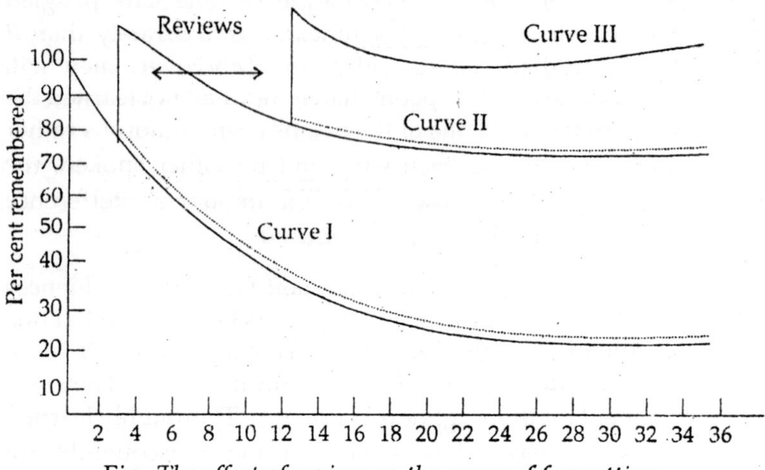

Fig. *The effect of review on the curve of foregetting.*

things for the first time, since he will seldom have learned all that is available during the previous exposure. In addition, new applications and understandings will be developed during the review.

The summary near the end of the class period, the review of yesterday's accomplishments before the beginning of today's problem, the examination, and the use of previous learnings to attack new problems—all are review activities that are under the teacher's control. And you will teach the child to review independently. You will teach him how to organise what he has learned and preserve it in notes and you will teach him how and when to review those notes. If you teach in the junior or senior high school, you may help the child to make a schedule of his study time. In such a schedule, time should be allowed at the end of each evening's study for a review of today's class notes and of the preparation that he has made for tomorrow's work. Also, an hour or two each week should be identified for the review of all the course notes for the semester or the year. When supervised study time is available, we schedule a regular portion of it for review and we have review lessons in our classroom whether or not we supervise the child's study. Frequently, we use such a review lesson before we begin a new unit.

Combining sensory experiences. Do we learn best by seeing or by hearing? The evidence is not entirely clear. There does, however, appear to be abundant evidence that the more sense organs we can use in the learning process, the better we will retain the material.

Hearing and seeing are better than either alone; and hearing, seeing, and saying the words that we hear are still better. One reason may be that when we undergo an experience through a combination of the senses it is more nearly unique and thus has fewer similarities to other learning situations. By emphasising the ways in which an experience differs, we can reduce the amount of interference with other learning experiences. For example, if a poem is to be learned, we can get different types of sensory experiences from hearing a recording of it as read by its author, from singing it individually and in a group, from reading it aloud, and from reading it silently.

The combining of sensory experiences is not limited to obtaining experiences from different senses. We can also obtain different experiences through the same sense. Motion pictures greatly extend the visual experience that a child can gain from his reading of geography, history, and literature. And he can combine his reading with many other sensory experiences. Classroom collections of insects, textiles, manufactured products of oil, iron, or coal, and visits to zoos, factories, and farms will reinforce learning through introducing touch, smell, and an entirely new visual and auditory experience.

Guided learning. Experiments have been conducted in which students were carefully prevented from making mistakes. For example, in teaching a child to write the letters of the alphabet, we might cut stencils of the letters so that by tracing with his pencil he will always obtain perfect letters. If we are teaching a boy to jump over a bar, we might tie him to a machine that would force his legs, arms, and head through exactly the right motions of the most approved type of roll. Such guided learning might conceivably be used to teach many different motor skills. Psychologists have tried to discover whether or not it is desirable to prevent errors in this manner. The conclusions are that it is not. Although the child may learn to trace perfect letters time after time, he will not necessarily show any improvement in his ability to write freehand. We must learn about our errors and how we can avoid them as well as learn the correct responses.

Obviously, we need to have examples of excellent performance both in the learning of skills and in our social learnings. We need to see how a good jumper or basketaball player performs; we need to see graceful and correct social behaviour. But much of our learning time must be given to the recognition and elimination of our own errors—errors that are peculiar to us and that the examples seldom bring to our attention.

This is a concrete application of the principles of motivation. The problem is an essential part of the learning situation!

Basic Principles

We have studied why and how people learn. We have examined many conditions that are favourable to learning and retention. Can we now identify common elements in the learning situations that we have discussed? Actually, psychologists long ago attempted to do this. Certain principles or "laws" of learning have been identified. You can gain a better understanding of the learning process by studying these principles, but if you merely memorise them as pet statements, they will be valueless to you in the classroom. However, if you orient your thinking around them, and use them as points of reference, they will help you to organise your knowledge of the learning process.

The law of effect. When a response to a situation is accompanied or followed by a satisfied feeling, that response tends to be repeated; but when it is accompanied or followed by an unsatisfied feeling, the response tends to be eliminated.

We have seen many of the applications of this principle. Our motives demand satisfaction. And when we are able to satisfy them, we have pleasant, satisfied feeling. When we fail to satisfy them, we have an unpleasant, unsatisfied feeling. We tend to adopt—to learn—any behaviour that leads us to goals that satisfy our motives. We tend to eliminate any behaviour that fails to lead us to a desirable goal. And we tend to eliminate behaviour that results in threats or punishment.

How does this law account for the many unpleasant tasks that we learn to perform? As we have seen, human needs are extremely complex. Our actions are seldom energised by a single motive. In striving to attain large goals, we often must identify and reach smaller, more immediate goals. Although our behaviour at any time may conflict with certain of our motives, we retain this behaviour if it satisfies other more powerful motives. And although a goal that we seek may itself appear unpleasant, actually it attracts us, for it marks a point on our journey toward some very attractive goal. For example, a child may find a scolding or even a spanking rewarding if it gains for him the much more important attention that he has been denied; a boy may find the rough physical contact of football or boxing satisfying in spite of the pain; and a girl may deny herself social engagements that she craves if in so doing she attains great satisfaction from good grades, the promise of a career as a singer, or the earning of money.

The law of exercise. When a connection between a situation and a response is repeated, the connection is strengthened, other things being equal; but when the connection is not used over a period of time, it is weakened. (This law is sometimes called the law of "use and disuse.")

The Ebbinghaus curve of forgetting demonstrates how this law operates when the connection is not used over a period of time. The value of review, and even the fact that learning takes place with practice, illustrate how the connection is strengthened by use. Note that the law does not say that the disuse causes the forgetting. If the connection is not repeated now and then, something happens that leads to a weakening in the connection. And we know that the repetition of the connection—the practice—does not necessarily lead to improvement. But when a response is repeated time and again, it does tend to become habitual. The child who is taught to brush his teeth following each meal finally comes to brush his teeth without being told and even feels some tension if he is prevented from doing so. However, if for some reason, he does not brush his teeth for a period of time, the habit dies. If a child meets numerous social situations in a friendly and relaxed fashion, that approach finally becomes a well-established personality trait. If he withdraws from one social situation after another, that trait too becomes habitual.

The law of readiness. Once an attractive goal has been identified, to attain it is pleasant, to fail is annoying.

This law has special implications for us as teachers because it emphasises the importance of preparing the student to learn. If he does not have a felt need to learn—in short, if he is not ready—it is unlikely that he will learn very much. Preparing the pupil for learning is the first step in good teaching procedure. It is for this reason that many skilled teachers spend so much classroom time in presenting assignments. They set the stage, arouse curiosity, and in other ways appeal to the needs of the child. Once the child feels a readiness to learn, the teacher may need to do little more than offer occasional guidance and encouragement.

The law of belonging. When we are able to perceive relationships, the speed of learning and the permanence of retention are greatly increased.

The recognition of cause and effect elements, the seeing of relationships between the parts and the total, and the perceiving of familiar elements in new situations—all these factors greatly increase the speed of learning and the permanence of retention.

If the child is to make real use of the information and skills that he learns in the classroom, they must be related in some significant way to his previous learning. They must "belong" to the context of learning that he has already experienced. Isolated facts can be learned only by rote; new facts and skills are meaningful only when they appear in the company of familiar facts and skills with which the learner already feels at home.

The learnability of materials. In addition to the four laws of learning, there are various determinants of the learnability of materials. A knowledge of how to use these determinants to influence the behaviour of others is an important part of the stock-in-trade of the politician, the salesman, the advertiser, and the writer. And they will be of practical value to you in preparing and presenting your classroom materials. Here they are:

Duration—The longer a person is exposed to new material, the better he will learn it. Though the ten-year-old child learns less rapidly than the 14-year-old, with sufficient time he can learn very difficult skills and concepts. And though the dull child learns less rapidly than the bright child of the same age, he too can learn and learn thoroughly. Since he must have more time, however, we must give him less that is new each day.

Frequency—The more often a child encounters a given body of material the more likely he will be to remember it. Notice how this rule is used by advertisers. A supposed characteristic of a product—an advertising slogan—is repeated many times on the same radio or television programme. And then this same slogan appears on billboards and in newspapers and magazines. Politicians and propagandists use this same principle. What they wish to have believed they state again, and again, and again! When we teach a child a new technique— the use of percentage, for example—we provide him with a number of problems all involving the same principle.

Recency—The more recently a child has studied new material, the more likely he will be to remember it. The child learns to review before an examination, we review our notes just before making an oral report, the pianist reviews a selection that he is to play in tonight's concert—in each case more effort is required to have the material fresh in mind than to gain new learnings or greater skill.

Contrast—The more strongly one portion of a situation contrasts with another portion of the situation, the more likely a child is to remember it. Thus, uniqueness of a part of a situation as compared to the remainder, or of one situation as compared to other situations, is an important factor in our learning of it. We remember a situation if it is different from those we usually encounter; we remember people who are different from others in the group. A part of the value that comes from using visual and auditory aids in our classroom situations comes from the fact that they make each situation stand out as different from others.

Vividness—The greater the impact of new material on the child, the better the chance that he will learn it. In the classroom we ordinarily use a sensory impact, though in life situations the vividness may come from the extreme pleasantness or unpleasantness of the experience. The advertiser uses colour, loudness, music, and humour to give vividness to his message. The effective teacher makes learning vivid with motion pictures, recordings, coloured charts, and three-dimensional models. His students perform experiments, learn in a social setting, go on field trips, see government in action, make collections, and prepare exhibits.

One important qualification: These general rules of learnability hold only when other things are equal. For example, a child may remember very vivid material that he studied many months ago much better than he remembers dreary, uninteres-ting material that he studied, as recently as yesterday. When we say that material to which we have been exposed twice is more likely to be remembered than material to which we have been exposed but a single time, we imply that both materials possessed the same or nearly the same degree of recency, duration, vividness, and contrast.

How do learning experiences in the school prepare children to solve the problems they will meet in later life? How successful are human beings in transferring the material they have learned in one situation to another?

At one time it was assumed that the function of education was to provide exercise for the mind. The idea was that schoo-ling would strengthen the mind and prepare it to meet success-fully any problem that might arise. What was learned in school was considered less important than the exercise required in learning it. Solving unusual problems in arithmetic, learning to spell difficult words, and memorising selections in Latin and Greek were accepted as educationally worthwhile, not because the problems, the words, and foreign language would be valuable to the child, but because it was believed that his memory could be sharpened and his reasoning ability would be developed in the process of mastering them.

We have discovered that education is not as simple as that. A child may memorise a thousand poems, yet his memory of what he reads in his books and sees in the world about him will not be improved in the least, and he can solve thousands of difficult mathematical problems with no improvement in his ability to solve social problems.

We now recognise that the materials to be learned in the school must be selected on the basis of their ultimate worth in preparing the individual for life. And we know that to make these materials most available to the child when he needs them, we must make the situations in which the child learns as life-like as possible. To be able to solve new problems in later life, he must not only know many things, he must recognise which of those many things applies to each problem. For example, we know that if the child is to remember and use—transfer—what he learns about percentage when he later is called upon to decide what interest rate he is to pay for a so-called "easy-payment plan", he must have learned percentage and how it applies to life situations. He must be given far more than the rules to memorise and meaningless exercises to solve. We know that if he later is to become able to talk effectively to a group of his fellows, he must practice speaking in a social situation—memorisation of grammatical rules alone is inadequate.

As you can see, to provide for maximum transfer we cannot make the learnings of the classroom ends in themselves. We must select the materials, skills, and habits that we will teach the child on the basis of their value to him in meeting his life problems. We know that if they are to be retained and used, learnings must be taught in a setting that is as near as possible to the life situations that he is preparing to meet. The learnings of the classroom must have belongingness in life situations.

This places a great deal of responsibility on us as teachers. And it has resulted in tremendous changes in curriculum and general teaching procedures. For example, we now teach the child to spell only those words that he will most often use. And we teach spelling in a situation as like as possible to the life situations in which he will use it—he writes the words rather than spells them orally and he uses them in sentences, pronounces them, and knows their meaning. We take this same approach in all our teaching—we select those materials, attitudes, habits, motor and social skills, ideals, and standards of life most needed for a happy and productive life and we teach them in a social situation.

Thus our modern school curriculum includes only such learnings as have maximum value for life, and the professional teacher sees that the child learns in problem situations and not by rote.

In the present chapter we have studied the learning process itself. We have a professional need for a knowledge of the learning process as a basis for the building of effective and efficient learning situations. And we must teach the child to learn effectively when he approaches learning problems without our guidance.

The general principles will of course be the same whether the child or the teacher decides the learning procedure to be used, for always it is the child who must do the learning. But let's summarise the conditions that are most favourable to maximum learning and retention.

The problems that the child solves as he strives to reach goals are the core of the learning process, because only through meeting problems does he change his behaviour. If we can set goals that challenge the child yet appear attainable, we are assured that he will meet problems. And we teach him to set goals for himself—to make questions on the material that he studies, to outline, to take notes, and to develop special interests and to pursue them.

Recall is a powerful aid to learning. We plan our lessons and units to make maximum use of recall and we teach the child to read, check (recall), and re-read. And a mental set to learn and to remember is important. Such a set will be present when the child learns in order to achieve goals that appeal to him. We choose for learning only those things that are most likely to meet the future needs of the child. But we make sure that these same learnings satisfy present needs for new experiences, recognition, and self-esteem. We plan out-of-school assignments so that they are interesting projects to be completed rather than an hour's reading to accomplish.

We know that the primary cause of forgetting is interference and that maximum interference occurs when learning experiences are similar to one another. But when materials are well learned they are less similar to other materials than they are when poorly learned. If we use a wide variety of sensory experiences the learnings will be less similar and thus interfere less with each other. And if we consider carefully the child's ability and govern the quantity of what he learns by his ability to. learn, we can encourage each child to learn thoroughly.

For maximum retention the child must see relationships—between old and new learnings and between cause and effect. We build new learnings on old and we teach the child to search for the relationships within situations and the relationships between what he knows and the new situations.

Time invested in review pays great dividends in cutting down on the speed of forgetting. We plan class activities so that review is guaranteed and we show the child how and when to review. But the ultimate test of what is learned in the school is its value to the child in later life. We recognise that not only must we choose wisely those things that he is to learn but that we must teach in a setting that is as life-like as possible.

The purpose of the present chapter has been to examine the learning process. We shall look for ways in which we can use this knowledge to build effective learning situations in classrooms.

Various Theories

Many a question. What goes in the process of learning? How do we learn? How can a child learn to solve mathematical problems? How does a girl learn to cook the food or sew the clothes? The answers to which need a thorough explanation of the phenomena of learning. Psychologists have tried to perform experiments for throwing light on the phenomenon of learning and as a result have developed various learning theories. Each theory, with its systematic body of knowledge, explains the nature and process of learning. Those theories represent broad principles and techniques of learning. The set of rules and the laws of learning, having wide applicability, are drawn from these theories. In other sense, these theories can put forth various methods of learning and suggest the teacher and learner to take proper steps for the effective learning.

Modern learning theories may be classified into two broad types, namely-

(a) Stimulus response - associationist type of theories.

(b) Gestalt field or field cognition type of theories.

The Conditions

Ivan Pavlov, a renowned psychologist of Soviet Russia won the Nobel Prize in 1909 for his work on the psychology of digestion. In his research on digestion, Pavlov used a minor surgical procedure that enabled him to collect samples of salivary fluid from the dogs that were his experimental subjects. During the course of experiment he found that the dog is not only salivating while taking food, but is also salivating at distinctly natural stimulus like sight of food, sound of the care-takers approaching with food, etc. This aroused his curiosity to conduct the experiments and ultimately propounded the conditioning theory of learning. Since Pavlov's observation is a classic example of animal learning, his experiment is called Classical Conditioning which represents learning at a very lower level. A great variety of our everyday experience are learnt through conditioning procedures. Conditioning is nothing "but the establishment of connection between a stimulus and a response which have no natural connection between them". It is learning at a very simple level, learning which we acquire mostly unconsciously. The basic principles of this learning process can be understood from the experiment of classical conditioning.

Pavlov demonstrated that a dog salivates when food is put into its mouth. This reflex of salivation is physiological and natural. But the dog can be made to salivate to any other natural stimulus say the sound of a bell, if for a few times the natural stimulus (food) is presented to the dog with the Conditioned Stimulus (CS) and Conditioned Response (CR) neutral stimulus (i.e., the sound of a bell). This salivation to the sound of a bell is unnatural and learned. Pavlov gave different names to the various type of stimuli and responses. The natural stimulus for salivation, i. e., food was called by him as Unconditioned Stimulus (US). The natural response to it, i. e., salivation ,while eating was called Unconditional Response (U R). The experimental stimulus which was natural before experiment is called Conditioned Stimulus (CS). Here it is the sound of the bell. The learned response (i. e., salivation) to the otherwise natural stimulus (i. e. the sound of the bell) is called Conditioned Response.

In a typical experiment on dogs Pavlov paired food and bell a few times. It was found that after a few pairings, the dog salivates even when only bell is sounded and food is not presented. This salivation is nothing but a conditioned (i. e. learned) response to an otherwise neutral stimulus i.e. bell. Thus, we can define classical conditioning "as a process in which a neutral stimulus by pairing with a natural stimulus, acquires all the characteristics of natural stimulus".

Pavlov also found that the amount of saliva secreted in response to the stimulus gradually increases showing the strength of conditioned response. To study it properly, he collected the saliva of the dog and measured, as the trial of pairing the CS and US went on. Then he plotted the findings in a graph which is called the Conditioning Curve or Acquisition Curve.

Pavlov noted that the strength of the response gradually increases with more and more pairing of US & CS. But gradually the curve flattens that is, after certain number of trials, an increase in salivation due to a particular trial becomes less than its earlier trial, like typical learning curves, where over-learning after a point gives 'diminishing returns'. Here also, more trial after a particular point results in diminishing returns.

The theory of conditioning propounded by Pavlov is based on his views on the mechanistic approach to learning. The behaviour which is learnt must have corresponding impact on the nervous system including the brain of the organism. Frank Restle explains the impact of conditioning process on the brain of the organism in the following way, "In Pavlov's thinking, the Conditioned Stimulus.

(CS) would set up a weak centre of excitation in the brain and the US - UR event would involve a strong centre of activity. When one centre of excitation proceeds to the other in time, the weaker centre becomes integrated with or drawn into the stronger activity and a pathway of some sort develops in the brain. At the same time presentation of CS initiates the activity US - UR complex and the animal makes the UR The theory states that the response original made to US becomes associated with CS and what is learnt is CS - CR bond of some kind".

This various phenomena discovered by Pavlov in his experiments of classical conditioning are explained below.

1. Higher order conditioning: Pavlov found that higher order conditioning is possible. It consists of several stages of classical conditioning. In the second stage, conditioned stimulus of the first stage of conditioning (CS) is paired with a new Conditioned Stimulus (CS). The trials proceed in the following stages:

(1) US	UR	(Food)	(Saliva)
(2) CS+ US	CR	(Bell+ Food)	(Saliva)
(3) CS	CR	(Bell)	(Saliva)
(4) CS+ CS	CR	(Bell+ Light)	(Saliva)
(5) CS	CR	(Light)	(Saliva)

Thus, in the end, the dog will salivate to a light on the face. It might seem that higher order conditioning has no limits. But actually it has limits that is because when the CS, is paired with CS2 it is paired without US. Hence, the conditioning response to it becomes gradually extinct. Upto a point such extinction can be prevented by interspersing trials, when CS, and US are repaired. By doing this and pairing CS with another stimulus CS3 Pavloy could condition UR to CS3 but he could go no further.

2. Contiguity: The contiguity in time of the CS and US is very important in classical conditioning. In conditioning, the conditioned stimulus is said to be reinforced by the unconditioned stimulus. To be reinforced, CS is to be continuous in time with U-S. But contiguity in time is a very vague term. How much is the inter-

stimulus interval? (Inter-Stimulus interval is the interval between the onset of the CS, and onset of the US). The inner stimulus intervals varies with the learner and also the response which is being conditioned.

However, in general, short inter stimulus interval ranging from 5 to 30 seconds are optimum.

3. Background Conditioning: Another point worth noting in this context is backward conditioning where Unconditioned Stimulus (US) is given before the Conditioned Stimulus. Pavlov found that it is not possible. But psychologists have proved later on that such conditioning is possible in case of human beings.

4. Extinction, Spontaneous Recovery and Reconditioning:

If the CS (Sound of the bell is repeated several times not being followed by the US (food), it means that there is nothing followed by the US (food). It means that there is no pairing, and consequently no reinforcement. Then what does happen? The dog starts secreting less of saliva with each presentation of the CS without the US until a point comes when it stops the secretion totally. This process is known as extinction of the learned response of secreting, saliva to the CS (bell). If the experimenter stops this experiment at this point, he will conclude that extinction is the erasure of the learning obtained by conditioning. But actually it is not that extinction is the process of inhibition or the response acquired is conditioning. It is new learning superimposed on the old without destroying the latter. This is proved from the phenomenon of spontaneous recovery and reconditioning.

It has been found that after the extinction of the Condi-tioned Response, if the animal is given some rest and then given trial by presenting it with CS (bell), it will again salivate to the bell, though not much. This proves that a Conditioned Response is called 'Spontaneous Recovery' and it proves that the old conditioning was not totally extinct after all. That in extinction, the original conditioned response does not become extinguished is proved by reconditioning. Pavlov proved that conditioning after extinction, is much more rapid than the original conditioning.

5. Stimulus Generalisation: Pavlov discovered that when the dog has learnt to salivate to the bell, it will also salivate to the all other sounds similar to the bell. This is stimulus generalisation. Many human responses and learnings are acquired through this process of stimulus generalisation. While explaining this phenomenon Pavlov wrote that when the brain gets excited its effect also radiates to the surrounding parts and points, because of the excitement of the surrounding parts, the other associate areas of the brain gets into activity and therefore other objects having similar characteristics and attributes also serve as conditioned stimuli. Pavlov called this phenomenon as "eradication of excitation", an important aspect of any learning process. Pavlov discovered that this is also possible. According to him, the animal can be positive conditioned to high tone sound and negatively conditioned to low tone. If the high tone is decreased with reinforcement and the low tone is increased without reinforcement, the dog can differentiate very small differences in pitch. But the difference between pitches should not be too fine, i.e. should not be less than a limit. If that occurs, the dog runs into temper-barks, bites, jumps, etc, which was called by Pavlov as 'Experimental Neurosis'. He thought in being positively conditioned to highest one, there is cerebral excitation in the brain, while negatively conditioned low tone produces cerebral inhibition. When the difference between the two tones is very fine, there is a clash between two excitations and inhibition joined simultaneously which results in experimental neurosis. Later on, Pavlov developed his theories of psychosis and neurosis based on this concept.

6. Motivational Factors: Pavlov found that the strength or ease with which the conditioning will be done also depends upon motivational factors like hunger, sex, etc. If the response of the animal is related to some organic needs, conditioning will be better.

Following the general procedure already described, Pavlov and his friends conditioned the salivary response of the dog to a variety of stimuli—visual, auditory, olfactory and cutaneous. Vladimir Mechterer, another, Russian psychologist also conducted classical conditioning experiments with so called "Protective reflex". In this experiment simulation is received inspite of the subject's reaction. The sequence of stimuli bell and electric shock remain, regardless of what the subject does. Gradually the subject learns to withdraw his paw, hand or finger, even when only the erstwhile stimulus (bell) is given. Thus, the bell becomes the conditioned stimulus and withdrawal in response to its conditioned response.

Scholars' Views

Pavlov brought a revolution in the field of study of learning process. His distinct contribution to psychology showed how a part of the environment can control a subject's response, though normally should have no connection with it. He experimentally proved in an objective way how learning can be acquired. He considered the process of conditioning as sufficient to explain all forms of learning. As he puts it "different kinds of habits based on training, education and discipline of any sort are nothing but a long chain of conditioned reflexes." Later on psychologists belonging to behaviour school used this concept of conditioning to explain all forms of learning. His emphasis on the objective behaviour of the subject rather than on its mental process were later followed by behaviourists like Watson to develop their theories of behaviourism and learning.

There is ample evidence of classical conditioning occuring in human subjects. A possible example in everyday observation is the situation of a child meeting a doctor quite undisturbed before the first inoculation, but crying at the sight of him before the second. More, systematically, Watson and Rayner established a fear of white rats in a nine month old infant named Albert. The child originally had no fear of these animals and would play with them quite happily, but he was frightened by loud noises. On a number of occasions the experimenters sounded a gong as Albert was handling a rat, after which they presented the rat alone again and found that he responded to it with crying and other signs of fear. Classical conditioning has even been reported in human foetus.

Effects of Theory

The phenomenon of conditioning does not limit itself to such laboratory experiments only. The day to day learning at home, school, etc, consists of plenty of examples where the child learns through conditioning.

Fear, love and hatred towards the subjects are created through conditioning. A mathematics teacher, with his defective methods of teaching or improper behaviour may be disliked by students or by a particular student. He, without caring to know the basic reason, always rebukes and punishes him while returning him the checked home-assignments. Gradually, the child begins to fear home-assignments of any sort. He also develops a distaste and hatred towards the subject of mathematics.

On the contrary, the sympathetic treatment given by the teacher and his interesting and effective methodology can bring a desirable impact on the students through the process of conditioning. They develop a positive attitude towards the subject and love their teacher as well as the subject.

The use of audio-visual aids in the teaching-learning process involves conditioning theory in making the students learn so many things. The child gets an idea of a particular object or phenomenon through this aid. For example, the teacher shows him the picture of a cat, along with the written word 'cat'. The teacher speaks out 'cat' and asks the student to say "cat" everytime when the picture is presented. After sometime the picture of the cat is not presented, only the written word 'cat' is shown. But the child responds to it by saying 'cat. He associates the written word 'cat' with the picture of the cat and the sound of the word.

In developing desirable habits, interests, attitudes, sense of application in the children, etc, the conditioning process may help the teacher and parents a lot. Not only it helps the development of proper behaviour in them but also, is helpful in removing many bad habits – unhealthy attitudes, superstition, fear and phobias – through deconditioning. A child who fears a particular object can be made to seek pleasure from it. Another child who thinks it is a dangerous sign if a cat crosses his way, can be made to give up his misbelief. In this way, the conditioning theory throws light on so many aspects of learning and helps the teacher and parents in their task.

Another Theory

E. L. Thorndike (1874 - 1949) was the first American S. R. psychologist who conducted a series of experiments on learning with animals. The theory of learning propounded by him on the basis of data from these experiments, is known as "the Trial and Error Learning" or "The Intelligence" published in 1898.

Thorndike experiments with lower animals have thrown much light on the learning processes. In one of his experiments, Thorndike confined a hungry cat to a cage.closed by door which could be opened by a latch. Food was kept outside the door so that it could be within the sight of the animal. The cat tried to come out of the cage by biting, crawling, scratching, etc. After 160 seconds, it succeeded in pushing the latch accidentally, and came out. Thorndike repeated this experiment several times. On the 24th attempt the cat took only seven seconds to come out. Similar experiments were conducted on rats, monkeys, rabbits, etc. Thorndike termed this method as 'trial and error' or 'hit and miss' method because prior to the learning of a task, the animal made many trials before it hit the right response. The preliminary responses were full of errors. Thorndike concluded the following from the above experiments:

(a) The animal in the learning situation resorted to random activity.

(b) As the learning situation proceeded there was gradual reduction of useless movements.

(c) After a number of trials the animals learnt to use the release mechanism without resorting to any useless movements.

(d) In learning the animal's improvement was regular.

Thorndike concluded that when confronted with a problem situation, the animal, in the earlier stages makes a series of actions and movements to achieve the goal. A large number of these movements are exploratory in nature. They are unnecessary and, to the observer, they seem to be just blind efforts, random in nature. Gradually, with the repeated trial the unsuccessful actions are diminished and the successful actions are increased manifold. Some contend that this type of learning is essentially and usually miscalled 'trial and error learning'. It should be called learning by 'selection of the successful variant', for it is by the selection of the right way rather than by the elimination of the wrong one that new response are learnt. The wrong one is usually eliminated because it cannot exist in the presence of the right one. Yet in hundreds of human activities, 'trial and error' method works successfully and it is considered as one of the most significant aspects of learning. Learning to play golf, to ride bi-cycle, to do typing, to drive a car, to skate, to swim, to write, to play a musical instrument, to model with clay, to paddle a canoe, and thousands of other human activities involve the process of trial and error. In learning sports skills, this method plays an extremely important role. Novices try a number of methods of kicking, hitting, throwing, catching, etc, before they succeed in doing so correctly. In everyday life, we make trial with many garments before we select one which fits well, many colours in painting before the right colour is found, even though we have enough knowledge and experience.

A few important concepts involved in this theory need a little more consideration. First, by trial and error method; learning is not instant, it is gradual and a function of time. Those expecting immediate results would generally criticise it. If the individual is given sufficient time for exploration, learning will proceed satisfactory. Second, the goal of activity in progress must be clear and be in sight of the learner. A clear goal or purpose invokes a more vigorous response from the learner who tries to achieve it as fast as possible. Third, the learner must be given an opportunity to understand the situation as a whole and not in fragments. Every component of a skill must be shown and presented as a the 'whole'. The piecemeal presentation of the situation creates stumbling blocks in the way of learning proper response. Fourth, the earlier stage of learning is the stage of exploration which necessitates wastage of effort and energy because the individual himself is to 'find out' the 'successful variant' unaided He is not guided, he is like a stranger who has to find his own way through the thick of the situation. Fifth, some pre-condition (s) must exist in the organism to receive the stimulus and try to respond. For example, a satisfied cat would not make efforts to reach food. Lastly, in all types of learning, trial and error is an essential element. If trial and error is rationally analysed, it is found to be an essential ingredient of our natural behaviour rather than a consciously-devised method! It is a descriptive process of behaviour. Establishment of stimulus-response bond, satisfaction or annoyance and practice are basic factors involved in trial and error.

8

Creative Learning

It is a way of acting, as all true learning tasks take into account some selective responses, it is not merely the summing up of all previous knowledge and experience; it is creative synthesis of all knowledge and the experience of the learner. Hence lies the difference between animal learning and human learning. In human learning the following mental processes are involved as cited by Crow and Crow (1954)

(a) Interest and attention are directed towards a goal direction

(b) Perception of relation and interpretation

(c) Selection and recall of relevant experiences

(d) Recognition of relationships among the component experiences insight

(e) Formation of new mental pattern creation

(f) Evaluation of workability of solution-criticism

True human learning should aim at the higher level of thinking i. e, creative and critical thinking.

Learning is not only individual but in a sense also social, because learning takes place in response to the social environment of the individual. A child's social interaction is of great significance to his favourable or unfavourable learning. An intelligent teacher takes note of the social climate in the classroom, the influence of peer group on a child, and so on.

Learning by Transformation

Transfer to a new task becomes more meaningful and advantageous to the learner when he has already discovered relationships between things and has learned to apply the principles within a given number of tasks. Learning is transferable in this way but the amount of transfer may vary. There is no wholesale transfer from one subject to another as had been supposed earlier by the theory of formal discipline. Transfer is possible between two situations, if there is identity of context, identity of procedures and identity of attitudes and ideals. In this way transfer takes place from one field of study to another and from the classroom situations to life situations. This transfer is also essential, as it leads to economy in learning.

Each learner is a unique person who has his individual needs and problems, interests and attitudes, purposes and aspirations. In some, learning may be quick and fast; in others the reactions may be slow, and still in others, it may be steady and deliberate.

Learning with an Aim

Human beings learn to achieve something, sometimes the teachers may not be aware of it at all. When the goal is more definite and explicit, the learning becomes more meaningful and effective to the learner.

Process of Learning

Learning is a form of activity and it largely depends on the learner. It is said that no learning can take place where there is no self-activity. That is why one psychologist has said: "No one can teach you but you may learn, your teacher can direct your learning, can show you how materials are derived or related and stimulate you to study. Whether or not you learn and what you learn depends upon what you yourself do, for learning an activity".

Individual's Role

Learning is unitary as man learns as a whole being. An individual reacts as a whole person to the total learning situation rather than to one single stimulus. Since each learner responds as a whole (physically, socially and emotionally) the various motivation factors within him which affect the learner must be taken into account for effective teaching. Again, as the learner responds to the total situation, all external or environmental factors which influence his responses must also be taken note of for favourable learning. Therefore, setting the environment for learning is very important.

Learning at a Higher Level

Learning and maturation are interrelated. But they are distinguishable. Maturation signifies the process of growth and development. It occurs in the absence of any sort of habit, training or stimulus. On the other hand, learning is the modification of behaviour, which is the result of experience and training.

At a particular age, every child starts to sit, crawl, stand and walk. This is the result of maturation. But when the child dances, sings, plays football, drives scooter or a car and swims in the river, it is called learning. Learning is dependent on maturation to a great extent. Unless a particular stage in the process of maturation is reached, learning of any sort cannot be taken into hand. A two months old baby cannot learn dressing himself and a two year old child is not capable of typing. So maturation plays an important role in learning new skills. It prepares one physically and mentally to learn. So the relation between the two is so intimate that one is often misunderstood as the other. But they are two separate concepts and maturation fuels the organism with capability to learn.

Meaning of maturation is not the same in every sphere. Social and emotional maturation refers to ideal and law bound behaviour. It depends fully on learning. Sexual maturation presupposes physical ability and learned skills. Physical maturation denotes a stage of physical growth. Sexual maturation is generally reached in between the age 13 to 16 and physical maturation may be reached at a later stage in life. In the context of learning, maturation implies physical growth and development.

Maturation does not mean only the natural organic growth of human beings, because before and after birth the organism is affected by environmental factors. Malnutrition and infectious disease during pregnancy leaves a negative effect on the new born baby. Again afterbirth if the child is not provided with opportunities to mix with others in society, his all round growth and development is affected. From various experiments, it is proved that children confined to the four walls of home show abnormal development of personality. Growth and development of children differ due to divergent environments, in which they are brought up.

The process of learning is affected by certain conditions. A knowledge of these conditions is essential for every teacher and parent, because by manipulating these conditions they can bring a required change in the behaviour of the child. Some of the important conditions are discussed below:

1. Readiness 2. Motivation 3. Interest 4. Attention 5. Drill or practice 6. Fatigue or boredom 7. Intelligence 8. Aptitude 9. Attitude 10. Emotional factors 11. Family and cultural expectations.

1. Readiness of Learning: When the child is not ready to learn, whatever method may be applied, he will not learn. It is applicable both for school and home. A number of students reading in the same class may be of a particular age level, but differ in readiness to learn, their readiness of experience, social and emotional stability, etc. The teacher should have a thorough knowledge about readiness in order to make his teaching effective. This helps the teacher in three ways. They are:
   - (i) Firstly he can develop the skill of his teaching and become aware of the change in the readiness of students.
   - (ii) He can try to intensify the readiness of the students and reinforce them for it.
   - (iii) Students who do not show interest in study can be tackled and interest in them can be aroused by the teacher.

2. Motivation for Learning: Motivation is one of the most important factors in learning process. Every man should

set a goal in his life. After a goal is set he is motivated to learn, because by learning only he can realise the goal. A poor student wants to earn his livelihood. So he is motivated for learning. A businessman wants to expand his business; so he is motivated to learn skills in business. But a student coming from a rich and affluent family is not so strongly motivated to learn as a student coming from a poor family. It is because he knows that without learning he can achieve his goal either by manpower or by money power. Without motivation the quality and pace of learning is hampered.

3. Interest and Learning: Interest is another important factor that accelerates the learning process. Different students are interested in different branches of study. So a teacher can make use of their interests and bring out the best result. During pre-childhood days, interest of the child is limited and does not last for a longer time. If now he is interested in one thing, the next moment his interest shifts to another thing. But as he grows up, his interest becomes stable and permanent. The teacher can evoke interest in students by making his teaching permanent and stimulative. This also decreases boredom, negligence and slowness of the student in his study. So he should adopt such methods as to increase the interest in the students. Only a learning with interest will enable a student to reach the goal and makes the student have interest in learning more and more.

4. Attention of Learning: Learning is impossible without attention. Qualitative and quantitative development of learning depends upon the quality and quantity of attention. When attention is diverted, learning is affected adversely.

5. Place of Drill and Practice in Learning: A simple matter is remembered easily. It needs no drilling. But in order to master complex matters, one needs drill or practice. So the teacher should bear in mind that practice makes learning perfect and act accordingly in the classroom. He should

develop the practice of reading, writing, etc, in students and drill them the different materials, that they come across during learning. But drilling should not be mechanical. In mechanical drilling the students lack understanding of the object. This promotes fruitless learning.

6. Fatigue and Boredom: Physical and mental tiredness is known as fatigue. Disinterest in doing a work is known as boredom. Learning does not cause fatigue. If the method of teaching is faulty, the students are bored. The environment and surroundings of school also bore the students. So these factors should be taken into consideration by the teacher.

7. Role of Intelligence in Learning: Intelligence brings qualitative increase in learning. Difference in intelligence is clearly marked among the students in a classroom. They can be broadly divided into three categories. Some are bright, some are average and others are dull. The teacher should adopt intelligence measurement test to evaluate the level of intelligence of each and every student and group them into categories. Then his teaching should take into consideration every category of students. He should see that every teaching material reaches the least intelligent student. Generally in our educational institutions teaching is rendered for average student and so the feeble-minded students are not profited from it. Again the feeble-minded students are divided into three categories. They are idiot, imbecile and moron.

8. Aptitude and Learning: Aptitude is a natural reinforcer of learning. When interest is aroused spontaneously, it is called aptitude. Remembering is long-lasting if the learning material is backed by aptitude. On the other hand, in the absence of aptitude, the student fails to remember his learning material. So the teacher should be aware of this factor also.

9. Attitude and Learning: Learning is also affected by the attitude of the learner. Interest, aptitude and readiness

correspond to one another. They make the learner prepared and fill him with potentialities to tackle the learning material. Attitude makes the students meet the problems with understanding, interest and smartness. If he is pressurised with much more material, he develops a negative attitude.

10. Effect of Emotional States: The last but not the least factor that affects the process of learning is the emotional state of the learner. If he is undergoing a pleasurable emotion, his learning is bound to be qualitatively better. On the other hand, if emotional states pressurise him and create tension in him, he develops frustration and lacks interest and readiness to learn.

Role of Emotions

(a) Unfulfilled requirements.
(b) Wrong attitude of parents in home.
(c) Quarrel, lack of security, inconvenience, plentitude at home.
(d) Frustration or inferiority caused by real or imaginary physical defects.
(e) Previous experience of failure in school.
(f) Neglecting behaviour by teachers and friends and avoi-dance by them.

11. Role of Family and Culture in Learning: Family and culture of the learner affects his learning to a great extent. Even his life process is affected by these two. Parent's hopes and desires count much in his life. Sometimes the parents set goals for their children. Hopes and desires of parents differ with the difference in culture and place.

    There are cultural demands, which affect the learning process. Social and educational environment reflect one's culture. So learning should be complementary to the learner's cultural demands and requirements. All such demands should be met with. For example, in a culture where democracy is a way of life, the learner should be imparted learning in consonance with democratic values.

Learning by Practice

When learning is associated with playing or merry making, it becomes more effective. It arouses interest in the learner. Teaching should not be only giving lectures to the students. They become bored by that. Secondly if while learning a skill, the learner does the work with his own hands he masters it without much effort. So now the modern methods of teaching lay stress on play-way method and discard the conventional reciting-in-classroom methods. Now the classrooms have turned into playgrounds.

Other Aspects

Learning is a process. This process depends upon a number of factors. If we categorise the factors upon which this process is based, we will find three main directions. They are

1. The internal condition of the learner - (such as capacity, motivation, age, sex, difference, experience etc.)
2. Nature of the subject to be learnt - (e. g. span or range of learning, complexity or simplicity of learning materials etc.)
3. Method of learning - (e. g. memorisation, analysis, drilling, recitation etc.)

Let us discuss these conditions of learning in detail.

1. Role of Age in Learning: Children fare well and better with adults. It is a general belief that learning ability decreases with increase in age. From various studies it has been proved that there is a fixed and definite age when learning ability of the child is maximum. Apart from this there is also a fixed age for better learning of literature, mathematics and science. Studies have been conducted by psychologists on the relationship between age factor and learning process. The results show that learning ability of new subjects goes on increasing till the age of 10 years. Then it remains constant till age of 20 years and after that it goes on diminishing and again becomes stable at the age of 50.

2. Role of Sex in Learning: Psychologist have been in the process of finding out whether there is any relationship between learning ability and sex. In some societies it has been found that children of a particular sex show more proficiency in learning than the other sex. Whether this difference is due to difference in sex or due to better facilities enjoyed by one sex over the other one, the findings are as follows:

(i) Difference in sex does not cause any difference in their intelligence.

(ii) While girls show more proficiency in literature, debates, songs, etc, the boys show more ability in social science, science, mathematics, etc.

(iii) Girls are more emotional, sociable and jealous. Boys are more influential, high minded, independent-minded and self-confident.

(iv) Girls have greater pronouncing ability, better memory and sounder sensitiveness. On the other hand, boys show good result in numerology.

(v) Girls are interested in service, home science and literature, whereas boys show interest in scientific, technological and ideological fields.

3. Role of Mental Stability in Learning: Effective learning and teaching depends fully upon a factor that is known as attention. Unless the learner is attentive to the process of learning, he can learn nothing. The learner should come in contact with the learning situation practically. That is he should attend by himself. Indirect participation yields no result. If the students are told that they will be examined after three days of the learning, it is natural that a greater attention will be paid towards learning; but if they are told that they will be tested after 6 months, they may not be serious on the subject. When the students point all their potentialities on a particular subject, learning becomes more effective and memorisation is accelerated

4. Role of Past Experience in Learning: New learning depends upon previous learning. Learning of one matèrial, backs the learning of another material. When a student fails in reading, writing or doing sums in classroom it should be noted that he had a defective learning before hand. Past learning enfuels present learning and present learning enfuels the future learning process.

5. Role of Family Background and Socio-economic Status in Learning: Village and town atmosphere influences difference in learning efficiency remarkably. Studies have been conducted and results show that town students are more fluent orally and in verbal expressions. Their way of talking is developed and disciplined.

   The difference marked between the town and village students in the field of learning depends upon their easily available level of stimulations. There are facilities of libraries, magazines and periodicals, books, schools, museums, T. V. and social works. These stimulants tend to increase learning ability in children. Another case of difference in learning ability in children is their socio-economic status. A child reared up in a luxurious environment is bound to be different from a child brought up in a poverty stricken family. There are some other social causes also, which include social customs and traditions, casteism, feeling of success and failure and its financial consequence.

6. Role of Experience of Success and Failure in Learning: A feeling of inferiority and hopelessness is marked in case of students who fail in examinations. Generally children having high hopes become successful in all walks of life. So success and failure have their respective impacts on the learning process.

7. Role of Knowledge of Promotion in Learning: Knowledge of promotion stimulates the learner and heightens his attentions. From group experiments it has been found that the experimental group, which had the knowledge of

promotion showed better result than the other groups which had no knowledge of promotion. From another experiment it has been established that further learning is impossible unless the learner knows the result of this last learning. So knowledge or result bring success in new learning. So the teacher should feel the importance of this factor.

8. Role of Meaningfulness of Subject Matter in Learning: It has been proved from experiments as well as observations that meaningful materials are remembered better than the meaningless materials. Meaningful material denotes those materials about which we have some previous experience. So the teacher must bear this in mind. The student should not be compelled to master unknown materials. The method of teaching should be from known to unknown.

9. Role of Complexity of Material in Learning: Before starting teaching, the teacher should consider whether the subject matter is simple or complex for the learner. At first a student should learn simple and easy subjects. He shows better results in this learning. Thus, when a complex subject is given to him his level of mastery decreases, but it surely adds to the development of his learning. So the teaching should be from simple to complex. On the other hand if he fails to show proficiency and his interest is hampered, he feels bored and neglects his studies. Fear complex is aroused and he displays escapist temperament.

10. Spread of Learning Materials: A question is often asked whether a long passage is remembered sooner or a short passage. Ebbinghaus has proved by experimenting that a long list of words takes a longer time to memorise than a short list. But it has also been proved that a bigger topic is remembered better and sooner than the shorter topic. This has been proved by psychologist Woodsworth in 1988. Hence the range of learning materials has a special role to play in the process of learning. If a longer subject is tried to be mastered as a whole from start to end., it needs much more time to remember. But if the teacher adopts the

method of dividing the long subject into small divisions and learned in parts, learning is effective and quick.

11. Role of Re-memorisation in Learning: Re-memorisation has a strong effect on learning and memorisation. Re-memorisation is often described as mental evaluation of learnt materials. Learning the material again is known in psychology as learning by closing the book. From the discussion below we can know how re-memorising helps memorisation process.

    (a) When re-memorisation is a conscious effort and not merely a bird's eye-view, it becomes fruitful.
    (b) The learner can measure his memorisation by this process. So he can be aware of his limitations and weakness in learning. He knows that he failed to remember and invents methods of remembering them again.
    (c) Rememorisation creates self-confidence in the learner.

    In this context drilling of a particular learned topic by the teacher is of prime importance. By drilling rememorisation takes place along with self-evaluation. But it should not be stereo-typed or mechanical. The same topic should be presented in various forms. By giving different tasks to students such as filling in the blanks, writing the summary, etc, rememorisation can be done and its effect realised.

12. Role of Over-learning: Overlearning sometimes brings good results. The topic which is remembered after the repetition of five times can be remembered better after the recitation of two more times. This helps the learner to produce the material more perfectly. Over-learning is something different from mere recitation or simple re-learning it again and again. Re-learning is required to memorise but over-learning makes the goal of learning felt. Drilling brings out the correct response out of the learner but over-learning confirms it.

13. Role of Time Gap between Learning Situations: Considering from a narrow point of view we see that the process

of learning is limited to a particular period of time. A topic can be read for 7 hours at length and it can also be read by dividing it into 7 parts and each part in one hour. Which of the two methods is fruitful is a question to be answered. In school curriculum the entire syllabus is divided into parts and taught day-wise, week-wise and month-wise. Experiments prove that by giving sufficient gap between two learning situations, efficiency is increased.

14. Difference between the Whole-method and Part-method: In past the part method was popular and learning was based on it. But later the whole method proved to be more effective and as such this was adopted by teachers. In part method, a longer topic is learnt in parts which makes the learning mechanical and the learner goes far from the root or basic point of the subject. Correlation could not be established among the various points of discussion. They were regarded by the learner as different topics and not as the points of view of only on topic. On the other hand, efficiency increased in whole learning and learning was still more effective. And if at all a vast subject is to be divided, it should be done in such a manner so that the divisions are interrelated and interdependent. In whole-method of learning stress is laid upon the totality of the viewpoint. The success of whole-method depends upon the past experience of the learner, his temperament and complexity of material. If the subject matter is understandably interdependent and smooth, it is learnt effectively. It is observed that intelligent students prefer whole method whereas students of lower intelligence adopt part method to memorise a material.

15. Recitation in Learning: It has been proved that recitation at the time of reading a material makes learning more effective. It is still more helpful in the learning of spelling, vocabulary and mathematics. Learning and recitation should go hand in hand.

16. Use of Audio-visual Aids in Learning: It is a belief of most of the people that by merely using audio-visual aids we

can bring about development in learning efficiency. But it is not correct Only showing these aids to students does not help them to learn better. There should be a complete plan as to the use of these aids. The teacher should make appropriate preparations for that. It has been proved from experiments that T. V. sets and cinema can teach students better than disqualified teachers, who do not make proper plans before using the aids. The teacher must create a suitable and stimulating environment in the classroom before using the audiovisual aids.

9

Laws of Learning

Various Laws

The law of effect which is Thorndike's primary law of learning takes place according to three basic laws. They are the Law of Effect, the Law of Exercise and the Law of Readiness.

1. The Law of Effect: The Law of Effect is Thorndike's primary law of learning. It stresses the importance of effect or consequence learning i. e. on the strengths or weakness of the connections between the stimulus and response. It says, "when a modifiable connection between a situation and response is made and is accompanied or followed by a satisfying state of affairs, that connection's strength is increased. When made, and accompanied or followed by an annoying state of affairs, its strength is decreased". Though the terms 'satisfying' and 'annoying' have subjective conno-tations, Thorndike tries to define them objectively. He says, " By a satisfying state of affairs is meant one which the animal does nothing to avoid, often doing things which renew it. By annoying state of affairs is meant one which the animal does nothing to preserve, often doing things which puts an end to it. Responses which are rewarded are firmly established and become more probable for recurrence. On the other hand, annoying responses, that is, responses which are meted out with punishment, are unlearnt and become less probable for recurrence. Thus, the Law of Effect of Thorndike is just another name for what the psychologists call the law of

rewards and punishment. The cat inside the puzzle box is rewarded in the form of food, when it makes correct response.

Therefore, it learns that response. Other random responses which are not thus rewarded are not learnt by it.

2. The Law of Exercise: This law explains the role of practice or repetition in learning. It states, "when any activity is repeated a number of times, there is a tendency for that activity to be firmly established and easily-learnt, while the activity seldom repeated becomes difficult for learning". This law has two parts. The first part is the law of use which states that if a situation is followed by a particular response, then a bond (S-R connection) is established. This bond between the stimulus and the response becomes strengthened by repetition or exercise. The second part is the law of disuse which states that when a given situation is rarely followed by a particular response, the bond between the stimulus and the response becomes weakened.

   Under this Law of Exercise, there are various sub-laws, like the law of frequency, the law of recency, the law of vividness of intensity. By frequency is meant the frequency of repetition of the particular response to a particular stimulus or situation. The sub-law of frequency states that a bond which has been recently established is less prone to error. The sub-law of vividness that signifies the active and interested exercise strengthens the bond more than mere mechanical exercise.

   Thorndike established a connection between the law of effect and the law of exercise by observing that the satisfying response is more often repeated and consequently becomes more permanently established.

3. The Law of Readiness: The Law of Readiness of Thorndike states, "when a bond is ready to act, gives satisfication and not to act gives annoyance. When a bond which is not ready to act, is made to act annoyance is caused. The

readiness and lack of readiness of the bond is the result of condition of the nervous system. The neurons of the nervous system, which are responsible for conduction of nerve impulses, are called the 'condition units'. The condition (readiness or lack of readiness) of the nervous system is ultimately dependent upon those of the 'conduction units'. All the conduction units are not always in readiness to receive and conduct nerve impul-ses, which are the result of stimuli acting upon the nervous system. They are not always in readiness to omit responses to the stimuli. When any conduction unit is in readiness to conduct, for it, to do so, is satisfying and not to do so, is annoying."

The readiness or lack of readiness in nervous system to participate in the establishment of a bond is dependent on various factors like maturation, attitude and the past experience of the learner.

(1) Law of Contiguity: This denotes that situation which occurs together either simultaneoiusly or in close succession tends towards receiving one another since one situation has association with many other situations or objects. It is also known as Law of Association. The temple of Sri Jagannath Dev reminds us of Puri, Nilamadhaba, King Indradumna, Gundicha Rani, Anangabhima Deva, Kanchi Abijan etc., because of their contiguity and association. Contiguity is one of the important factors in associational learning theories. Associationists believe that although reward will aid association to proceed more rapidly and will perhaps, strengthen the connection, association will occur, regardless of reward, if the stimulus and the responses are contiguous. The greater the affinity between the stimulus and the responses, the faster would the learning proceed. Learning of poetry i. e. memorizing a poem is easier than cramming prose because the words in the former are rightly and oppositely associated with one another which is not the case with prose.

(2) Law of Multiple Response to the Same External Situation: Here the connection is that the individual makes several responses and not one to the same situation or the external stimulus. A chance word or observation, sets off a train of thoughts which runs for a long time. Some external stimulus seems to be necessary in the beginning but in a series of the further internal or external activity i. e. one reaction leads to a number of further reactions in sequence. There are, then multiple responses to a single stimulus. In this process, the desirable responses may be selected and practised and the undesirable ones eliminated. The higher the animal is in the hierarchy of the evolutionary scale, the greater the number and the variety of responses. This hints at the variability of human behaviour. This law is also called concomitant or, Attendant Learning. During an athletic class, the learner not only learns the activity pattern but also how his coach explains the procedures, how he dresses up; what techniques, what peculiar word or sentences he used to make teaching more effective. All these factors ultimately decide whether the learner would give response wholly or partially. By this way the habit of concentrating on the activity of paying attention, initiative, etc, may be cultivated. This means that one learns many things in one single situation.

(3) Law of Attitude, Set or Disposition: What response shall an individual make to a given stimulus depends upon his attitude or his disposition at that time. Further satisfaction or annoyance would also depend on this factor. The attitudes are acquired from the previous experience, and the state of affairs of the individual at that time. An inexperienced and a seasoned athletic differs in his attitude towards a particular learning situation. The former is well set mentally to practise drills, skills, etc. The latter is well disposed to take to the whole game. Thorndike says that a well-fed cat goes to sleep in the cage while a hungry one would strive to get out of it and reach for food. In the same way, the mental and the physical disposition of the individual at that time determines as to what extent, he would respond to the new stimulus.

(4) Law of Partial Activity: "A part, or an element or an aspect of a situation may be prepotent in causing res-ponse, and may have responses bound more or less exclusively to it regardless of some or all of its accom-paniments". A student who had solved a number of puzzles or gone through a number of intelligence tests "gets on to the thing" more quickly than the one who has not had similar experiences. Similarly, the situation in the sports field also demands the distinction to be made between the raw hand and the one who knows something. The latter would look for more complex activities while the former remains stuck up with simpler ones.

(5) Law of Associative Shifting: This is a 'conditioned' response. A response may be shifted from one situation to another which is presented at the same time. In the process of motor skill acquisition, the situation is gradually transferred from element to element until the whole complex skill becomes clear. Conditioning is so universal that it might truly be said that the teacher can get any response of which a student is capable and is associated with any situation to which he is sensitive.

(6) Law of Belongingness: According to this sub-law, if the connection between the stimulus and the response is natural, learning would be more effective. Motor skills based on natural activities of running, jumping, throwing, etc, are learnt faster. Artificial activities are difficult to learn. For example, it is harder to try running backwards with the same arm foot co-ordination.

(7) Law of Intensity of Stimulus: Learning depends much on the intensity or strength of the stimulus. The stronger the stimulus, the stronger will the response be. For example, a player who is getting an opportunity of participation in the national or international tournament, will practice hard and more seriously. Most often the strength of a stimulus is intensified by using extrinsic and intrinsic devices of motivation.

(8) Law of Primacy: This denotes that the situations which are presented at the outset, elicit a more lasting response. That is why it is said that the first impression is the best impression. Teacher's first day appearance, his turn-out, his speech, the condition of the playground, the equipment, etc, go to make the fast impression on the students. This ultimately will determine the quantum of satisfaction or dissatisfaction which a learner derives therefrom At the end of a serious activity-practise class, the physical education teachers are advised to provide a recreative game so that the students forget the primary painful experiences of forced skill-practice.

(9) Law of Recency: Experiences received recently are revived easily and very often such experiences are more vivid than others. They can be recalled without much effort than those occuring in the middle of the activity. If first impression is the best impression, best impression is the last impression. If at the end of the class, the last act is satisfying, the impression will linger on in the minds of the students.

(10) The Law of Assimilation and Analogy: This law states that when the learner is faced with a new situation for which he has no natural or learned response, the response he makes, will be that found useful in a similar situation in the past. In other words, the law states that the responses to new situations and problems are made on the basis of the past experience.

At first, Thorndike called his bond theory of learning as blind and mechanical. But subsequently, he modified his theory to such an extent that it could hardly be termed as blind mechanical. The modification of his laws of effect and exercise were necessitated in the light of further experimental evidence. In 1929, he admitted before the International Congress of Psychology that his law of exercise and effect needed revision. Then, soon after that, he published his revised laws.

(1) Revision of Law of Exercise: He revised this law as a result of his experiment on human learning. According to the

revision, the law of exercise is not considered as an independent law. Mere repetition of a response or practice is not enough. Repitition or practice brings improvement, when other factors like rewards are present. Connection gets strengthened when recurrence is rewarded. Simple recurrence does not strengthen the connection.

(2) Revision of the Law of Effect: He also revised his law of effect. The original law of effect had given equal importance to the effects of rewards and punishment. But later on Thorndike discovered that the effects of rewards and punishment do not weaken to that extent.

(3) The Principle of Polarity: He also introduced a new concept called the principle of polarity which means that "connections act more easily in the directions in which they are formed than in the opposite direction."

(4) The Concept of Spread of Effects: Another concept introduced by him is the concept of spread of effects. This concept suggests that the effect of reward and punishment is not confined to a particular connection but it has a "spread". It also affects-adjacent connections which are there, both before and after the rewarded connection.

(5) The Concept of Belongingness: He also introduced the concept of belongingness into his learning theory. A connection is more easily learnt if the response belongs to a situation i. e. fits perfectly into the situation. This concept merely states that an appropriate and useful response to a situation is more easily learnt than in appropriate one.

(6) The Concept of Motivation: Another important revision of his learning theory is the admission that motivations are very important for learning. Motives like hunger, sex, thirst, etc, determine which are to be avoided. They also provide the basis for repetition and confirmation of the responses already made.

The Assessment

Thorndike is the first S-R theorist. He placed much importance upon the need for experimental evidence and objective verification in psychology. According to W. F. Hill "Thorndike was no less a pioneer of objective psychology than Watson. Indeed his original contributions were quite likely more important than Watson".

Hill also hails him as "the first real reinforcement psychologist" as "he incorporated within the objective psychology the law of effect". The theory of reward and punishment was very clearly explained by him for the first time in the history of psychology. He explains that acts that are rewarded tend to recurr and acts not reinforced or punished tend to become less probable of recurrence. His law of effect has also called attention to the importance of motivation, belongingness, etc, in learning.

His theory of learning propounded very important laws in relation to learning process. It has much implication for the teachers and the students. For example the law of exercise stresses the need for practice for better learning. The law of disuse explains the process of forgetting. The law of attitude or disposition brings out the importance of the attitude of the learner on his learning capacity. The law of assimilation or analogy brings out the principle of transfer of learning.

But the learning of theory of Thorndike has certain short-comings also. First, his contention that learning is only a connection between the situation and response is not true. His argument is that the cat only learnt physiological movements, cannot be accepted as true. A cat that has learnt to pull the loop will, on the next trial go to the place where the loop was, even though it has been removed to another place. But when it discovers its new locations, it will no longer go to the former place. Thus the cat has certainly got acquainted with the cage, the outlet, the locations and the use of release mechanism. It has not learnt only physiological movements or connections. Rather it has learnt the cognitive map of the problem environment and also its solution. Secondly, the law of exercise of Thorndike is too mechanical. It does not take into account factors of learning. Thorndike should have known that mere repetition without understanding does not improve learning. However the latter revision of the law made by Thorndike nullifies much of the criticisms against it. Thirdly,

Thorndike explains the law of readiness with reference to connections between neurons. The law of readiness is useless, unless it refers to mental readiness. He also does not explain this law clearly. That is why some psychologists interpret this law as natural readiness. Fourthly the law of effect cannot be explained without reference to mind. Guthrie disproves this theory. He suggests, what is learnt is what is connected not what is rewarded. Tolman's theory of latent learning proves that the law of effect is not an essential law, as learning can also take place without reward.

Implications and Effects

Thorndike's theory of trial and error has enough educational significance. It tries to explain the process of learning, carefully on the basis of actual experiments performed not only on the animal's but on human learning also, which to a greater extent, follow the path of trial and error. A child while confronted with a mathematical problem, tries so many possibilities of its solution, before he arrives at the correct one. Even the discoveries and inventions in the various fields of knowledge are the results of trial and error process.

For example, let us take the discovery made by Archimedes in the form of his well-known principle. He was confronted with a problem given by his emperor. There was a drive that he will be beheaded if he could not get the solutions to the problem. There was a block as he could not think of any solution. The problem was difficult. He went on experimenting and made a number of attempts (trials) for the solution of his problem. One day while taking his bath, he got chance success in one of his attempts and this led to the formation of the law of floating bodies.

But the excessive use of the method, trial and error, without caring for the development of understanding should not be encouraged in any circumstances. We cannot reduce the human learning as mechanical and blind-folded as advocated by this theory. It must be supported by reason, understanding and insight. Trials and practice coupled with insight, will make the process of learning more effective than either of the methods adopted alone.

As far as the Thorndikes laws of learning are concerned, it goes without saying that Thorndike has done a valuable service to the field of learning and teaching by providing these laws. These laws state the following things in general.

(1) In the process of teaching and learning the main task of the teacher is to see what things he likes to be remembered or forgotten by his students. After this, he must try to strengthen the bonds or connections between the stimuli and responses of those things, which are to be remembered, through repetition, drill and reward. The connection should be weakened through disuse and annoying results.

(2) The child must be made ready to learn. His interest, attitude and mental preparation is essential for the smooth sailing in the teaching learning process.

(3) It is also emphasized that the past experiences and learning give an adequate base for the new learning. Therefore the teacher should try to make use of the pre-vious knowledge and experience of the students. The child must, also, be encouraged to see similarities and dissimilarities between the different kinds of responses to stimuli and with the help of something in one situation to the other similar situation.

(4) The child should be encouraged to do his work independently. He must try the various solutions of the problem before arriving at the correct one. But every care should be taken to see that he may not waste his time and energy. He should not be allowed to repeat his mistakes and proceed blindly without using his reasoning and thinking powers and utilize the past learning experiences.

In short, Thorndike's theory and laws of learning have contributed a lot to educational theory and practice. It has made learning purposeful and goal-directed and has brought motivation to the forefront. It has also given impetus to the work of practice, drill and repetition and realized the psychological importance of rewards and praise in the process of teaching and learning.

Learning by Wisdom

The term psychology has been defined in different ways. Particularly three definitions have been predominant: Psychology as the science of mind, of consciousness and of behaviour. Psychologists who advocate learning by insight accept the last definition of psychology as the science of behaviour. This group of psychologists are known as gestaltists. The gestaltists lay more emphasis on insight or understanding in the learning process.

Kohler, a German psychologist, is the exponent of this theory. He conducted a number of experiments on higher animals like chimpanzees, monkeys, etc. After a long obser-vation, he came to certain conclusions which later on became the main-stay of cognitive theories. Kohler believed that no discussion on learning, without reference to 'insight' could be complete in anyway. Learning could not take place in the absence of insight'. By 'insight', he meant inner-sight i. e., seeing or penetrating deep into problematic situations. Insight, he said, involves 'foresight' as opposed to 'hind-sight' in trial and error theory. The crux of trial and error learning is the 'after thought' whereas in learning by insight "the problematic situation is reviewed as a whole, and the solution at once comes vividly before the mind in the form of foresight'. The right solutions is foreseen before the action is initiated. That is to say that in trial and error theory, thinking succeeds action while in learning by insight thinking precedes action. In the former case, the learner is bound to try a number of responses before selecting the correct-one, while in the latter case, the 'trial' is made internally at mental level so that at the end only correct response occurs.

The Experimentation

To prove the above thesis, Kohler conducted certain experiments on such animals which are higher in the biological hierarchy. In one of his classical experiments, he put a chimpanzee in a cage with iron bars and kept food (bananas) at some distance from the cage so that the food could be pulled into the cage by the chimpanzee by using the bamboo sticks lying near the cage. At first the chimpanzee, to reach the foodstuff, made frantic efforts and showed hectic activity. Then it sat in a corner just brooding over the whole situation. With a sudden start, it took one stick and tried to reach the food but failed. He then took another stick fixed it into the broader-end of the other and ultimately pulled the food into the cage with the lengthened stick.

From numerous experiments of this sort, Kohler concluded that when 'insight' is gained into the entire situation, the animal abruptly gets hold of the correct response to be given. However, this kind of learning requires understanding of the situation as a whole. The goal of the activity must be clear to begin with and the learner must posses the power of 'generalisation', along with that of 'differentiation'. Lower animals posses neither power of generalization nor of differentiation; they cannot retain experiences nor store knowledge; their behaviour is a mass of thropisms and reflexes. Whether they have 'foresight' except the instinctive danger-signaling mechanisms, is a matter of guess.

In a contrived learning situation, the problems are so structured that the significant features are perceived in proper relationship, with distraction or confusing features and aspects being subordinated or kept in the background. The use of 'insight' leads to the solution of problem. Children especially young ones, cannot perceive the problematic situation as a whole, without guidance from parents and teachers. In school, the teacher has to play the role of a guide, helping the child to perceive the situation as a whole so that the use of insight is frequent and direct. Unless the learner is capable of putting the problem situation in proper perspective, the use of insight becomes redundant.

Insight may be particularly important in human learning. We have all had the experience of quite suddenly seeing the solution to a problem after a period of puzzlement, and it then seems so obvious that we cannot understand why we had any difficulty. Often such sudden insight appears to be triggered off by some new perception-seeing an object, hearing a remark, or remembering something which gives us a fresh perspective on the situation. The process appears to involve recombination of past experiences and understanding of the relationships or principles underlying the solution, features which have been demonstrated experimentally with human subjects.

Wertheimer, before presenting one of his problems, taught his subjects how to find the area of a rectangle. They were told the product of two adjacent sides formula, and were also shown why this formula works by dividing a rectangle into squares and demonstrating that the area is the number of squares in a row times the number of rows. Wertheimer then asked his subjects to find the area of a parallelogram. Some replied that they could not do this without being told how. Others blindly applied the formula for the area of a rectangle. But some understood how to use their knowledge about areas of rectangles in finding the area of a parallelogram. One five and a half year old boy, for example, cut off one end of the parallelogram and fitted it against the other end to make a rectangle. This sort of solution involves a restructuring of the problem and an understanding of how existing knowledge can be used to solve it. From this type of inquiry Wertheimer concluded that children should be taught to understand how problems are solved rather than to apply rote learned solutions.

Important Elements

Now it should be clear that this was not just a random response. It makes more sense to say that the chimpanzee had insight-he perceived the box as something that can be climbed upon in order to seize something high. What happened does not look much like the gradual elimination of errors and the gradual strengthening of a correct response hit upon by chance. Once the insight has been attained, the problem is mastered. It can be solved immediately the next time. After the principle is understood, quite a few changes in the situation can be made without causing any difficulty. Then it matters little whether the lure is banana or orange, or just where the box is located, or its shape or size, (of course, there are limits to how big the changes can be without causing trouble). In other words, learning generalizes (or transfers) widely, once the principle is understood. This is one of the important characteristics of insight in learning

Kohler also found that some chimpanzees were able to solve more complicated problems, like stacking boxes so as to get bananas placed even higher or fitting two sticks together to make them long enough to reach food placed outside their cage. Typically the solution came rather suddenly, usually, after a quiet period in which the chimp looked over the situation.

In the Gestalt view, we solve a problem in this way. We think of various hunches (hypotheses) about what to do. Practically never do we fumble blindly, although some of our hunches may be very poor ones. What we try helps us to know which hunches will not work. It is as though we are testing our hunches, although we usually are not very systematic in doing so. Merely by thinking, we may perceive some possibilities and their probable effects without our doing anything overtly. Finally, either all at once or piecemeal, we get insight into the principle. We can use it to solve not only this problem but many others like it.

Certain factors may make it easier or harder to get insight into a problem. For one thing, past experience with similar problems may be helpful. A person with an engineering background, for example, is more likely to get insight into an engineering problem than someone without such a background.

It can also make a difference whether or not the various parts of the problem are handicapped in that the mechanism is largely hidden. Therefore, the insight into the relationship between pulling the string and the opening of the door is not possible. That is why his learning must be a fumbling, trial and error process.

Another factor having bearing on insight is strong preconceptions. We can feel so strongly that the solution lies in a particular direction that we are blind to other possibilities. All our efforts go into the wrong ideas. For instance, so long as we think that the way to get a stuck door open is to force it, then all that we can think about is how to bring enough force to bear on it. We might end with an ingenious arrangement of jacks and levers that finally break the door down, when unlocking it would have done the job! Even in our stupidity, however, our behaviour is not random or automatic. The lesson for all of us is clear; we should not get stuck on a premature hunch but should look over the problem in order to get a variety of hunches. Then we shall be less likely to waste our time in a blind alley.

There are some fundamental difference between Thorndike's Trial and Error-learning and Gestalt's insightful learning. Firstly in Thorndike's experiment the lever to open the door of the cage is out of sight of the subject. So the subject can't see it. Hence it is difficult on the part of the cat to under-stand the situation and apply its insight to solve the problem. According to Gestalt Theory the role of understanding and organisation of perceptual process is the most important in learning process. A problematic condition should be studied as a whole in the start and then it should be divided into interrelated parts. Then the situation is reorganised into a whole. This leads to the solution of a problem. All learning processes progress in such a manner. In short, perceptual comprehension is essential in learning process. In the process of perception it is marked that the perceiver completes the incomplete task by himself and considers the figure as a whole. It is clearly understood from the experiment of Kohler. The chimpanzee in the cage after some unsuccessful trials used two sticks by putting one in another to get the banana. Here the distance between the place of chimpanzee in the cage and the position of banana was judged by him and it used the two sticks to reach his goal. This became possible by the cognition and insight of the chimpanzee. So there lies the main difference between the trial and error learning and the insightful learning.

Trial and Error Learning	*Insightful Learning*
1. Dependent upon effort and labour.	1. Dependent on nature's gift.
2. Available to all.	2. Available to only higher animals.
3. Stress on physiological efficiency.	3. Stress on psychological efficiency.
4. Based on sensory-motor co-ordination.	4. Based on perception.
5. Goal directed activity.	5. More work done by sub-conscious brain.
6. No transfer of training takes place.	6. No transfer of training takes place.

10

Learning Made Easy

As a teacher, you will be interested in how motivation influences the acquisition of skills and knowledge in a school situation. We shall look closely at the problem of learning in the classroom. Here we shall discuss some aspects of motivation that are not directly a part of the classroom situation.

"Plateaus" in learning. Over a long period of time, the development of a motor skill, such as typewriting, working on an assembly line, or sending code messages, follows a fairly predictable pattern. At first, the individual shows a rather rapid increase in efficiency. This is followed by a period of slow improvement and then by a long period in which little or no improvement is made. When a secretary first learns to typewrite by means of the touch system, for example, her speed develops during the first year of practice from zero to perhaps 50 words per minute. The next year or so of practice may bring her speed up to 60 or 65 words per minute. After that, she will probably maintain the same level of skill for many years, with slight day-to-day fluctuation. This will be true even though she receives a certain set fee per page typed and it is to her advantage to type as rapidly as possible. We might decide that she has reached her physiological limit. However, psychologists discovered long ago that although individuals do reach a level beyond which they do not progress as long as their need remains the same, a substantial increase in need will result in progress far beyond what originally appeared to be their limit. When sufficient additional motivation arises, further improvement takes place and the individual may continue to improve for a substantial period of time.

If our typist, for example, is promised a promotion that involves prestige and money if she can attain a level of speed well beyond her present maximum, there is a good chance that she will succeed – assuming, of course, that the goal is not actually beyond her abilities. Habits of working at a speed that satisfies the individual's present motivation will not be broken until his motivation is substantially increased. He is content with his present performance even though it is well below his physiological limits. Each individual's level of performance is determined by a combination of his abilities, his level of aspiration, and the habits of work that have proved adequate to satisfy his current needs.

Of course, the ability to attain various levels of skill does vary from person to person. But regardless of our real physio-logical limit, we seldom come very near to attaining it. And the nearness with which we do approach it is determined by the extent of our needs.

Although we have been talking here only of simple motor skills, there is evidence that other types of learning, problem-solving, and competence in doing complex tasks, such as reading with speed and understanding, also depend on the amount of motivation furnished by our present needs.

The use of incentives. Rewards designed to influence behaviour are often called incentives. To influence behaviour significantly, however, the reward must be needed. It must serve to satisfy some motive. In the school we offer the child interesting experiences and opportunities to satisfy his curiosity and to achieve status and self-esteem. For example, a child can have numerous incentives for reading about the pioneers. His curiosity concerning what solution they will find to each problem acts as an incentive. And he identifies himself with Daniel Boone or David Crockett and obtains interesting experiences. He is able to share his experiences with his classmates and gain their attention and approval. He gains a word of praise or a sense of security from his teacher. His reading may result in a better grade and heightened self-esteem and esteem in the eyes of his parents.

In business and industry a bonus or a promotion may be offered as a reward for extra effort. In any situation, the most successful incentives are those that appeal to one or all of the psychological motives.

Positive and negative incentives. Educators have stated repeatedly that praise is stronger than reproof. But before we accept such a broad generalisation, we should look closely at what is known about these common incentives.

Both praise and reproof are strong drugs. If praise is administered constantly over a period of time, it loses much of its potency. In addition, how effective it is depends a good bit on the personality of the person who administers it. We expect praise from some individuals and accept it almost as we would accept silence from another. And if we hear little but praise from everyone, we grow to value it less and less.

The same is true of reproof. If a teacher constantly berates his students, they come to expect it. In fact, if a student fails to receive his fair measure of reproof for the day, he may lose status with his fellows. And so it is in the home. A child who receives little but reproof from his parents comes to expect and accept it. Its sting becomes dulled. But give such a child an unexpected word of praise and he will grasp it as a jewel. He will treasure it as a rare source of satisfaction.

Both praise and blame, like certain drugs, lose their effectiveness as we become tolerant of them, but our tolerance varies in relation to the individual from whom we receive them. We strive for a word of praise from one person either because he rarely gives praise or because his good opinion is necessary for our security. A word of reproof from another person may fail to stir us either because we have come to expect it or because his good opinion is of little importance for our feeling of security. If praise or blame is to affect our behaviour, it must either satisfy or threaten our security, our self-esteem, our esteem in the eyes of others, or some other motive.

The varying effect that praise and blame have on different individuals has been well demonstrated by experiments. During one learning experiment, a group of introverted children and a group of extroverted children were praised at certain times and blamed at others. The extroverted children made more improvement when they received blame than when they were praised, but the opposite was true of the introverted group. Other studies suggest that the extrovert tends to come from an environment where praise is more common than blame and that the opposite is true for the introvert. Typically, the introvert's development has been marked by strong repression whereas the extrovert has been encouraged to express himself and has often been the center of favourable attention.

Other things being equal, then, which has the more powerful effect on classroom learning—praise or blame? As you might expect, praise seems to be somewhat more powerful in actual practice. However, the evidence indicates that both serve to stimulate learning, since either one seems to produce better results than no comment whatsoever.

Praise and blame are examples of positive and negative incentives. Although individuals may react somewhat differently because of different past experiences, it is more pleasant to all of us to strive for positive rewards than it is to escape from negative threats. We strive either to improve our status or to prevent loss of our present status. Which motivation will result in greater effort depends somewhat on the nature of the individual and on the nature of the promised gain or possible loss.

Quite apart from the actual effort induced by different motivating situations, we as teachers must also be interested in the mental health of each child. Striving for advancement, particularly when it leads to success, is accompanied by a happy, pleasant feeling. Striving to prevent a threat to our present status, however, even if it is eventually successful, is accompanied by an unhappy, unpleasant feeling and by worry. The maladjustment evidenced in "nervous breakdowns" is more closely related to overworry than to overwork. Positive incentives in themselves, then, contribute more to the mental and emotional well-being of children than negative incentives do.

Product of Motivation

Interests are a specific type of positive incentive. They are capable of arousing and sustaining concentrated effort. For this reason, we shall want to study them carefully. How much appeal the classroom material has to a child's interests determines to a considerable extent how hard and how long he will be willing to concentrate on it. For the most part, study fatigue is created by nothing more than disinterest or boredom.

Why children differ in interests. Since children learn new things in order to satisfy physiological and psychological motives, biological factors have a strong influence on the development of their interests. If a child is large and agile, he is likely to gain selfesteem and the esteem of others from physical competition; if he is small or awkward, his security and prestige are likely to be threatened. If a child finds that experiences in the classroom nurture his security, he comes to enjoy being a student and to spend more time and effort in studious pursuits. If an adolescent girl finds that boys admire her, she is likely to enjoy dancing and similar activities in which she can receive their attention; if boys do not seek her out, she will find other activities to nurture her self-esteem.

Most interests are the product of past experiences. The goals that a child discovers to be approved by his family and his community, the experiences he has had with books, movies, companions, and teachers, and the experiments he has made in the world about him determine the direction that his interests will take.

Some differences in interests are caused by differences in chronological age. If for no reason other than the desire for social acceptability, the boy of 16 must shun some activities that are quite appropriate to the boy of eight.

Other differences in interest are related to sex. The fact that parents tend to approve one type of play activity for girls and another for boys is especially important to younger children. A girl receives favourable recognition when she spends time with dolls, plays house, or learns ballet dancing, but a boy who does the same things finds that his security and self-esteem are threatened.

Since girls, on the average, reach maturity at an earlier age than boys do, they show an earlier interest in dancing and in other activities that involve the opposite sex. Also, individual differences in physical maturation among members of the same sex have a strong effect on interests. As we have seen, some boys of 14 are sexually mature and others are immature. For both boys and girls, the attainment of sexual maturity results in new forms of motivation and in new problems. It is reflected in their choice of reading matter, conversational topics, heroes, movies, and radio and television programmes.

Actually, the specific interests that a child develops depend directly on how clearly he has been able to identify the types of activity that satisfy his motives. His desires for security, self-esteem, the esteem of others, and new experiences, and the success or failure that he meets in attempting to satisfy these desires, play a major part in determining what his interests will be. In other words, psychological motives, as well as physiological motives, are significant.

And once interests are formed, the habit motives tend to perpetuate them. A boy may retain an interest in coin-collecting, fishing, football, or photography long after they cease to satisfy the motives that they originally satisfied. Habit motives and the desire to be with friends who have the same interests may be sufficient. Or, as we trace interests throughout life, we may find that an activity remains the same but that the motives satisfied by it change greatly. For example, a boy may take up golf because it makes him feel mature and because it has social prestige; as a young man, he gains group and self-esteem from his proficiency; later he continues the game for the business contacts that come from it; and still later he follows it for reasons of health and to satisfy habit motives.

As a teacher, you will need a deep understanding of what interests are typical of both sexes at each developmental level, and of the range of interests that you can expect to find within groups of the same age and sex. Then you can translate your information into specific, practical terms, such as the games, books, movies, and songs that will be most appealing to a particular group of children.

What techniques can we use to determine specific interests? And how can we use interests in developing an effective learning situation?

Leisure-time activities due to interests. When children work and play under the direct supervision of adults, they have a natural tendency to display the interests they feel are expected of them. They are more interested in winning approval than they are in following their other inclinations. But in their freely chosen, leisure-time activities, they unwittingly provide us with valuable dues to what their interests really are. So you will want to take advantage of every opportunity to observe children after school hours, to talk with them about how they spend their evenings, and to enter into their social activities whenever you can do it unobtrusively and without embarrassment to the children and to yourself.

Try to find out what books they like to read, what radio and television programmes appeal to them, what movies they go to, what friends they spend their time with, what hobbies they follow, and what they do when they are with the family group. In the classroom itself you can gain insight into children's interests by encouraging them to exercise self-direction in attacking problems or in choosing assignments.

Each time you discover a new interest, remember that it has real importance in the life of the child. It represents to him a possible way of finding satisfaction for his motives and a solution to his problems. If you can manage to accommodate classroom activities to a real interest that the child himself has shown, you will succeed in creating a stimulating, effective learning situation. The secret is to enlist children's interests in the classroom rather than to oppose and reject them.

With the information you gather by observing children's leisure-time activities, you can do more than just appeal to their current interests. You can encourage them to enlarge and extend their interests in new, more rewarding directions. Since interests are the child's way of satisfying his motives, he will welcome sincere attempts to help him develop more satisfying activities. Of course when you attempt to build up new interests, you will have to be much more careful than when you appeal to interests that already exist. But once a child has discovered that a new activity provides him with satisfaction, he will readily adopt it as a new interest.

Some Suggestions

Never worry about creating motivation in children. Every child has a tremendous amount of motivation that he is eager to satisfy every hour of the day. If you can suggest desirable educational goals that appeal to the child's motives, and if you can give him frequent opportunities to succeed in his attempts to reach those goals, you will have harnessed one of the most powerful learning forces known.

Since frustrating problems are as essential to the learning situation as motives themselves, you will want to be careful not to remove every difficulty from the child's path. Problems are a nece-ssary condition of learning. They must be great enough to call forth serious effort, but not so great that they lead to defeat and a retreat from important goals.

As you help children in their attempts to satisfy their motives, always remember that individual children vary in their ability to achieve. No child will strive after an impossible goal for very long. He must find his tasks challenging but not discouraging. They must be tailored to fit his individual abilities. By providing him with opportunities to succeed in winning security, self-esteem, the esteem of others, and new experiences, you will make the classroom the scene of significant learning.

Be careful about how you approach the needs and interests of the child. Your task is not so much to let each child do just what he wants to do, but rather to encourage him to strive for significant long-range goals by appealing to the needs and motives that he already possesses. In short, you will help the child to choose what he is to learn. You will not force him to do things that he finds objectionable, but you must guide him in the directions that the curriculum-maker and the school as a whole find desirable.

There is much for the child to learn, and only a short time in which to learn it. You can increase both the speed and the quality of his learning by appealing to the motives that he brings with him into the classroom.

Process of Learning

Another question. How does learning take place? What are the conditions which favour learning? What external conditions result in improved performance by an individual? These questions are of great interest to the teachers, parents, students and the educationists. Psychologists have defined learning as any relatively permanent changes in behaviour as a result of practice or experience. It modifies or changes the behaviour of the students in terms of achieving the goals. It is the process by which the student profits from past experiences. It is an inference from behaviour and must be distinguished from it, for learning can occur without behaviour being affected. We may learn that a certain petrol-station is open twenty four hours a day without influencing our observable behaviour, unless and until we need petrol-station during the night. It is inferred that learning has occurred if in such circumstances we patronise the petrol-station concerned whereas previously we would not have done so. Thus learning is a change in behaviour potential rather than in behaviour itself. Such changes can occur for many reasons, including maturation, fatigue, injury or the effects of drugs. But the term learning is applied only to those resulting from past experience. Further, it is restricted to changes of relatively permanent nature. Once having learned to ride a bicycle or drive a car, we quite soon regain former attainments in these skills after even long periods of disuse. Long term changes in behaviour potential of this sort are to be distinguished from shorter term changes which are often the result of temporary states in the learner such as variations in motivations.

Learning Conception

From the above discussion, it is understood that learning is the modification of behaviour potential as a function of experience. A simpler definition, most frequently found in ordinary dictionaries, is that learning involves the acquisition of information.

This is often the case, but there are a number of situations in which individuals learn without acquiring any new information. This is obvious in the development of certain motor skills where practice rather than information leads to gradual modifications in behaviour.

In addition, affective learning (learning involving emotional behaviour) does not necessarily involve the acquisition of information as it is ordinarily defined as a behaviour change due to experience including all affective motor and cognitive (intellectual) changes that do not result from other causes. For example, behaviour can change as a result of fatigue, drags or maturation; but these changes are of a transient nature resulting from genetic forces, or are induced artificially. They are not considered to involve learning.

Man learns new methods and skills to successfully do, think reason and adjust to any forthcoming problem. Learning is associated with acquisition of new behaviour or modification of old behaviour. Psychologists from their own viewpoints have defined learning in various ways. Let us discuss some important definitions given by eminent psychologists.

While a student wants to learn more and more new ideas, a teacher tries to make his teaching effective and fruitful. Simi-larly, a doctor is interested to know about new medicines, and an engineer wants to invent new ideas of construction. An industrialist puts into use new methods of production. A politician sticks to new methods of propaganda to attract people towards him. In the same way a housewife prepares new items of food, while children want to make themselves attractive by wearing dresses of new designs. Priests and prophets adopt new tricks to make their views popular. They manipulate methods to attract more and more persons and to have more and more followers. So it is clear from the above discussion that everybody is inclined to learn new methods for his way of life. Then a question arises spontaneously as to, how does learning take place? What is learning? What is nature and what are its principles? Now let us discuss the definitions and nature of learning.

Definition of Learning

Learning can be defined as any relatively permanent change in behaviour which occurs as a result of practice or experience. This definition has three important elements (1) learning is a change in behaviour, for better or worse. (2) It is the change that takes place through practice or experience, changes due to growth, maturation, or injury are not learning. This part of the definition distinguishes learning from innately controlled, species specific behaviour of the sort. (3) Before it can be called learning, the change must be relatively permanent, it must last a fairly long time. This rules out changes in behaviour due to motivation, fatigue, adaptation, or sensitivity of the organism.

According to Skinner, learning is not acquiring knowledge or skill by mere mechanical repetitions. It is a process in which the learner organises different elements and experiences to reach a particular goal.

In the view of Hilgard, learning refers to the change in a subject's behaviour to a given situation brought about by his repeated experiences in that situation, provided that the behaviour change cannot be explained on the basis of native response tendencies, maturation or temporary states of the subject (e g, fatigue, drugs etc).

In the opinion of King Ley and Gray, "learning is the process by which an organism in satisfying its motivation adopts and adjusts its behaviour in order to overcome obstacles or barriers."

According to Eason, "learning includes changes in behaviour that are determined primarily by the individuals interaction with his, environment."

H. J. Klausmeireir writes, "Learning is a process whereby a change in behaviour results from some form of experience, activity, training, observation and the like. change in some behaviour which results from such forces as bodily injury, disease, fatigue or use of drugs is not considered learning".

According to Cronback learning is shown by a change in behaviour as a result of experience.

Blair, Jones and Simpson are of the view that, "any change of behaviour which is a result of experience, and which causes people to face later situations differently may be called learning".

According to W. C. Morse and G. M. Wingo "Learning can be defined as changing one's potential for seeing, feeling and doing through experiences partly perceptual, partly intellectual, partly emotional and partly motor".

According to Morris L. Bigge "Learning is a change in a living individual which is not heralded by genetic inheritance, it may be a change in insights, behaviour, perception or motivation or a combination of them."

Guthrie in Psychology of Learning says learning is "The ability to learn, that is, to respond differently to a situation because of past response to the situation".

Hall opines, "the essential nature of learning process may, however, be stated quite simply. Just as the inherited equipment of reaction tendencies consists of receptor effector corrections, so the process of learning consists in the strengthening of certain of these connections as contrasted with others or in the setting up of quite new connections".

One of the shortest definitions was given by J. P. Guilford. It reads, "Learning is change in behaviour resulting from behaviour."

According to Garret, "Learning is an organization of behaviour, It is the activity by virtue of which we organise our responses with new habits".

Murphy states that "Learning is a modification of both behaviour and the way of perceiving".

Man not only learns but also trains the lower animals. For example in a circus, wild animals like tiger, elephant, and bear perform many tricks. So also a pigeon can be trained to carry letters from one place to another, and a trained dog can identify a thief. Psychologist Hays brought up a chimpanzee from his babyhood just like a human child. By providing him with special learning experiences certain changes in his behaviour were marked.

As a result of his learning in his latter days he preferred more to live among human beings than among other chimpanzees. He was able to clean the dishes, polish and colour the furniture, clean the room and sharpen the pencil, etc. He was even able to attend psychological non-verbal tests with human chiidren of his age. But in spite of all the attempts of the researchers, he could not develop his skill in language. It is because, the vocal center of animals lacks something, which human beings possess. While human beings are able to read, play, dance and gather knowledge, about various things, the animals fail to do these. The mind of human beings is a developed one and that is why' they are able to master the knowledge of higher level. What learning does for a human child and how it affects his lifestyle is clear from the following discussions.

1. Learning is Modification of Behaviour: Learning produces change in behaviour. Learning is often described as the modification of behaviour. The child learns ideas, rules, customs, etc, from his surroundings in order to adjust himself with his environment and different required behaviour and predicted activities though no one teaches him to do so. Gradually this modification of behaviour becomes permanent and goes on developing and changing day by day.

2. Learning Helps to Reach the Goal: Learning not only brings change in behaviour but also helps one in meeting the desires of one's life. Again, goals and ambitions can be achieved only with appropriate and positive learning in a particular direction. It directly or indirectly helps the individual to reach his goal. Learning of speech, learning to laugh, cry in the case of a child, is organised deliberately. They are not accidental. Hence learning is accepted by all as an internalising process.

3. Learning Creates Interest to know New Things: A deep desire or thirst for knowledge is often marked in some individuals Even in case of children, it is observed that they show interest and are anxious to do new works to

find out new facts and engage themselves in small and simple researches. This helps them to learn more and more.

4. Environmental Influence brings Difference in Learning: All children are not reared up in similar environments. A particular child is brought up in different environ-ments during his lifetime. Hence learning process and its effects on one child may be different from that of another on the basis of their difference in environment in which their learning experience takes place. Children coming from adverse environments such as poverty, sometimes show amazing results in learning. So also the ones coming from a proper environment sometimes show the same originality in learning. Children coming from villages and undeveloped localities, In spite of their intelligence, fail to become successful in learning due to their undeveloped environment. On the other hand, children in urban areas, In spite of their low I.Q. are successful in better learning performance. It is because their environment helps them learn better. Hence it can be said that a proper and adequate environment is very much necessary for a fruitful learning of the child. Especially the house and the school should provide the necessary stimulus for learning experience.

5. Learning is a Problem-solving Activity: Society is dynamic. An individual has to adjust himself with every change and he has to face many novel and unexpected situations. There are some problems that cannot be solved by means of age old customary methods. The novel situations should be met with new ideas, and at this point learning helps him. Changing problems in changing circumstances can only be solved with new forms of learning.

6. Learning is a Matter of Habit: From this proposition one may conclude that doing a work habitually is learning. Learning is the display of mastered personal reaction to a given situation. Man has to react in the right way to his stimulus. By habit formation, he can do away with incorrect ways of reaction formation. Secondly, learning makes habit

not only to be formed in the correct way but also be organised.

7. Learning is an Automatic Process: Learning takes place when the child becomes active. He has to indulge himself in the process of learning. In course of performing daily activities he automatically gathers experience. And that is the process of learning. When he himself becomes aware of his requirements—mental, physical, social and emotional, etc, he becomes active. Its requirements stimulate his will and produces response. If he is easily motivated by some other factors, then learning can also take place even without a teacher. The child learns when he feels the requirement for it. So this process is always directed to a particular goal.

8. Learning is not Knowledge about Subjects: Learning is not confined to the four walls of an educational institution. Reading and remembering books is also not learning. All round development of a person is learning and by learning only, one's personality matures. Studying different branches of knowledge in schools and colleges is generally termed as learning. But apart from this there are so many things such as knowledge about God, language, literature, philosophy, art, sculpture, social values, personal traits, which are also learned by human beings. So it should not be misunderstood that learning implies only reading books.

9. Learning may be Correct or Incorrect: Though learning is defined as modification of behaviour, the modification itself may be correct or incorrect. It may be socially acceptable or unacceptable. We learn both good behaviour and bad behaviour in our day to day experiences. But true learning warns us against bad behaviour and this is right learning.

10. Learning Occurs both in Formal and Informal, Situations: Process of learning starts from the birth of a child. He learns many things through social interaction with others in his environment. New habits are formed and skills

mastered. Many novel ideals also occur in his own mind. New choices, new beliefs and new interests are aroused in him. Then he comes to school and learns what he is taught. He is aware of what he is learning. So all the above learning processes can be termed as formal learning. Apart from these, he also learns informally from his various other experiences. Various institutions such as family, club, gymnasium, religious place, playground, excursion, etc, render informal learning to him.

11. Higher Learning depends upon Capacity of Individual and Complexity of Learning Material: For successful and effective learning, so many personal factors are responsible. They are our individual capabilities. They include our memory, interest, understanding, emotion, controlling capacity, etc. To make learning effective, the child takes the help of two processes. One is that he tries to solve some of his problems with already acquired knowledge and skills and the second is that he discovers new methods and skills to face some personal problems. In order to solve some complex problems, he needs higher and more learning.

12. Learning is a Function of Maturation: Learning to an extent is also a function of maturation. One cannot teach a new born baby to walk or to pick up any object with his fingers however much one may try. Before anything is learnt by a person, his sensory, motor and also the nervous system including brain must reach a certain level of maturity.

    The predetermined sequential stage of maturity of the sensory motor and nervous system of an animal is called maturation. Individuals of different species undergo different sequential patterns of development and maturation. It has been observed that unless an individual attains a particular level of maturation, he cannot learn a particular skill of learning. Different learnings require different levels of maturation. Acquisition of simple motor skills is possible in early infancy. But complex activities like reading and writing, etc, which require a developed brain has to be postponed for pre-school and early-school period.

Important in this context is the concept of "critical period" for learning. If it has not been learnt at a particular stage of child's maturational development, it becomes difficult for him to master it at a later period. Harlow made an experiment in 1962 on monkeys regarding this. He raised some monkeys in isolation, without letting them to mix or play with other monkeys. He found that if the isolation is upto 90 days the resultant abnormal social and sexual behaviour is short-lived, but if isolation is more than that period, the abnormality persists throughout life. This made him conclude that the first 90 days is the critical period for learning of social and sexual behaviour in monkeys.

13. Learning is Dependent on Nervous System: Learning is also dependent on the nervous system which includes the brain. It has been found that the animals with more complex nervous systems learn faster and acquire more complex skills than those with simpler nervous systems. An experimenter reared a chimpanzee just like a human baby soon after its birth. He also gave it special training whenever necessary. As a result of this she learnt to perform simple acts like dusting, washing dishes and painting furnitures, etc. But she could not talk because of the deficiency in the language or speech center of her brain. Thus, limitations of the brain is an important factor in the learning ability of a child or an animal.

    As to human learning, the growth of cerebral cortex plays a very important role. Growth of learning ability during childhood and adolescence is directly related to maturation of the cerebral cortex. The decline of learning ability in old age is probably due to the decay of the tissues of this part of the brain.

    Lashley conducted an experiment on white rats. His three important findings about learning and the brain are that learning is related to the amount of cortical tissue, available inside the brain of the subject. The greater the amount of cortical tissue, the quicker will be his learning. He proved this by taking away various percentages of cortical tissue from the brains of rats and then making them learn the maze. The second conclusion is that learning is related to the location of specific cortical tissues in the brain of the subject. He proved that the removal of specified cortical tissues led to the loss of sensitivity to visual details, removing another, to the loss of sensitivity to different odours, and so on. Thus, there are functional specialisations inside the brain. A brain has different centres for different abilities. If the subject's brain lacks a particular centre, say speech centre, he cannot learn that ability. Lashley also came to another conclusion. He found that if a particular centre in the brain of the subject, relating to some particular ability is destroyed, then it results only in temporary loss of the ability. Gradually other parts of the cerebral cortex take up the function of the destroyed centre. Hence the lost ability of the subject reappears from this. He propounded his theory of mass action, which means that cerebrum functions as mass.

14. Learning is a Self-acting Process: Learning is also a self-active process. Learning involves the subject. If a child has to learn, he has to be involved in the process of learning. He has to participate in his experiences and has to learn from them. There cannot be any learning without the involvement of his self. To learn, a child or a subject has not only to involve his senses but he has also to use the higher centre of his brain, which will impart pattern, meaning and significance to his sensory inputs.

We can conclude that learning is a process that provides impetus for a new behaviour or through interaction with the environment brings change in the already existing behaviour. Learning brings a permanent change in behaviour. Hence the changes in behaviour caused by regular exercise, games, habitual walks, are permanent change. The intensity of emotion may also bring change in behaviour. So it is right to conclude that human behaviour is the central point of learning process. Here behaviour does not mean physiological activities only, but inner processes like thinking, memory, power, causality and emotional reaction.

The sort of change in behaviour, which can be termed as learning may also be necessary or unnecessary. This change may occur inside the school or outside it. It may occur knowingly or unknowingly. W. R. Mescaw in his book *Educational Psychology* has given details of the characteristics of learning process. They are:

The Change in Situation

Learning in case of human beings, is a matter of pro-gressive change in behaviour. It is result of a felt need from within the organism. Unless there is a strong urge in the body to adopt a particular response and to modify its pattern, learning would not take place. Heredity and environment affect learning and the capability of the learner in a very big way. Some animals are more educable than others and similarly some individuals get more opportunities of learning than others. Learning and process of maturation are strongly related. It is the level of maturity in the individual that determines whether he would be able to make a particular response or not. More complex responses and more intricate activities cannot be acquired unless one has matured to do so. Thinking stabilizes as the level of maturity goes up. Higher intellectual activities are not possible without greater maturity. The native behaviour is less refined in comparison to the acquired one. In fact the acquired behaviour gives definite shape to the inherited behaviour, it is a sort of mere ornamental process which refines and brightens the inherited raw response. Learnt behaviour is an embellishment to the personality. Throughout one's life, not only does one learn to sit, to stand or to turn or to speak but also to dress well, to think deeply and to acquire knowledge. The home, the school, the club, etc, are the temples of learning. The child learns by himself; he also has to learn a number of response patterns in the company of his friends, parents and teachers.

Learning may be defined as relatively permanent change in behaviour potential occurring as the result of past experience. It is an inference from behaviour and must be distinguished from it for learning can occur without behaviour being affected. We may learn that a certain petrol-station is open twenty four hours a day without this influencing our observable behaviour, unless and until we need petrol during the night. It is inferred that learning has occurred if in such circumstances, we patronise the petrol-station concerned whereas previously we would not have done so. Thus learning is a change in behaviour potential rather that in behaviour itself. Such changes can occur for many reasons, including maturation, fatigue, injury or the effects of drugs, but the term learning is applied only to those resulting from past experience. Further, it is restricted to changes of a relatively permanent nature. Once having learned to ride a bicycle or drive a car, we quite soon regain former attainments in these skills after even long periods of disuse. Long-term change in behaviour potential of this sort are to be distinguished from short-term changes which are often the result of temporary states in the learner such as variations in motivation. A convenient fourfold classification of learning is outlined in the remainder of this chapter.

The Cooperation

Learning is not an individualistic process; it is a co-operative process too. The child learns by impulse and he learns by compulsion; he learns by imitation and he learns by initiation, and he learns by adoption and he learns by assimilation. Philosophy, religion, science, architecture, etc, are the results of human learning and the capability of the human child to retain experiences. Man has developed media through which experiences are stored and transmitted from one to the other generation. Ability to retain experiences, is the key note of learning. Learning is an institutionalized and formalised affair in modern education. The child does not go to school to learn, reading and writing but he has to learn to adjust to the environment.

11

Evolution of Personality

Evolution is a continual process. The study of growth and deve-lopment helps people to understand what life means. That is, one must study the changes that normally occur in body, thought and behaviour over the course of a life span. Right from the time of conception to death at a ripe age, the human organism runs through various stages of growth; each stage being a ladder-step taking to the final goal of life. An infant and an adult are paradoxically "like and unlike" each other in very many ways: one is erratic, impulsive and playful and the other seasoned, reasoning and thinking and artful; one is waxing and the other waning, one is like a rising star and the other a setting star. Biologically, it takes a long span of time for a neonate to become an adult, to become big, to grow in height and acquire weight although all the physical organs are already present at birth. Growth is a natural tendency with all organisms.

Growth and development are generally used inter-changeably though the scientists consider growth to be one aspect of development. Ordinarily the term growth refers to the 'increase' caused by the biological process in which the organism becomes bigger in size, and heavier in weight. Starting his life almost from an invisible dot, the human organism grows to be more than five feet in height and more than 150 pounds in weight. Growth indicates the enlargement of cells, fibres and muscles, elongation of the skeleton and increase in the general volume of the body-parts and organ-systems. Growth brings about perceptible changes in one's structure and form: it is quantitative in the sense that can be measured in inches, points and dynes. Marked structural changes are noticed as the orga-nism advances in age. Day after day and year after year, as the child looks different in appearance, we conclude that the child is growing.

'Development' is a wider term indicating advancement, more unfoldment, a progressive change - a sort of growing forward to a greater maturity; it is a process of qualitative transformation which brings about maturity and functional improvement.

Gessel stresses "Development is more than a concept. It can be observed, appraised and to some extent even 'measured' in three major manifestations: (a) anatomic (b) physiologic and (c) behavioural...... Behavioural signs, however, constitute a most comprehensive index of development states and development potential"

Development is growing up characteristically. It is related to growth in as much as that it denotes more specifically the changes in the character and efficiency of the organs, organ-systems. For example, the bones as they grow, they become larger but changes also take place in their ossification, hardness and the ability to bear weight and shocks; elasticity gives way to solidity which gives strength. Similarly the heart grows, becomes bigger and it also undergoes qualitative transformation when it becomes capable of pumping out more blood and thus stand the rigorous of vigorous exercises. Filling up the soft-parts of the brain, elongation of the axons and dendrites of the nerve cells are instances of development in which the internal physiological processes stimulated by them are integrated (or responded to) in a way which enables the individual to master further anew environmental stimulations. The better the child develops, the stronger he becomes to fight knowledge of the environment and the environmental hazards like diseases. Development is an interactive process causing the organism to acquire physiological capacities and psychological capabilities.

Growth and Development

"Many people use the terms "growth" and "development" interchangeably. In reality they are different, though they are inseparable. Neither takes place alone.

(i) The term "growth" is used in purely physical sense. It generally refers to an increase in size, length, height and weight. Changes in the quantitative aspects come into the domain of growth.

(ii) Growth is one of the parts of the developmental process. In strict sense development in its quantitative aspect is termed as growth.

(iii) Growth may be referred to describe the changes which takes place in particular aspects of the body and behaviour of an organism.

(iv) Growth does not continue throughout life. It stops when maturity has been attained.

(v) The changes produced by growth are the subject of measurement. They may be quantified and observable in nature.

(vi) Growth may or may not bring development. A child may grow (in terms of weight) by becoming fat but growth may not bring any functional improvement (qualitative change) or development.

Development, by contrast; refers to qualitative and quantitative changes. It may be defined as a progressive series of orderly, coherent changes. *The Webster's Dictionary* defines 'development' as "the series of changes which an organism undergoes in passing from an embryonic state to maturity". These changes refer to physical, emotional, intellectual changes which we shall discuss under the following points:

(i) Development implies overall changes in shape, form or structure resulting in improved working or functioning. It indicates the charges in the quality or character rather than in quantitative aspects.

(ii) Development is a wider and comprehensive term. It refers to overall changes in the individual. Growth is one of its parts.

(iii) Development describes the changes in the organism as a whole and does not list the changes in parts.

(iv) Development is a continuous process. It goes from womb to tomb. It does not end with the attainment of maturity. The changes, however small they may be, continue through the life span of an individual.

(v) Development, as said earlier, implies improvement in functioning and behaviour and hence brings qualitative changes which are difficult to measure directly. They are assessed through keen observation in behavioural situations.

(vi) Development is also possible without growth as we see in the cases of some children where they do not gain in terms of height, weight or size but they do experience functional improvement or development in physical, social, emotional or intellectual aspects.

Hence when observed in minute details, both growth and development show differentiation. But in a wider and practical sense both terms are used to denote any changes in the organism's physical as well as functional behaviour. These changes which cover physical, emotional, intellectual and social aspects of human life are roughly divided into four major classes by Mrs. Hurlock: (i) Changes in size, (ii) Changes in proportion, (iii) Disappearance of old features, (iv) Acquisition of new features.

All the types of changes have qualitative as well as quantitative aspects and hence generally growth and development go hand in hand. And it is in this sense, that the two terms are to be used collectively. Both, taken together explain the total changes-functional as well as constitutional changes in the body and behaviour of the individual with the lapse of time after the conception.

However, growth and development are so closely linked that at times it is hardly possible to clearly distinguish between the two. Nature has set limits to the extent of growth of every animal and hence no animal would grow beyond those limits. Macy and Kelly declare that "physical development does not necessarily mean increase in size. There are modifications of the body composition taking place constantly. In the body, for example, gain in weight comes partly from increase in neural, glandular, and muscle tissue; in childhood the gain comes principally from bone and muscle tissue; while in adult years, the gain is from an accumulation of fat tissue". No boundaries are set for development. Normally the growth may stop by the time a boy or a girl crosses further, depending upon one's pro-fessional work and labor. Not only does one develop physically but also socially and intellectually. Acquisition of new skills and assimilation of more knowledge constitute those qualitative changes which characterise 'development'. Quantitative measurement of the structure may reveal the pattern of growth a child is following and it is nowadays very easy to find out from the school health records whether the child is growing or not. Similarly tests have been devised to objectively measure strength, an indirect-index of the qualitative change in muscles and bones - and determine the extent of the development. In the same way, intellectual capacity and ability which are the indices of mental development, can be noticeable in the players and athletes who day after day give better performance in activities involving strength, speed, cardiovascular endurance, etc. Ordinarily when children reveal their motor skills, intellectual ability, etc, differences in their growth and development can be spotted without much difficulty. Physical development is prominent in athletes who regularly take exercise while people with sedentary habits lag behind in this sphere. Simi-larly voracious readers show signs of mental development. When athletes behave wonderfully well during play and do not lose mental equilibrium when defeated, we normally say that they have developed emotionally too. Social development is purely qualitative in nature because it reflects one's adjust-ment in the environment.

Regardless of individual background and concerns, it is desirable to examine our purposes in studying growth and development. We want to acquire the following abilities:

1. The ability to recognize individuality. This implies the ability to recognize the uniqueness of each child's traits and view of life.

2. An understanding of the theories and principles of growth and development so that one can understand develop-

ment in terms of the varied hereditary, environment and self influences usually involved.

3. An increased effectiveness in observing and interpreting the pattern of individual behaviour.
4. The ability to differentiate and evaluate the effectiveness of varying points of view in child study.
5. The development of a point of view and set of principles basic to guiding children more effectively in the learning and adjustment processes.

Thus, the student of child development should be involved not merely with learning a number of facts, but also with developing skills which can help him both personally and professionally throughout his life. This necessitates the continuing and purposeful observation of children in action, to supplement regular class study. As time goes on, he will be able to apply his knowledge and experience to interact more effectively with children.

Basic Elements

Development psychologists believe that an accurate picture of the principles of growth, and development is essential for the teacher. They are as follows:

(1) Growth in Some Direction is Inevitable: All living organisms have to grow come what may. Propensity to grow is inherent in the organism. Because of malnutrition or some other environmental factors, the functional capacity of the child may not improve. Yet he has to grow and become bigger to the extent to which his heredity has set limits. It has been found that mental development is not much affected by malnutrition in childhood, provided the child received normal diet later on and that unfavorable conditions are not allowed to continue. All persons gain normal height even if they are not subjected to any special diet and physical exercises. Only those who exercise shall have better physical functional ability. There is, in each individual, an urge to grow and become bigger. Some

individuals strive to grow into athletes, others into Mathematicians. The inner urge for growth will certainly take some form or direction.

(2) Mental Growth is Dependent upon the Changed Structure: Along with increase in child's physical proportions, his ability to experience things enhances because physical growth and mental activity go hand in hand. When a child is found to be poor at perception and comprehen-sion, it is because various organs of perception are not fully developed to receive cues from the environment and he is not in a position to sift the wrong from the right. Gradually the brain also becomes capable of accumulating experiences. A child and an adult differ from each other in physical as well as mental growth. Perception and execution of complex motor skills involving a very high degree of neuro-muscular coordination is beyond the mental limits of the child while an adult having richer experience of years, takes little time in picking up hints and behaving accordingly. Qualitative mental activity is not possible without proper growth of the nervous system.

(3) Characteristically, Children are Ego-centric and Adults Socio-centric: A child's behaviour is motivated by the intra-organismic drives which lead to the achievement of biological ends. When the needs connected with this process are not satisfied, the child revolts. As the child matures, he also learns to consider "other things" before his self. Much of his instinctive behaviour gets modified because the society demands certain norms, standards, customs and traditions as well as etiquettes to be observed and followed in the manner of walking, talking, dressing up, eating and the like. The adult behaviour is guided more by social norms and standards. Childhood, in fact, is a state of animal-hood. The child does what pleases him and what strengthens his ego. In infancy, for example, all activities of the child, including play, are individualistic in nature. Childhood is not bound by the shackles of social norms and standards.

(4) Growth is a Creative Process: Right from the time of conception to adulthood marked differences in structure and form appear-thus resulting in behavioural varia-bility. Transforming a infinitesimal zygote into a child, is the nature's highest form of creativity. As a child advances in age, year by year marked changes become visible in his behaviour. Instinctive behaviour which hitherto was more or less fixed, starts giving way to variability. Behaviourally what a child is at the age of one year, he would not be so at the age of five and the child at the age of fourteen is entirely different from the one at five. The process of growth creates novel, cogni-tive, conceptual and motor forms of behaviour as the child marches ahead in time.

(5) Heredity sets Limits for Development in terms of Potential: Even if environmental factors such as food, air, exercise, etc, are abundantly available, the organism would never grow beyond the limits nature has already set on various animals and their respective species. Even twins may differ on anatomical characteristics. Certain races are tall while others are short statured.

Similarly short children born of short parents would not gain height despite the best nutritional facilities and physical exercise. No teacher of physical education and sports should hope to increase the height/size of the individual which is already determined and demarcated by his hereditary forces. Many parents and teachers still erroneously believe that certain physical exercises can help children gain height. The teacher of physical education has to take special note of this fact. The activity programme has to be framed keeping in view these facts concerning the anatomical structure and its developments. Similarly many other hereditary traits cannot be developed beyond a certain limit. A born imbecile will never become a genius despite all efforts. Effects of certain congenital defects and deformities might be attenuated. Yet the total cure is impossible.

(6) Different Aspects of Growth, Develop at Different Rates

Some children start toddling earlier than they start babbling; some start articulating sounds before they step into the phase of upright locomotion. Parents often worry when there is some delay in the appearance of a particular trait or characteristic at a particular period of time. Children characteristically speak three to five words at twelve months of age but in the next three or four months they seldom use words and often even forget the ones they knew. Language growth slows down for the time being because the child's physical energy and enthusiasm for learning are thoroughly occupied with the thrills of upright locomotion. Physical growth proceeds rapidly during puberty. Children probably learn more new things in the first five years of life than at any comparable period during the rest of their lives. In most of the children there is no synchronization between the physical and the mental growth. Some children become psychologically mature earlier while some excel mentally earlier than others. Ultimately all aspects of growth catch up by the time maturity is reached.

(7) Various Organs of the Body grow at Different Rates: Each organ reaches its maximum extent or dimension at different times. But within this chaos, a definite order has been found by the researchers. They speed up first reaching their peak growth rate only after about three months after the adolescence spurt has begun. In other six months, it is the turn of the calf muscles. Four months later, the hips and chest begin to broaden at an accelerated rate followed by the shoulders. In both sexes, the length of the trunk and the depth of the chest reach peak growth last of all.

(8) Growth is Characterised by Fluctuation: Many factors may be held responsible for fluctuation in growth. Generally infancy or pre-school years are periods of accelerated growth while later childhood and late adolescence are periods of slackness. They are, in fact, periods of consolidation. After adolescence, the growth tapers off. Some psychologists have found certain individuals still

growing-though imperceptibly-even at forty. Nutrition, physical and mental stresses and strains and other environmental factors influence the rate of growth. Some time, with all other factors there is still fluctuation in growth with certain children. For this, some internal and external factors may be responsible. Fluctuation in growth is not a drawback but an internal law and can easily be spotted if periodic check-up is made and proper records are kept. A month-to-month and year-to-year study, through pschomedical and ability tests, can reveal fluctuation.

(9) Any Breaks in the Continuity of Development will generally be due to Environmental Factors: Given an adequate environment, development will ordinarily take place in a relatively predictable way. Infants will grow physically as do most other children in the culture. They will learn to crawl before they walk. By the age of two they will have a rough working knowledge of the language that surrounds them; and toward the end of childhood they will experience rapid physical changes culminating in sexual maturity and adulthood. Motor, or intellectual development may be impeded in cases of severe childhood diseases or as a result of certain maternal diseases while the child is still in embryo. In much the same way, diet, drugs, and illness can affect children directly at various stages of their development and stunt both physical and intellectual growth. And, according to a principle already stated, the effects of these conditions will be most pronounced during the period of most rapid growth.

(10). Correlation and not Compensation is the Rule in Development: It has often been assumed by grandmothers that nature makes up for deficiencies in some areas by compensating for them in others. Thus, children who develop with frail and uncoordinated bodies, will most likely be given exceptional minds to make up for it. Only rarely will mother nature give the same individual both a superior body and a superior mind.

In reality, mother nature is probably not responsible for such events. Striking incidents of compensation that can be gleaned from personal experience or anecdotal evidence are probably most often the result of considerable direct effect on the part of the individuals concerned. Because all individuals have a need for acceptance by others. Children who are unsuited for the competitive aggressive sports of their peers because they are significantly smaller, may naturally become more interested in intellectual or other matters. The point is that the compensation is not a natural pheno-menon, but results instead from the individual's activities motivated by whatever needs are predominant at that time. That correlation rather than compensation is the rule is supported by evidence from a number of studies of gifted children.

(11) Development usually Proceeds at the Rate at which it Started: Children who learn to walk and talk at an early age are likely to be advanced in all areas of development throughout their childhood. This does not mean, of course, that they are more intelligent and better developed physically than children who mature more slowly. Although their biological clocks may be faster, they are not necessarily programmed for more superior development.

(12) Development is a Life long Process: Generally growth and development go hand in hand. When the boy or an individual child grows in structure it also develops in function. But it is not the universal truth. A time may come when he may grow but does not develop or he may develop but does, not grow. Again growth may stop at a particular period, but development continues after growth has ceased. Development thus, is a continuous process. An individual changes both physically and psychologically and encounters new adjustment problems throughout his life.

(13) Development Involves Changes: The life of an individual is dynamic in nature. It is never static. From the moment

of conception to the time of death, it undergoes changes. At each stage of human development, changes take place, whether for good or bad, as a result of accumulation of experience. The aim of such developmental changes are achievement of genetic potentials or self-actualization.

(14) Early Development is more Critical than Later Development: Milton, the world famous poet once said, "The childhood shows the man, as morning shows the day." Right from the beginning of the early childhood, one can predict the future of an individual. Freud, in his study about personality maladjustment emphasises on the significance of early years of life. Erikson also opines that "childhood is the science of man's beginning as man". Thus, most educationists and the psychologists feel that the early development of the child is very critical. Early pattern of life is relatively unchanged as time goes on. The early impression of the child remains for all times to come. Therefore, the first five years of the child have been called "The critical period". From this age onwards the foundations are laid for future life. The environment in which the child lives during this period has strong impact on his hereditary patterns. Hence guidance is most needed in the early stage of life.

(15) From Infancy to Childhood each Individual has his own Rate of Growth: The rate of development varies from individual to individual. While some develop rapidly others develop slowly. Dull children continue to be dull and the bright children maintain their brightness. Children having mental defects stop growing at an early age in comparison to the normal children From physical point of view, a child who is tall and heavy for his age, will continue to be tall and heavy to his age, and a child who is weak for his age, will continue to be so. Such rate of growth is a tendency and it may be influenced by environment.

(16) The Pattern of Growth is Continuous and Gradual: Behaviour of an individual does not become mature and perfect soon after birth. It is a slow continuous and gradual

process. To enter into a stage or level, it takes time. Early childhood lays the foundation for later childhood and later childhood for adolescence. Therefore, it is not possible to demarcate sharply the different stages of development. It is a continuous process. Physical growth and mental and social development is also a conti-nuous process. The process of continuity is maintained even in the development of traits.

(17) Growth is a Process of both Differentiation and Inte-gration: People vary in their behaviour because of differen-ces in their genetic constitutions. From birth till the end of life man's behaviour changes at each progressive stage. This change in behaviour pattern occurs due to new discrimination and generalisation of different factors. Now we shall discuss how the child discriminates and generalizes mental processes.

The complex mental processes are the combinations of simple processes like sensations, feelings and images. Behaviourist also build complex behaviour patterns from simple reflexes. At the first stage of life the child is in a state of confusion but gradually according to his age and mental ability he is able to discriminate things properly. For example, when the child utters the words mummy, daddy, etc, he may use the same word 'mummy' for every woman. But when his intellect develops properly he uses the same word for one person only. At first the child does not know the actual relationship with different people. But gradually he learns to distinguish between them. Again another example may be stated that in early infancy emotions begin as undifferentiated generalized excitement. But day by day anger, fear, love, and delight begin to be distinguished from each other. In the social development the child also selects his friends, peer groups, and companions through the process of discrimination.

In growth and development integration and co-ordination of different physical parts, mental activities are more important as differentiation because the growth and development of every individual is a process of integration. Staging a drama, appearing at a competitive examination, playing cricket, giving a lecture, writing an essay, organising a social function are seen as simple unitary responses but all the activities require some mental and physical capacities in an integrated way. For example, we expect more achievement from a three or four year old child when he starts his first alphabet learning. But until the proper movement of his hand, and proper mental development he cannot write a single letter. Therefore without proper integration and co-ordination among different organs, no success is possible.

From the above discussion it has been found out that growth is both differentiation and integration. These two processes happen together. Both are important and fundamental aspects of growth and learning. Thus, we must keep these two in mind while framing the curriculum and selecting methods of teaching.

(18) The Effect of Training Varies with the Stage of Maturation: In the process of growth and development the role of maturation is more important. But what do we mean by maturation? It is appropriate inner growth which develops readiness for learning. Without proper development of inner organs of the body, the child is unable to acquire new skill by guidance or training or education. Therefore training and teaching will not be fruitful unless actual maturation has taken place. But from our day to day experience we have seen that many parents don't have any knowledge about this inner growth. They lay much emphasis on education and training and expect notable results. Now psychologists have conducted many investigations upon this factor of growth and development. The outcomes of their studies indicate that the teacher or the parent cannot put new things into the child until he is mature for that. Real matured child can learn easily. Therefore proper training or instruction should be given at the right level of maturation and that may produce

right results. In the process of teaching the subject matter for curriculum, and evaluation procedure, the level of maturation of the child must be taken into consideration.

(19) There are Wide Individual Differences in Growth Pattern: Individuals differ in respect of their physical appearance, mental ability, school achievement, height, and weight, habit and skills, temperament etc. This individual difference occurs due to genetic factors, environmental influence and many other reasons. But in the process of growth and development children vary in their rate of growth. It implies wide individual variations both in their rates and pattern of growth. From our modern research it has been found that growth is a creative force which results in new experience and ability. According to one's own intelligence and ability, and influence of his own environment he is capable of making a unique pattern of growth. Thus, this variation occurs spontaneously in growth pattern.

(20) Both Rate and Pattern of Growth can be Modified: Both rate and pattern of growth can be modified by the conditions within and without the body. Although the patterns of growth are family definite for all children yet 'some' modifications can be envisaged. When environment does not offer equal opportunity to all, the natural flow of growth is modified. Amount of activity, psychological challenges, learning facilities, security, affection, discipline, etc, are a few factors which determine how fast and to what extent the potentialities of the child will have opportunity to develop. Children living under abject poverty and constant mental strains when freed, will show positively modified growth patterns. Growth brings differentiation as well as integration in behaviour. The processes are closely knit. It is impossible to understand the 'physical' child without understanding, at the same time, the 'thinking', the feeling and the 'impulsive' child. Likewise it is impossible to understand a mentally 'matured' child without evaluating his social development.

There is a close relationship, for example between his total adjustment at school and his emotional growth, his physical health and his intellectual adequacy; his intellect is related to his physical health and his intellectual adequacy; his intellect is related to his physical well being: his physical growth and health are deeply affected by his emotional development; his emotions are influenced by the school success or failure, by his physical health and by his intellectual growth. His growth – physical, intellectual and social - is a product of his family history, his personal history and his current satisfactions and strains. Differentiation is a marked sign of growth; each organ, each aspect of the child's personality reaches its fullness by the process of differentiation; integration aims at synthesising all aspects to give the individual a sort of uniqueness and "wholeness".

(21) Developmental Process and Education: Opportunity for good education and learning help developmental processes – being an inextricable aspect of an individual's personality. Acquisition of knowledge, experience and motor skills clearly point out the direction and the pa.tern of an individuals growth. Gesell claims that innate capacity for growth "is a gist of nature. It can be guided, but it cannot be transcended by an educational agency". The patterns of behaviour which develop through learning, clearly indicate the cultural influen-ces. Generally, children studying in public and convent schools seem to-be maturer than children studying in ordinary schools. Urban children seem to behave in a more mature manner in the field of sports than do the children from rural areas.

The above generalizations about growth and development serve as a sort of directive principles of programme-planning in educational setting. Generality may solve a great number of problems of education and yet 'individuality' may always pose itself as the biggest problem to the educationist and the psychologist alike.

Pattern of Change

Developmental changes are continuous and gradual. The importance of these continuous changes among children has been highlighted by research in the field of child psychology and child education. Because of these developmental changes certain characteristics emerge in the life of an individual, which put a permanent stamp on his whole life. Besides these, the ultimate success or failure of his life are determined largely by the way he happened to have spent his early infancy and childhood period. It is the real period of learning. During this period, the most significant patterns of thought and behaviour are formed. Therefore, the study of early infancy and childhood in human development is the most significant.

Life begins at the moment of conception, when the ovum (the female reproductive cell) is fertilized by the sperm (the male reproductive cell). Not only before birth, but also after birth for many years the child is a helpless organism until and unless he is helped by the continuous process of growth and development and attains maturity. When one attains maturity he ceases to be an adolescent and labelled as an adult member of the society. He is supposed to play a responsible role in the society. Before being called as adolescent, he is named as child or infant, etc. All of these names—infant, child, adolescent and adult, etc, are linked with various stages of growth and develop-ment through which the child passes from birth to death.

There are certain common developmental or practical characteristics belonging to each stage. The human organism shows peculiar quantitative and qualitative changes in his body and behaviour with the help of which we can say at what parti-cular age an individual belongs to which definite stage of his life.

The life span of an individual can be divided into the following stages.

Name of the stage	*Period and approximate age*
1. Pre-natal (pre-birth) stage	From conception to birth,
2. Stage of infancy	From birth to five years.

3. Childhood stage	From 6th to 12 years or in strict sense up to the onset of puberty.
4. Adolescent	From the onset of puberty to the age of maturity (generally from 13 to 19 years)
5. Adulthood.	From 20 years and beyond or from the age of attaining maturity till death.

Psychologists studying child behaviour tend to discern distinctive phases in the development of the child, and they conceptualize the whole development process as consisting of certain identifiable stages. Though logical objections against stage concepts are strong, the concepts may be useful for practical purposes.

There is no single scheme of stages of development. Depending upon the aspects of behaviour studies, and the investigators frame of reference, there are different schemes of developmental stages. It is not possible to discuss here all the schemes of development stages.

Dr. Earnest Jones has divided human development into four phases.

1. Infancy	(1 to 5 years)
2. Late childhood	(6 to 12 years)
3. Adolescence	(12 to 18 years)
4. Maturity	(18 years onward)

James Ross deviated a bit from the above divisions. Instead of four, he says, the stages of development are five in number.

1. Infancy	(Birth to 3 years)
2. Early childhood	(3 to 6 years)
3. Later childhood	(6 to 12 years)
4. Adolescence	(12 to 18 years)
5. Adulthood	(18 years onward)

Dr. Earnest Jones tells us that 'we grow up twice achieving a pseudo-maturity before puberty. At this age. "nature seems to undo most of her pioneer work and begin again the process of building up and consolidating." In his opinion adolescence and adulthood arc recapitulations of infancy and late childhood respectively. Before adolescence, each year of growth brings rapid changes and each year itself is a separate stage of development. Reckoning the span of each developmental stage is more a matter of convenience than a rule.

Since we all have similar beginnings, it is interesting to ask what makes us all so different as we grow older. One answer is that, except in the case of identical twins, we have different heredity. Another answer is that we have. different environments. There is further more a constant interplay between heredity and environ-mental influences and our physical and mental characteristics are the complex results of both factors.

Each of us begin life at the moment of conception. Conception is the moment when the ovum (the female repro-ductive cell) is fertilized by spermatozoan (the male repro-ductive cell). Thus a single cell smaller than the head of a pin, later multiplies and become many cells. This cell results from the fertilization of a female's ovum by a male's sperm. Heredity is determined by complex organizations of chemical materials within the nucleus of the fertilized cell. These chemical materials are contained in nuclear structures which are known as chromosomes or coloured bodies.

Microscopic studies have shown that there are forty six chromosomes in every body cell. Within each sex cell whether male or female, there are 23 pairs of chromosomes before the maturational process takes place. Within each chromosome there are strings of microscopically small particles, the genes. The genes are the physical substances passed on from parent to offspring. Those are the carriers of hereditary traits.

The moment of conception is regarded as one of the most important moments in the life of an individual for the following reasons.

(i) The first important reason is that at the moment of conception, when the ovum is fertilized by the sperm, is the determination of the newly born child's hereditary endowment.

(ii) Whether the child will be male or female is determined once and for all at the moment of conception only. Nothing after this moment can change the sex of the child.

(iii) The third important condition determined at the time of conception is whether the child will be single or multiple. Thus number of offsprings is also determined at this moment.

(iv) The fourth condition determined at this moment is the ordinal position in the family; whether the child will be first born, second born in the family has a lifelong influence on the behaviour pattern of the child and his personality development.

Since the combination of genes an individual receives from his two parents is a matter of chance, only in rare situations will two children get identical combinations and hence identical heredity. This is only possible in case of identical twins (or identical triplets, identical quadruplets, and so on).

Identical twins develop from the same, zygote. If a zygote divides into two cells, each separately goes to form a new individual.... Since each cell has the same genes as the zygote, the heredity of the two individuals will be identical. These are known as identical twins; they are always of the same sex and are identical in many other respects.

Not all twins, however are identical. Host twins are fraternal twins; they develop from two separate eggs of the mother and hence begin as two zygotes formed independent by the union of two different sperms with two different ova. Fraternal twins are no more alike genetically than ordinary brothers and sisters (siblings) born at different times. Fraternal twins may or may not be of the same sex.

From the foregoing, we come to know that we have different heredity. Therefore, we differ from each other. The diagram on the previous page will give us a clear picture about the influences of heredity upon the life of an individual.

Significance of Environment and Nature

Like heredity, environments also plays an important role in growth and development of an individual. It is everything, other than heredity, that influences an individual's growth and development. It starts from the period of gestation in the mother's womb. Of course, it must be pointed out at this juncture that it is a mere superstition that everything the mother does affects the unborn foetus. Some ladies spend the months of pregnancy visiting art galleries in the belief that they are improving the child's mind. While malnutrition of the mother or disease or any such factor can affect the uterine environment of the foetus, external factors like visit to beautiful places or listening to music cannot have any direct effect.

The environment influences an individual all through his life from "womb to tomb". Environment refers not only to the physical surroundings but even to the thoughts and attitudes of others which exert an influence on the individual. It is very difficult to study the environment because it is also unique to each individual. Let us take the case of two brothers playing in a room. Though the physical environment is the same for both, the psychological environment is not the same. One boy is older and is playing with a younger brother while the latter is playing with an older brother. Their past experiences too cannot be identical and therefore their reactions to the situation are also different. Hence psychologists are faced with many problems when studying the effect of the environment because it is impossible to keep it constant and introduce a few variables.

Heredity and environment influence human development. For example, differences in eye color are hereditary, differences in social attitudes are largely environmental, and differences in intelligence have both hereditary and environmental origins except in the case of identical twins, where they are purely environmental.

Hereditary and environment in interaction with one another, produce the wide range of individual differences observed among people. Heredity gives a predisposition for high intelligence of activity level, but the extent to which the potential becomes a reality is determined by the interaction of genetic endorsement.

Nature and nurture are jointly responsible for the development of personality characteristics, abilities and skills of an individual. In this connection we shouldn't treat Nature and Nurture separately in determining their contribution to particular type of behaviour. Therefore the issue in Nature versus. Nurture should not be raised. Nurture, or the environment, seems to determine whether the potentialities will be realised. For instance, a person has the genetic potentiality to be educated, but his potentiality may fail to be expressed because of poverty or illness which comprise the environment. The potentiality always acts through the environment and the result of the joint of Nature and Nurture is the behaviour of the persons as seen by others. The greater the potentiality and the more favourable the environment, greater will be the result of the joint action. Thus an individual is the product of an interaction between nature and nurture.

There is always a controversy between the psychologists, biologists and educationists whether heredity or environment is a more important factor for growth and development of an individual. This controversial issue is very significant for the teachers. If we say that heredity is responsible for the growth and development of an individual, then the teacher has nothing to do. He has simply to watch how the innate potentiality of the child gets unfolded. If, on the other hand, we consider environment to be responsible, for the growth and development of the child, then the role of teacher becomes very important. When he becomes the sole moulder of the students according to his own ideals, he can shape or pattern the life of the students in the way he likes. Thus, he occupies a pivotal place in the process of growth and development. Role of heredity and environment in the process of growth and development from the external point of view is not at all desirable. Those who support heredity to be the only factor responsible for growth and development argue that nothing can be done to improve the individual beyond the limits laid down by heredity. On the other hand, those who support the role of environment to be the most important factor are guilty of exaggerated optimism that there are no limits to the growth and development of an individual.

But it is not possible to have a watertight compartment between the two factors of heredity and development to work for the growth and development of the child. It is not possible to point out the traits which are exclusive hereditary or environmental. Besides this, most of the modern psychologists are of the opinion that because of the interaction between the energies inherited by an organism and development of an individual, it is impossible to estimate the amount of contribution made by heredity and environment for the growth and development of an individual. Nor is it possible to have watertight compartments between the two factors. From the moment the child is conceived in its mother's womb, the two factors work hand in hand and continue to play their roles throughout his life. A study of both the points of view brings us to the conclusion that heredity or environment alone cannot be the sole determinants of the status of an individual. The combination of the two factors in obvious and implicit ways makes the individual what he is.

A child is purely a product of heredity at the time of conception. He receives this heredity from his father and mother, who are having different traits, qualities and characteristics. Each of them contributes to the heredity of the child through genes. A child becomes a distinct individual with distinct characteristics of his own because of the interaction of genes. Hence the teacher cannot change the influence of heredity on the child. A child who has inherited poor intelligence cannot replace it with superior intelligence by the help of a teacher. A teacher can only help in the development of his intelligence within the given limits.

The influence of heredity of the child begins from the very beginning of life. Soon after conception, the organism comes in contact with the environment. The effect of this contact becomes apparent only after the birth of a child.

It becomes very easy to understand the influence of environmental factors because of the marks left by the forces operating in the environment in which the children live. Being influenced by environment they learn different attitudes, values, etc. Malnutrition for a long period and poor hygienic conditions develop certain functional deformities and diseases which leave a permanent mark in the life of an individual. The teacher plays an important role in moulding the environment of the child. In order to become a successful teacher, he needs to understand the concepts and role of heredity and environment in the life of a child.

Learning Process

Maturation is considered as the chief competitor of learning as a modifier of behaviour. Maturation is regarded as those stages of growth and development which takes place from within the subject without the help of any special training, practice, experience or stimulation. For example, at a particular stage, a child starts crawling or sitting or standing or walking. At a particular stage of its development, a tadpole starts swimming and a bird starts flying. All these changes in behaviour are the result of maturation. But the ability to talk by a parrot, the ability to drive a motor cycle or to swim in a river, etc, are the products of learning.

Learning sometimes depends upon maturation. A child can learn a thing better, only when he reaches a particular maturational level. For example, during the age from 1 to 5 a child can learn the language better, a stimulus response function. All our sense organs are bombarded by the stimuli of the environment and we respond to them. The sense organs help us to understand and to interpret the environment, to discriminate between good and bad stimulus, to decide to welcome which stimulus and to avoid which one. All these are stages or processes of learning activity.

Different senses contribute differently to the learning process. This is illustrated by an interesting experiment by C.H. Hongik. A number of white races were divided into 5 groups to learn a maze. Some learnt it with all senses intact. Others learnt after being blinded by operation, some others after being blinded and deafened. Another group after being blinded and rendered anosmic (made intensive to adore). The last group was deprived of all these senses.

Learning to an extent is also a function of maturation. One cannot teach a new born baby to walk or to pick up tiny objects with his four fingers, however much one may try Before anything is learnt by a person, his sensory-motor and also the nervous system including brain must reach a certain level of maturity. The predetermined sequential stages of maturity of the sensory-motor and nervous system of an individual comprise the "critical time" for that learning. Similarly there is critical time for other important tasks like toilet training, reading, learning socially approved behaviour, etc. If a child is taught a behaviour before the critical time i. e. before he attains the maturational level for the task, he fails to do so. If he is taught that task after the critical time, he also fails to master it effectively as is proved from the language problems of the wolf-children.

To be successful in the teaching-crafts, a teacher, therefore, must have a thorough knowledge of the process of child development. A mere bookish knowledge of child life, however, will not be of much help to a school teacher. Descriptions and researches contained in the literature on child development are, of course, very enlightening for a teacher. But unless supplemented by concrete observations of and experimentation with children, a mere bookish reading will be of little value in actual school or home situations.

A sound knowledge of various characteristic features of child development through infancy, childhood and adolescence is indispensable for the teacher owing mainly to the following reasons.

1. It gives him the most authentic knowledge regarding the human staff that he deals with the children.

   It enables him to understand the root causes of their good and bad behaviour.

2. It helps him to match his teaching techniques and standards with the developmental level that a child has actually attained. He is thus enabled to avoid being too difficult, too easy or too common place in the classroom.

3. By enabling him to understand his own infancy and childhood periods it facilitates him to understand his own self This self-understanding proves immensely helpful for him in becoming a better teacher and a better person.

12

Mental Development

It is a well established fact that in a whole class, an emotionally disturbed child is like a fly in the ointment. He soon affects other students and the peaceful atmosphere of the whole class. So it is the first and foremost duty of the teacher to point out the emotionally disturbed children when they are a handful in number and take possible preventive measures to eradicate the problem from its beginning. He should render special interest towards them and help them to solve their personal problems. If all children are emotionally balanced then he should maintain a pleasant, adequate, cooperative and mutual atmosphere in the classroom by which there will be no room for emotional disturbances. If the teaching process is heart-touching, classroom work is sensitive and facilities for extra-curricular activities are available easily, the student will be less prone to emotional disturbances. And in case any student shows such problematic behaviour, the teacher should be cautious enough to take up the measures discussed below.

1. Re-Education: While the teacher applies a particular method of teaching and finds that some students show the symptoms of disturbances, he should at once change the method and again start teaching the same topic from the beginning. It is necessary to make the students understand why a particular person, place or topic is boring. He should know the cause of boredom. He should be given chances to solve complex problems for himself. The student should be taught and directed as well as reinforced as to adjust himself with the difficult, proble-matic situations and persons. Re-education immensely helps the child in

regaining his mental strength to overcome the emotional difficulties.

2. Insight: The root cause of emotional ill-health of the child is his disturbed thinking process. If at any rate the student is enabled to analyse his own problem with greater insight, most of the anger, aggression, mental pressure and temptations can be brought down. Things and events that pressurise a child's mind and give birth to high emotions should be arranged according to their intensity and importance, in order to help the child in restoring his mental health. It should be a unique feature of the child that he should always be attracted towards positive aspects of life. Only when the teacher has a clear unders-tanding of his students character, behaviour, thinking process; language and temperament, can he arouse insight in them.

3. Removal from Disturbing Environment: It has been said that when an emotionally disturbed child is transferred from one school to another or when he is separated from one section of friends and included in another section of students some development occurs in his emotional level. This brings a change in the social environment of the child. The students get chances to adjust with new people and new events.

4. Developing Emotional Immunity: A particular condition that produces fear and annoyance, if repeated again and again, arouses excitement at a diminishing rate. For example, if a person wearing the mask of an animal appears before a child, he is annoyed. Then, if the same action is repeated, the child will not be afraid of it. This is because the child develops familiarity and becomes accustomed with that condition. Likewise if the child is inattentive and fails to perceive a certain stimulus, there is no reason that he should be emotional.

5. Catharsis: Catharsis means removal of an emotion or release from a tension. It is a common fact that emotional disturbances originate from mental tension. If there is any outlet for emotional tension, disturbances disappear. For

example, if a violently angry child is given a chance to express his anger verbally, or in any socially acceptable way, he does not show disturbances. Wrestling, boxing, debating are the various means through which the child expresses his anger, annoyance, disgust, etc, and his tension is eliminated. There are examples of many children giving up their disturbing behaviour and becoming great men in their future life.

6. Emotional Education through Sports: The child never applies all of his strength in performing a task. He retains some extra energy. When he does get any facility to apply this extra energy, he lays stress upon his mind and generates excitement. Hence to use this energy fairly and constructively, sports should be introduced in schools. When the emotional disturbance of the child is manifested in games and sports, it leaves a favourable and positive impact on his personality. So it is the foremost duty of the teacher to note that the students showing emotional disturbances take active part in sports and games in the school. Secondly the teacher should keep a watchful eye on the health of students. In case any decrease in the health of certain student comes to his notice, he should lose no time in advising him to build up his health. He may take the help of parents in this regard from time to time and inform them about their children's physical weakness, irregularity, inattentiveness, illness, etc.

7. Maintaining Democratic Set up in the Classroom: Children, in common, need love and affection of the teacher. So the teacher should have respect for the individual personality of every student, and should take into consideration their individual differences while teaching in the classroom. He should make arrangements for fulfilment of minimum requirements of students.

Along with psychological aspects, the teacher should impart moral and ethical education. The behaviour of the students should be ideal in every respect. He should know about the great men in history and follow them. The social development of the child should be balanced and positive and should be well acquainted with his circle of friends and take active part in every group activity. Feeling of loneliness is not good for the emotional health of a child.

8. Influence of Teacher's own Emotional Health: A teacher suffering from emotional disturbances spoils the child's emotional balance instead of doing him good. A violently angry, aggressive and extremely strict teacher causes similar emotions in the minds of students. So every teacher should, at the first hand, be cautious of his own emotional balance. He should have patience and be democratic in his approach.

9. Taking Preventive Measures: It is said that prevention is better than cure. It means that we should not wait for a problem to arise and then try to solve it. We should give no chance to the problem to arise. At the first sight of any kind of emotional disturbance in a child we should put our efforts into action and eliminate it. Otherwise it will get multiplied and trouble us a lot. The child, may be anti-social and cause problems to the society. Hence both the teacher and the parents should take preventive steps from the beginning. In no circumstances the emotional disturbances should be given any chance to grow.

10. Treatment: In case the emotional disturbances go beyond control, the teacher should suggest the child to be sent to mental clinic. Timely treatment may help the child to restore his emotional balance and help him in future.

The students showing emotional disturbances need personal care and sympathetic treatment with a good understanding of their problems. By showing them the right path, rendering correct guidance and timely treatment, their living in the society can be clean and disciplined. Carelessness makes them face more and more complex emotional problems and their abnormality goes on increasing. Hence they become the victims of various physical and mental frustrations. They are defeated at every step of their life and every defeat adds a bitter experience and intensifies their abnormality. So the teacher should try his best to save the children from such a condition and immunise them from any mild emotional disturbance by acknowledging their capacity and limitation. The individuality and personality of the children should be encouraged, the genius in them be aroused and cultivated and self-confidence be strengthened. By this the teacher fulfils his professional commitments and serves as society's strongest pillar.

Each one of us is changing from conception till death continuously due to the impact of biological processes as well as owing to the influence of our environment As time passes the physical growth occurs and a human child becomes a full grown adult. This can well be visualised. But side by side the other developments go on continuously. Those developments are rather felt than seen. For example, during the first year of age, the child who is unable to speak, uses sophisticated language when he grows up. This happens due to his rudimentary ability to solve problems of communication with others. So the sophisticated language of intellectual skills differentiates our species from all other forms of animal life. Changes occur in physical, mental, social, emotional and such other levels. A child reared up in a good social environment, can develop a sound personality and can overcome the bitter outcome of feelings of fear, anger, anxiety, etc, with an ability of better adjustment to the complexities of life.

By the 1920s, concept of the development of child was dominated by the thought of John Watson, the father of behaviourism. His impact, along with that of Freud, Binet, Hall and many others lead to the establishment of clinics to assess children and advice parents. Till then much was not known about children's thought, language and intellectual functioning. Watson discarded those internal events as in appropriate topics for research. But after using the concept of mediation it was learnt that the external behaviour of human beings and the reaction shown to the environment to know the ability of the child to build internal models of the world and to inculcate those models in order to learn from the past experience are necessary to draw conclusions about the future. The development of such ability in the child is known as intellectual development.

Intelligence is a concept rather than a thing which can be observed directly. It is the ability to think in terms of abstract ideas. It refers to mind in its cognitive aspect, particularly to the higher thought process. These higher thought processes are conception, comparison, generalisation, reasoning, etc. The topic "Intellectual Development" therefore, includes an account of the growth of these mental functions at different stages of development along with other allied mental functions.

Evolution of Mental Abilities

Some people opine that the scholastic achievement of a child is his intellectual development. Though intellectual achievement includes scholastic learning, it is not limited to it. It is a well-known fact that the mental growth of the child is not solely dependent upon his pursuit of school subject. Intellectually, he learns a lot of things. But we cannot make a survey of the various aspects of intellectual development of the child in a single chapter. Therefore, here is an attempt to highlight in brief the salient features of some significant aspects of intellectual development during infancy and childhood.

As discussed above, mental or intellectual development takes into consideration the development of various mental abilities and capacities. How these abilities grow and develop from birth onwards is an interesting as well as useful thing to know. Though the development in the areas of various abilities proceeds simultaneously and is continuous, yet the studies have revealed possibility of the differences in the rate of overall mental development at various ages. Similarly it has been also noted that there is a possibility of greater growth and development in one aspect or area of mental activity than in another at one or the other stage of life.

As far as the general characteristics of trend or mental growth and development of various stages is concerned we have already discussed it in chapter two of this book. Now in the following pages we will try to discuss the changes and development in some of the important mental abilities or aspects of mental power of a small child as he grows older and older.

1. Sensation and Perception: Both sensation and perception are considered important aspects of mental development. Sensations are the elementary impressions gathered by sense organs. When these impressions are interpreted and some definite meanings are attached to them, they take the form of perception.

In the beginning, the child lacks in sensation as well as in perception. His sense organs are not developed. As a result, he cannot discriminate between things and understand their meaning. Focussing of the eye towards the lamp, bright coloured objects, etc, can be said to be the beginning of an infant's perceptual growth. Later on, he distinguishes people from objects and then familiar people from strangers and in this way his environment gradually becomes differentiated into perceived objects. Those perceived objects become later on, associated with a verbal sound that he can recognize when heard.

When he is able to use his sense organs, he becomes increasingly conscious of the things around him and begins to ask a series of question such as why, what and who. At this time he has a poor perception of space, time, form, movement and distance. For example, due to lack of perception of the size of distant objects, the train when viewed from a distance, may appear to him as a toy train.

But gradually, his ability of perception gets developed. As the individual passes through the year of his adolescence, the sensory acuity reaches almost its peak and perceptual patterns become most organized and refined. His perceptions now become more definite, rich and detailed. They are now beginning to be influenced by his beliefs, opinions, ideals, etc, besides his needs, interests and mindset. They now need not be associated necessarily with concrete objects.

2. Concept Formation: Acquisition of concept is the generalised meaning that is attached to an object or idea. It is the result of one's perceptual experiences and involves both discrimination and generalization.

Discrimination begins early in life, sometimes after the child tries to generalize his perpetual experiences and thus begins to acquire concepts. Experience is a great factor in concept formation. In early childhood, the concrete experience in the form of actual objects helps the child in the formation of concepts. He tries to develop various contents from direct experiences.

In the later period, various experiences offered by reading, movies, lectures, etc, also provide the base for concept formation in the later years. It is not that only new concepts are formed; the old concepts may also get a new shape. They may be broadened, developed or the wrong concepts can be altogether abandoned. Normally, in development, concepts go from concrete to abstract, from vague to clear and from inexact to definite on the type of experiences one receives as he grows older.

In this way the concepts of the child in the beginning are characterized by vagueness, indefiniteness and inadequacy. For example, the child has very poor time concepts. As Crow and Crow put it "Time as such means little to the young child. He cannot distinguish among 'today' 'tomorrow' and 'next week' except as they represent words rather than actual duration of time."

Similarly his concepts of social relations and distance and depth are very vague and inadequate in the beginning. Gradually, as a result of learning and maturation, they became clear, specific and definite.

3. Development of Language: Development of language adds to the mental growth and development of an individual. The growth and development in speech, vocabulary and length of responses are some of the important aspects of language development.

At birth the child can utter some crying sounds. By the age of one and little later he may learn to speak a few words. After this, his vocabulary increases rapidly. Much of the speech pattern that the child learns is the result of imitation of others in the environment. During the course of learning to speak, it is possible that certain speech disorders like omissions, stuttering, stammering, etc, may develop. Therefore the parents as well as the teachers of small children must remain very cautious about this.

The vocabulary of children in the beginning is too limited. There is a continuous increase in the size of one's vocabulary during childhood. Later on, as the result of environmental needs and opportunities, the vocabulary goes on developing. Maintenance of the past and addition of the new words in one's vocabulary may continue even upto the period of old age depending upon their reading habits and interests.

In addition to the change in vocabulary and speech, the pattern of giving responses also changes with age. In the early childhood the child's responses are characterized by the "one-word response." Later on, gradually, he begins to use descriptive words like adjectives and adverbs and his responses include a large variety of words and almost every form of sentence structure.

Power of Memory

Memory is also an important aspect of mental development. At birth, there is little memory, but gradually with maturation and experience, memory increases. The developmental schedule as discussed by Hurlock and Schwartz indicates that "memory of an impressionistic kind appears in the first half of the year and instances of true remembrance appear by the end of the first year. During the first year memory is only aroused by sensory stimuli. With the learning of speech, the child is able to remember additionally by the end of the second year. During the first and second years the memory is stronger for persons and objects than for situations. During early childhood, from 3 to 6 years, situations become significant factors in the child's memory. Also the emotional quality of the impressions influence memory. By 3 years the child can recount the story heard a few days ago and he can also give information about past experiences."

Therefore the child shows signs of memory from the early childhood. The memory which the child possesses in his young age is generally a rote memory. He enjoys repetition and seldom uses logic and a selection process of remembering and forgetting begins to operate. In the later years of childhood memory tends to decrease. But from which age the downfall begins, it is difficult to say with certainty. It varies from individual to individual and generally besides the age and health, the situation and stimuli which are associated with a particular kind of memory affects significantly, in remembrance or forgetting.

5. Development of Problem-solving Ability: Problem-solving ability is an important constituent of mental development. An individual needs this type of ability in discovering the solution of the problems faced by him. Both thinking and reasoning powers are used in problem-solving. Therefore problem-solving ability depends upon the development of thinking and reasoning. Thinking and reasoning powers begin to grow from as early as two and one half or three years. However reasoning at this stage is confined to concrete and personal things from the child's immediate environment. The younger child deals more easily with the concrete than with the abstract. We cannot expect from him to solve complicated problems which require abstract thinking and more developed reasoning. But gradually, he shows increase in the ability to deal with abstract as he grows in age. He begins to compare and evaluate the ideas and solve the problems through the utilization of verbal symbols and imaginary concepts.

It follows from this discussion that in the beginning children should be provided with the simple realistic problems depending on concrete situations related to their own experiences and environment so that they can store them with insight and understanding. With the increase in age the more complicated problems requiring abstract thinking and widened experiences may be given to them. In this way, gradually, the children should be made to increase their problem-solving ability.

In addition to these aspects, mentioned above the other aspects of mental growth and development include attention, imagination, decision-making, ability of interpretation, etc. Like other aspects they also change, grow and mature with the increase in age due to maturation and learning.

Mental growth and development is controlled by both the hereditary and environmental factors. An individual's mental abilities, at any age of his life, are the products of his heredity and environment. The child is what he gets from his ancestral stock through his immediate parents at the time of conception in terms of mental traits or characteristics and mental apparatus. But the environment which he gets afterwards for the development of those innate abilities is no less significant than the social and cultural experiences, learning opportunities and education which he avails for the developmental process as he advances in age.

In fact, maturation and learning are responsible for controlling the process of mental growth and development which in turn affects the process of mental growth and development. Brain and the nervous system play a significant role in this direction. At birth the brain and the nerves that lead to it, are not fully developed. Their growth and development rapidly increase after birth and get matured in due course. As the nervous system advances towards maturity, the mental powers of the child also go on developing. Therefore, organic growth of the nervous system is the basic factor in mental development.

Learning is a form of experience and education helps the developmental process and in fact intensifies it to reach to its optimum level. It is said to play the same part as exercises play in developing physical skills and power. As Sorenson puts it "A child's legs, arms and body are made stronger by healthful play. We can deduce that the mind with its organic counterpart, the nervous system, improves and becomes better equipped because of use and exercise in the form of reading, calculating, memorizing, speaking, imaging and other mental activities."

Study of intellectual development during infancy is based on approximate guess work. Most of the time of the new born baby is spent with events connected with his immediate bodily needs, e.g. hunger, affection, etc.. Events like sounds and sights do not have any importance for him. Therefore, through approximate guesses, we try to study the intellectual level of the newborn baby.

When the infant, sometimes after birth, is able to fix at or follow a moving object with his eyes, we mark some early sensory responses. The vision and hearing play an important role in the study of early intellectual development of the child.

Faculties of Mind

The intellectual life of an infant, when he turns his head and follows a person, rings a bell to get amusement out of the sound, displays signs of recognising and remembering certain objects and persons. It has been observed that the infants from birth to twelfth month, show remarkable signs of progress in this discrimination of visual form. At two or three years, they are able to identify differences in position.

Experimental evidence shows that at this stage of development, infants develop ability to discriminate colour, sound, weight, time, space, etc. The perception of colour develops rapidly before the child becomes two years old. At the age of four they can discriminate loudness of sounds. After this age, the auditory discrimination becomes more prominent.

Infants are capable of paying attention at a very early age. Observation has proved that the beginnings of attention can be seen even during the first week of the life of an infant. During this period his eyes follow bright or moving objects. He develops the ability to watch people before he is three months of age. The infants develop likes and dislikes, interests and preferences during the second year.

Intensive observation has revealed that by the third month a baby can recognize his milk bottle. He can also recognize his father and mother even earlier. He can distinguish between a familiar and strange object by the age of six months. An infant can name several objects from seeing pictures at the age of two. At the age of three and four, they can identify pictures correctly, which are mixed up with others.

Creative Ability

The early creative work is the source through which we can study the intellectual growth of the child. The earliest specimen of the creative work of the child is drawing, which most children start. It is the sign of early creative alertness. The choice of lines and colours shown in the drawing of the children, help us to study their intellectual level.

If we listen to the talk and watch the behaviour of the children we can develop an insight into their power of rea-soning and judgement. F. D. Brooks states many interesting cases of reasoning among the infants. A little boy of two was pulling his daddy's hair. The father says: "Don't Danad it hurts daddy". To this, the little boy says "It didn't hurt grandpa".

Another father hurt his hands while working. His three and a half year old daughter told him: "Little girls daddies should not hurt themselves, because little girls love their daddies."

Thus, with the increase of age, the power of reasoning and judgement of the infants develop.

Evolution of Languages

Language development is an intellectual process. It involves all types of mental ability like experiencing, perceiving, reproducing, memorizing, associating, etc. We can study the intellectual development of a child through the medium of language. Thus language becomes an important instrument for studying the intellectual life of a child.

During infancy, many children learn to use words. A study made by Smith suggests that active vocabulary at ten months is one word, at twelve months three words; and at fifteen months nineteen words. However, his passive vocabulary, (the words he can understand) is much larger at every stage of language development. When the child becomes 16 months old, he makes varied use of language. He uses words to name people, action and things. He asks questions about things, people and action. Thus he adds new words, and his active vocabulary becomes 300 words. At this stage of development, the child's language consists of "one word sentences". For example when he says, 'milk', he may mean 'I want milk to drink'. Usually, the words used by him are nouns.

Thus, the infant's achievement in language is the most amazing. The same helpless child, who faces a lot of difficulties to utter a single correct word, uses several thousand words in the later stage of his development. The growth of vocabulary during the first five years of the child is rapid and interesting.

The moment the child enters school, his intellectual horizon gets widened. His social contacts and scholastic learning bring further development in language skills. Besides this, he also attains intellectual growth in other fields. Let us now discuss some important aspects of his intellectual development.

When the child grows older, his vocabulary undergoes further development. Intelligent children have a larger voca-bulary and greater skill in its use than the backward children. Children, who develop speech at a relatively later stage of growth, are not necessarily sub-normal.

In language development sex plays a very important role. Girls seem to excel boys at the age of the appearance of the first word. They also begin to talk earlier then the boys. Environment and training also contribute considerably in language development.

Children at the beginning of school stage use language for narration more extensively than before. They also express complex thought and reasoning. At this stage, they ask a series of questions on 'What', 'Who' and 'Why' and about fear. They also ask complex questions about God, death and sex. When they become three or four years old they use some 'dirty' words. They like very much the 'toilet' talk.

Ability of Speeches

Some studies done on bilingualism reveal the fact that bilingualism has a retarding influence on the language development of the child. From a study of bilingual children (English and Chinese); it was found that bilingual group had below-average vocabulary as compared with monolingual children. A child for instance, in Orissa, who speaks Punjabi, Sindhi, Pushto or Bengali at home, receives school instruction in Oriya or English, faces a lot of difficulties in his linguistic development.

From various studies it has been proved that the development of reading ability in a language other than one's mother tongue is not very difficult to learn. But so far as its pronunciation, grammar, phrases, and idioms are concerned it becomes relatively difficult to master.

The linguistic environment in which the child lives, plays an important role in developing his grasp of context, vocabulary, sentence structure, articulation and grammar. Slow maturation, inadequate learning and emotional tension at times accompany speech defects and disorders. Children may develop incorrect or unintelligible speech habits due to slow maturation or inadequate environmental stimulation. Poor and wrong patterns of spoken and written language should be kept away from his environment from the very beginning of infancy. Expert surgical treatment should be made in case of an organic impairment of speech mechanism like tongue tie, cleft palate, etc. To overcome emotional factors in speech defects, attempts should be made to encourage children to overcome emotional inhibitions impeding the clear and spontaneous use of language.

Throughout childhood, the ability to reason goes on developing. This reasoning process of children functions much in the same way as that of adult, but there are a lot of differences between the children and the adults. Problems faced by the children are related to their own immediate concern. They cannot phrase their thoughts and conclusions like adults. They do not have much experience and relevant information at their disposal to develop thinking and reasoning. They are also less responsive to the demands of the society. Even when they face new problems they usually resort to trial and error. The following are the main differences between the reasoning processes of the child and the adult.

(i) Like the adult a child does not posses the adequate language to phrase his thoughts and conclusions adequately.

(ii) The child lacks the wealth of relevant information and experience that an adult usually possesses.

(iii) The child possesses lesser capacity for sustained attention and lesser power of concentration than an adult.

(iv) He is more pre-occupied with his own immediate environment. Consequently, he is less capable of reasoning about problems that do not directly concern him or are too complex for him.

(v) A child reacts more and arrives at fewer solutions than the adults.

Power of Imagination

Beginning from infancy, children remain engaged in imagination. 'Make-believe' plays an important role in the process of development. Imagination helps children to think beyond time and space. When they remain engaged in imaginary activities, they express many of their unfulfilled wishes, and release their emotional problems. Afterwards, imaginary activities include more adventurous themes. But too much involvement in the world of imagination causes unrealistic ambitions and experience of failure.

To provide intellectual diet to the children, books magazines, music, drama, good cinema programmes, and radio programmes play an important role. Therefore, the teachers and parents should try to provide opportunities to their children to use the aforesaid things effectively. Children should remain away from dangerous comics, sex and terror films, obscene reading materials etc. All these may obstruct the intellectual development of the children.

The Effects

To achieve healthy growth, proper intellectual development is very important for the infants, children and the adolescents. Let us now discuss certain educational implications in the following.

(i) The Problem of Grouping and Classification: It is commonly an accepted psychological fact that individuals differ from each other in every respect, including the intellectual. It is, therefore, very important for the teachers to group or to classify children into different sections.

It is not wise to classify children merely on the basis of intelligence tests. These tests cannot measure the total intellectual development of the children. For example, a child may have high ability in one field and low in another. Therefore, it is not reasonable to classify children in this manner.

The most reasonable way of classification would be on the basis of maximum homogeneity in intellectual growth. Such scientifically based classification is desirable both for the students and the teachers. Teachers can group children on the basis of homogeneity and facilitate teaching and guidance.

(ii) Intellectual Growth through Pleasant Instructions: "Filling the minds of the students with facts is not education." The mind of the child is a growing organism. We cannot pack it ruthlessly with alien ideas. But we should provide knowledge in such a way that it would help to provide natural food for developing intelligence. Hence to make the food of education palatable for children, the method of instruction should be so pleasant that the child feels quite at home in the class. In such a situation, he learns a great deal without a feeling of boredom.

(iii) Treatment towards Intellectually Handicapped Children: There are some children, who are intellec-tually handicapped. Some of them are dull and back-ward and others suffer form specific backwardness in some school subjects. In our school system, we either ignore them altogether or push them too much. But such attitude towards these children is undesirable. The teachers and parents, therefore, should treat them properly and avoid the load of bookish instruction on them, which is not within their innate capacity.

(iv) Encouraging Creative Pursuits: For the growth of intelligence, creative pursuits should be encouraged. Some such pursuits include poetry, drama, literature, radio programmes, journals, magazines, developing cultural association with intellectuals, different hobbies, ideal cinema programme etc. The teachers and parents should encourage the students to take part in these activities.

(v) To Provide Maximum Scope for the Development of Language: The role of language in the development of intelligence is indispensable. Therefore, in the centers of learning maximum opportunities should be provided to the children for language development. Such development could be achieved by giving the child frequent exercises in reading, spelling, writing, etc. Besides this, opportunities should be provided for conversation, listening and repeating stories, participation in debates, discussions, symposia, etc. Teachers and parents should do their best to provide the children with healthy language environment at school and home to facilitate maximum language development.

13

Utilising Emotions

(i) Knowledge of the pattern of physical growth and development can help a teacher in knowing what can be expected normally from the children at a particular age level. In turn it can help us to arrange school programmes like curricular and co-curricular experiences, methods and techniques of teaching, timetable, textbook and material, seating arrangement and learning environment, etc.

(ii) The contemporary age has witnessed an evergrowing interest in the welfare and education of children. It is on account of the period of childhood that the present age has sometimes been called "the children's century". Therefore knowledge of the health and proper physical development is very much essential for a teacher in a modern classroom. Modern schools have to play a decisive role in the task of growth and development process and can render valuable help in this direction.

(iii) Knowledge of physical development will help a teacher to be aware of the physical deviates, their psychology and problems of adjustment. Consequently he can help them in their social and emotional adjustment as well as in school learning.

(iv) Psychologists are of the opinion that the needs, interests, desires, attitudes and in a way the overall behaviour of an individual is controlled to a great extent by physical growth and development. Hence at a particular age level what would be the expected behaviour of the child growth and development pattern? For example with the study of the trend of the physical development in adolescence one can be aware of their growing physical, emotional and social needs. Accordingly, adolescents can be helped by the teacher in the adjustment to their rapid development and changes.

Since physical development plays an important role in the life of children, the parents and the teachers should pay attention to certain significant educational implications.

A child can become efficient in all fields of life, if he possesses a good physical health. Therefore physical development during infancy and childhood days deserves attention. In every school, there should be a regular programme of health education. Children should get enough of opportunities to participate in games, sports and physical exercise. Necessary information about physical culture, personal hygiene, food values, cleanliness, etc, should be provided in an interesting way. Interesting talks and film strips introducing the children to the various developmental stages should be arranged in schools. As a result of which they can develop a correct picture in their mind about their own changing selves and role in life. Besides this, it will work as a safeguard against the development of irrational worries regarding abrupt development, which take place in the children's bodies.

Emotion is the magic word that makes human life dynamic and makes him a multicoloured shell on the shore of the sea of society. It is like a battery charged by the nature in the organism that provides him with great primeval forces of great power to adjust and cope with the environment. Emotions add colour, spice, lyric and adventure to our lives. Along with this, it connects the mental and physical activities of man together. Between the hide and seek game of happiness and sorrow, human life becomes a daring adventure. Emotions control most of our activities. The best achievements as well as the worst deeds of human beings are the product of different emotions at different times. History is sufficient proof to project that starting from Mahabharat war till the wars of today, the root cause of all the destructions, is nothing but human emotions. While some emotions make our life horrible, others make it happy. Hence, for human beings it has become a necessary evil and so it occupies an important place in curriculum of psychology and education as well.

Emotion is a very complex phenomenon. So its study raises a number of difficulties. Almost all psychological phenomena notably perception, memory, learning, etc, except thinking and reasoning are involved in its study. Many types of emotions like pleasure, frustration, love, affection, fear, anger, sorrow, jealousy, hate, etc, make life happy and at times sorrowful being controlled by different types of emotions. At different times man may become a God or a monster in different situations of life. Emotions, not only influence our behaviour but also control our style of living, social adjustment and development of personality. One fault of our educational system is that we do not take into account seriously the emotional condition of the child while imparting education to him. If we can steer the emotions of the child in the right way, it will act as a constructive element in human personality.

If studied comparatively, emotions play a more important role in the life of a child than in the life of an adult. Child's power to think on a particular problem is limited. So he takes the help of a few emotions like fear, astonishment, anger and disgust to express his mental conditions. If the emotional state of children moves in a negative direction they do not become interested to learn; rather they fail to adjust themselves properly in the society. For example, if the child suffers from emotions like fear and anxiety all the time, his mental health is hampered and bitter introvertism and inferiority complex develops in him.

Emotion may be defined as a stirred up state of the organism. In all emotions there is a strong disturbance of the whole organism which involves visceral disturbances and other internal changes producing definite external signs. Bodily manifestations like clenched fists, biting of teeth, shivering of the whole body and loud laughter, etc, often take place in emotions. As the term emotion is derived from the Latin term "emovere" which means to stir up, to agitate or to excite, to move outward, the feeling of an emotional state seeks an outlet in the form of an overt action. The intensity of such a feeling changes in proportion to change in the strength of an emotion.

Mainly three types of outer stimuli arouse emotion within us. They are person, object and situation. There are some other inner stimuli such as mentality, interest, ideal, health, self-respect, self-awareness, self-control, etc, which cause emotion. An emotional state continues till the stimuli function within or without us. In order to down or control the emotion we have to get rid of the particular stimulus responsible for it. A particular stimulus may create, a strong emotion at one time and a weak emotion at another. Secondly a particular stimulus may arouse emotions of different intensities in different persons. Both the outer and internal stimuli work in a particular emotional stage. For example, when a person of our age or a friend of ours ridicules or passes comments on us, we are not angry but when the same activity is shown by a younger one we become angry.

Emotions have a strong link with our urges, needs and interests. If they are satisfied, an individual is said to be enjoying a happy life and he is emotionally stable, balanced and healthy. But if they remain unfulfilled, frustration grows and the individual suffers from failure in adjusting himself with his environment.

Instinct is the source of emotion. Different instincts give rise to different emotions. Again, the same instinct may give rise to so many types of emotions in different individuals and in different situations. Psychologists give divergent opinions regarding the number of original instincts. According to Descartes, the human child, at his birth carries six instincts. They are amazement, hate, sorrow, love, happiness and wishes. But according to McDougal, fourteen instincts cause twenty eight emotions. Some others opine that anger, fear and love are three basic and primary instincts. On the other hand, American behaviouristic psychologists do not agree on the point that instincts that cause emotions are inborn. By experimentation they have proved that the child takes birth with only one instinct that expresses itself through different types of behaviours in different circumstances. This changing style of behaviour is considered by us as different emotions. They also proved that by conditioning, the emotional state can be expanded or controlled.

Significant Elements

1. It is a stirred up state, that shows both internal and external disturbances.
2. The emotions vary in intensity, from person to person and situation to situation.
3. Instincts work as stimulus to emotional responses and if they can be controlled, emotions can also be manipulated in a desired direction.

Various Kinds of Emotions

The emotional response of the new born infant cannot be defined well or identified specially. But two distinct patterns are clearly noticeable in the reactions of the infant. They are pleasant and unpleasant responses. If the position of a new born is changed suddenly, if a sudden loud noise is produced or if the movement of the infant is obstructed, unpleasant response is elicited. The new born in unable to feel the degree or intensity of a stimulus. So his emotions of same intensity to all in the mother's womb lie dormant and does not show any emotional responses. As Backwin has stressed, "The ability to" respond emotionally is present in the new born as part of the developmental process and does not have to be learned.

After two weeks of birth, the infant enters into babyhood. During this stage, emotions can be well differentiated and they are aroused by different stimuli. Some observable emotions such as fear, anger, distress, delight, elation and affection, etc, are remarkably developed in the baby. During this stage the emotional state is short-lived and one emotion gives way to other emotions. Emotions can be conditioned easily at this time as the level of intelligence is very low. "A baby who has been frightened by the pain of an inoculation, for example, is likely to be conditioned to fear the doctor. Because he wears a white coat the baby's fear may spread to anyone wearing a white coat, such as a barber and in turn, he will fear having his cut."

1. Anger: Anger is the most common emotion of a baby. When the movement of the baby if interfered with or wish thwarted he cries in order to show his anger. For example, if the child wants to have a particular toy and advances towards it but some one obstructs his advancement or sometimes the baby wants to be picked up but nobody gives attention towards him, anger is aroused within him. If the child becomes physically unable to reach a particular object he wants, he becomes angry. The baby often tries to express himself through speech. But he is unable to do so. In such a case also he feels angry.

The anger response of the child is shown by an outburst of energy in screaming, kicking the legs and waving the arms in a random fashion. Sometimes they hold their breath, jump up and down, throw themselves on the floor, or hit or kick anything within their reach.

How to Handle Anger: Anger aggravates matters very frequently and causes distress. Therefore the teachers and the parents should take the following steps to handle anger.

(i) When a child is angry, the adults should try to distract the attention of the child from frustrating experiences and direct it towards some other situation.

(ii) When an older child is angry, the adult persons should discuss about the situation and help him to have a correct view of the situation.

(iii) The parents, teachers and. other adult members should try to avoid needless restraints, tedious repetitions and inconsistent demands.

(iv) There must be a provision to develop the required skill in the children which will help them to overcome an angry situation.

2. Fear: Generally babies are protected by the parents from any type of fear provoking stimuli. Even then, they learn to fear through imitation of those who are afraid or by remembering some unpleasant experiences. The most fear provoking stimuli in babyhood are loud noises, animals. darkroom, high places, sudden

displacement, being alone, pain and strange persons, places and objects. Fear of stranger persons is one of the outstanding features of the emotional growth of the baby. It happens because the baby is not ready to see an unknown person approaching in place of the familiar person. So every situation of novelty or strangeness arouses fear in him. If a familiar person dressed in an unfamiliar fashion approaches the baby, he is frightened but when the unfamiliar dress is removed the fear is also removed off the baby's mind.

The responses shown by the baby in fearful situations are those he tries to avoid or withdraw himself from, namely the fear provoking stimuli. Whimpering, crying, temporary holding of breath are the other responses made by the child in such situations. Generally a fearful child turns his head and hides his face and if capable runs and hide himself in a place he thinks safer. Towards the end of babyhood his curiosity is aroused to see what is happening when he hides himself, and so he peeps out of his place to look at the person or object that aroused his fear.

When fear safeguards against harm, it is valuable. The child should avoid dangerous situations by the help of fear. But fear becomes dangerous, when a person cannot do anything because of the fearful situation. Such type of irrational fears are called phobias. Phobias cause much sufferings to an individual. Complete prevention of fear is not possible. But by the help of the following methods one can prevent fear.

(i) By the method of verbal appeal, an individual can get rid of fear. Such verbal appeals suggest the children how to develop the power of reasoning and how to build confidence.

(ii) The second method of prevention is negative adaptation. It helps to give an opposite response to the fear response. For example, when a child is afraid of a dog, he can overcome the situation if he is allowed to play with it.

(iii) Social imitation is another method where the child observes his friends and relatives acting in a fearless manner in a fearful situation.

(iv) Distraction is also a helpful method by which the attention of the child can be diverted towards an interesting feature of the feared object.

Affection: Affection of infant and baby is directed towards a person, an animal or a thing. "The baby fixes his gaze on a person's face, kicks, holds out and waves his arms, smiles and tries to raise his body, because these movements are so uncoor-dinated at first, he cannot reach the loved one. He can, however, usually reach the loved one by the age of six months. Affection of a baby manifests in his warm regard, friendliness, sympathy and helpfulness, mainly in action and less in words towards a person who takes care of his bodily needs, plays with him or gives him pleasure.

During the second year, the arena of affection of the baby includes objects, especially his toys. Along with human beings his affection is directed towards the "love object." Animal pets are also included within the love objects. With a family pet the baby can play without fear and feel warmth with a family pet.

The babies generally love those who give close physical contacts. The love reactions shown by the baby are hugging, patting or kissing the love object or person.

The baby's love for a person or a thing is influenced by his learning. His learning, mostly the conditioned learning makes him determine whom to love and how much to love. Only for this reason the baby's love for the different family members varies. In general, they love their mother more than any other member of their family due to constant companionship with her.

During Childhood

In comparison to infancy and babyhood, the emotions during childhood are more common, more intense and more distinguished in character. During this stage, the child does not like to be under someone's guidance and control; rather he wants to enjoy himself in his own style. So irritability rises frequently at this time. Sometimes emotionality occurs from fatigue caused by strenuous and prolonged play. The main causes of emotion during childhood are psychological rather than physical as they were during babyhood. The level of aspiration of the children is very high. They think that they can do what their parents think impossible on their part. But the parents do not allow them to do that. At last when they fail to do what they thought, emotional state is aroused in them. Emotions and tensions grow in number and degree, when children enter schools, where they have to adjust themselves with dynamic and different social conditions. In such a situation the children make problems for their parents and peers and hence they try to avoid children for their unreason-able and constant emotional outbursts.

Different factors influencing emotionality during childhood are: health condition, differences in environment, patterns of emotional behaviour established during the babyhood days, undivided attention of the mother, sex and ordinal position of the child within the family, age difference with the sibling and the standard set by the parents for the child, etc.

During babyhood maximum of pleasant experiences and minimum of unpleasant experiences occur. But during earlier childhood, the situation is just reversed. As the child tries to come out of the closest guidance of parents and tries to lead an independent life, his emotions are intense. Sometimes he is frustrated. If he learns to tolerate frustrations, a balanced emotionality is developed and it helps the child in later age in not becoming aggressive.

Intelligence checks emotion. In late childhood he knows that if he expresses emotions, especially unpleasant emotions violently it will be socially unacceptable. "Hence a child acquires a strong motivation to learn to control the outward expressions of his emotions." He becomes careful about his expression of emotions outside the house. But inside the house he lacks that carefulness. So his parents often punish him for "not acting his age".

On the whole in late childhood, the emotional expressions are somehow pleasant. The child, through various activities shows that he is happy in his adjustments with his environment. Though most of the emotions are pleasant, unpleasant emotions often occur. The child sometimes suffers from anxiety and feelings of frustration.

A survey of some common emotions shows that they are also experienced by adults. But the stimuli and the manner of reaction are different. We will emphasize the difference on child.

Anger: The child in his early childhood comes across many anger provoking situations in his life. Secondly he thinks it is a better way to get the wish fulfilled by becoming angry. The anger provoking situations are quarrel over playing, dissatisfaction over toilet and dressing, obstruction caused to other interesting activities, unpleasant attack from other children and taking away the plaything, etc.

In the later childhood the child faces more anger-provoking situations than in early childhood. This is caused by his desire for more independence than he had when he was undergoing the period of early childhood. The various situations that arouse anger are interruption in course of an activity, constant criticisms, unfavourable comparisons with older children, blame or punishment based on misunderstanding, accusing him of lying and failure to achieve the goals set by him.

The younger child expresses his anger through 'temper tantrums'- that is, by crying, screaming, stamping, kicking, jumping up and down, striking, throwing himself on the floor, holding the breath, stiffening of the baby or making it limp, etc. The older child expresses his anger through sulkiness, negativism, refusal to speak, quarrelsome, fussiness and being generally disagreeable to everyone about everything. But older children have more controlling capacity over their emotions than that of younger children. Temper tantrum behaviour is eliminated when the child reaches the school going-age. The degree of frustration is more in case of older children. So some become aggressive in nature and some others become withdrawing in nature.

Fear: Fearfulness increases in early childhood. The child recognizes some situations which he fails to take into notice before hand. His intelligence is increased so he tries to understand a novel situation. If he fails to understand it he is frightened. When the novelty wears off the fear decreases. Fear is a painful experience for the young child. It becomes more specific in late childhood.

Fear responses of young children are running away, hiding, avoiding physically and verbally, crying and whimpering, etc.

There are various reasons why fear develops in young children. Conditioning, imitation and memories of unpleasant experiences are the main factors contributing to arousal of fear. If the child hears some fearful sounds on radio or sees a fearful scenery in cinema he fears any sight and sound that bears similarity with that. Imitation plays a prominent role in the development of fear in young children. They see how their mothers are fearing a particular stimulus; so also they develop fear for the particular stimulus.

When the child is a little older, he tries to understand a situation Secondly he does not want to be ridiculed by others as he thinks to fear is a cowardly behaviour. Thirdly he develops a negative attitude towards the thing he feared or he develops a liking for it. So during late childhood fear decreases considerably. The child tries to understand 'what is the fact' and why it is happening, etc. Definition of fear for the child changes at this time. The most common fears in late childhood are fear for fire, darkness, illness, disease, doctors, operations, being bitten by a dog, etc. Girls show fears more frequently than do boys.

Concrete stimuli decrease and abstract stimuli join strength during late childhood. The fears are imaginary, fanciful, supernatural, etc. Children fear their losing self-prestige and try to hide their personal limitations. If a child is afraid, he does not show his fear. It is expressed in different forms such as shyness, worries, anxieties, etc.

Affection: The child expresses affection towards those persons and objects which give him pleasure and satisfaction. For the first time the child establishes a love-relationship with any particular person in his environment. Love is stimulated by the activities of other persons towards the child. During this stage the child should get love from his family and outsiders. If he does not get it he becomes 'self-bound' and feels stress in his emotional activities. As Garrison has explained: "Love seems to be a two way affair and grows best when it is both given and received. A constant rejection in the home may leave the child's capacity for giving forth affection undeveloped, or may cause him to seek affection from individuals outside the home. Over affection and indulgence may have an undesirable effect as lack of affection or rejection....... There is therefore the danger that over affection for one or both parents will tend to exclude affection for children of the child's own age level".

So it is clear from the opinion of Garrison that too much of affection is as dangerous as lack of affection for the child. If parents love is not there, the child thinks himself secure, On the other hand, in case of over-affection, self-confidence is eliminated. He may be too introvert and may fail to establish friendly relationship with other children.

Children express their emotion of love both physically and verbally. They hug, kiss and pat the loved person or object. They opt for the companionship of the loved one for a longer time. They express their dissatisfaction when he leaves them. They imitate what he is doing and follow his styles and activities. This is also the same in case of pets and toys whom the child loves. During this stage girls are more affectionate than boys, and both choose children and adults of their own sex for the expression of their affection.

During late childhood the expression of affection is indirect rather than direct as it is during early childhood. The child does not like to be kissed or embraced especially in public. They feel grown up which forces them to be undemonstrative in their relations with others. But indirectly they keep the company of those whom they love. They try to help him in all possible manners. The love in its direct way bursts at unexpected times

Growth and Development

Educational institutions play an important role in the emotional development of children. Child's emotions can be steered either in positive direction or in negative direction by family and school. Some factors in educational curricula may make the child unhappy instead of making him happy. In traditional system of education the child gathers more unpleasant experiences than pleasant experiences. Some common emotions, that are negative in nature, and experienced in the traditional schools are anger, fear and jealousy. They do not help the child to maintain a healthy emotional growth. On the other hand, the pleasurable emotions help the children to develop love, affection and fellow-feeling towards others in the surrounding and ultimately an adjusted personality in future life.

There is no surety that the child, in his future life, will always face pleasurable situations. Rather he is sure to face both pleasure and sorrow in the long run. He must know how to adjust when situations of emotional tension arise. Only by that he can maintain his mental balance. He must tackle the dangers and problems that he confronts during his life. He must have tolerance, which he should put into use in adverse situations that arouse anger, worry, anxiety, frustrations etc. On the whole, if the pleasurable experiences in his life are more than the sorrowful sequences, balance in mental and emotional level can be maintained effectively. In case the sorrowful events come thick and fast, even a bold person can break down and lose his balance of mind.

1. Avoidance of cause or source of a particular emotion is the best way out in maintaining emotional stability. One must take into consideration what causes emotion in the child and then take preventive measures not to allow those things to happen to the child. Hurlock has pointed out five causes of arousal of emotion in children. They are:

(a) Tiredness: Physical tiredness makes a child to show anger, disgust and other severe emotional reactions. So when the child is tired he should not be given any task to work out.

(b) Ill-health: Ill health is one of the most important causes of frequent emotional outbursts.

(c) Relationships with People of Severe Emotions: There are people who are thick-skinned, furious and angry. If children are allowed to mix with them, they try to imitate their behaviour and develop such nature.

(d) Submerged Wishes: If the child is regulated under a strict and controlled atmosphere and rigid authority is imposed on him, wishes are not expressed freely which make his emotions arouse violently. So the wishes of the child should not be repressed in any way.

(e) Embarrassment:

1. If the child faces a particular situation, for which he was not ready, emotions arise and the child feels embarrassed.
2. The children should be taught about the proper way of expressing their emotions. Young children express their emotions in natural ways but adolescents are expected to express their emotions in a socially acceptable manner.
3. Some societies impose such rigid restrictions that the child does not get any chance to express his emotions. The society does not allow him to do certain things. But this is not good for the mental health of the child. He should be facilitated to express his emotions, at least verbally.
4. The educational institutions should help the child to find out the cause and understand the nature of unpleasant emotions. While undergoing an emotional stage it is not possible to change the behaviour of a child by injecting judicious thoughts into his mind. The only way out is to have a knowledge of the problems and wishes of a child and then provide him with measures to overcome them.
5. The child should not only be helped to express his emotions in an acceptable way but also he should be taught how to control them. Especially the emotions which are likely to cause embarrassment to others or destructive in nature, should either be avoided or controlled. This can be achieved by paying respect to the sentiments of the child.
6. The child should be directed and taught how to develop his capacity of internal control more than the external control of his emotions. This can be achieved by continuous endeavours.

7. The teacher plays an important role in educational system and hence apart from teaching lessons in the classrooms, he should be careful about the emotional growth of children. The teacher's care, sympathy, affection, help and pity, etc, help the child to maintain a balanced emotional set-up. The teacher should have proper knowledge of emotional growth of the child. By this he can build a healthy atmosphere in the institution and the child will be able to gain a lot from it.
8. Judicious and rational thinking is the most effective in preventing emotional outbursts. So educational institutions should steer their curricula in such a direction that it will strengthen rationality and morality in children. Once the child is able to judge every problem in a disciplined way, unpleasant emotional outbursts will decrease as he knows what should be done and what should not be done. So his emotional growth moves in the right direction.

It is clear from the above discussion that a lot can be done by parents and educational institutions for the sound emotional growth of children. So in every sphere of family and school, proper attention should be paid and adequate steps should be taken to maintain emotional balance of children.

Exceptional Children

Children showing emotional disturbances create problems for teachers in the school. They are generally naughty, destructive, aggressive and indisciplined. Sometimes, such behaviour crosses the limits and they go beyond control. Their temperament is wayward. After studying and analysing the behaviour of such children, a famous psychologist of London University opined that at first all emotion, which is opposed to the social customs and traditions, emerges in the mind of the child in the beginning. Opposed one after another, many anti-social and contradictory emotions emerge in different situations and make the child temperamental. As a result, the child expresses such aggressive behaviour. If this process continues, the future life of the child becomes an inflammable packet of Chinese crackers. Such a child creates innumerable problems for the teacher as well as for the school. If there is such a child, his temperament and mental problems should be understood correctly and measures should be taken to eradicate them for the benefit of the institution and the child himself. Hence it is a must for every teacher to have knowledge about the sources and causes of emotional disturbance of children.

There are some internal and environmental causes of such types of disturbances. They are discussed below:

1. Organic Factors: Some organic disturbances cause various emotional difficulties in the organism. Irregular secretion of endocrine glands is one of these. In some cases the physical structure and health condition of child hamper his emotional balance. If the child suffers from prolonged illness, if he feels much physical pressure on his body or if there is insufficiency in proper diet, emotional disturbances often occur. As a result of which angry, aggressive, and quarrelsome behaviour arises.
2. Mental Factors: At times some mental pressures force the child to show emotional disturbances. If long cherished hope is hampered he becomes frustrated.
3. Social Factors: For the healthy and sound emotional growth of the child the financial and temperamental environment of the family plays a significant role. The family, in which the parents lead an emotionally disturbed life and always quarrel with each other, can never create an ideal emotional background for the child. This affects the emotional growth of the child. Any child, (if unluckily,) is brought up in such a family, will show symptoms of emotional ill-health.

   Likewise there are divided families where the father and the mother live separately. They produce children of emotional difficulties. On the other hand, a child always gets proper care, affection and protection from an emotionally balanced family.

Besides family and parents, social environment may also affect the emotional growth of the child. The locality, where the child resides, the schools where he reads and the friends with whom he is in constant touch make an element of social surrounding. If at any place the child comes in contact with the traits like suspicion, worries, anxiety, rivalry, anger, jealousy, etc, - they are reflected in the child's own emotional and physical behaviour.

4. Sociological Factors: The emotional growth of the child bears the mark of the geographical surroundings and the climatic environment within which the child has been brought up. A convenient, healthy and beautiful atmosphere always accelerates emotional growth of the child in a positive direction. But on the other hand, an unhealthy place with drains producing stink, dirty lanes, houses like cattle shed, crowded locality, etc, - create abnormal emotional symptoms.

5. Economic Factors: Poverty is one of the most important causes of emotional disturbances. A hungry person is always aggressive. Children living in acute poverty cannot maintain their emotional balance.

So it is proved that the causes of emotional disturbances of a child are many in number. Sometimes more than one factor pressurises the child's mind at a time and he is abnormally tempted and forced to show emotional disturbances.

14

Art of Motivation

This theory brings the following important facts into limelight:

1. The whole is greater than the parts and therefore, the situation should be viewed as a whole.
2. The use of blind fumbling and mechanical trial and error should be minimised. The learner should try to see relevant relationships and act intelligently.
3. The purpose or motive plays the central role in the learning process.

Based on the appeal of this theory, teachers are required to pay attention to the following aspects.

(i) Subject matter (learning material) should be presented in Gestalt form. While teaching the topic 'parts of a flowering plant' the initial start should not be made by presenting the different parts. The plant or flower as a whole should be represented before them and later on the parts should be emphasized. The problem of mathematics requiring solution should be presented as a whole; it should be tried for the solution.

(ii) In the organisation of the syllabus and planning of the curriculum, the Gestalt principle should be given due consideration. A particular subject should not be treated as the mere collection of isolated facts or topics. It should be closely integrated into a whole. Similarly the curriculum, comprising of different subjects and activities should reflect unity and cohesiveness.

(iii) This theory has brought 'motivation' to the forefront by assigning purpose and motive, the central role in learning process. The child should be motivated by arousing his interest and curiosity and he should be acquainted well with the specific aims and purposes of his learning.

(iv) The greater contribution of the insight theory of learning is that it has made learning an intelligent task requiring mental abilities instead of blind fumbling and automatic responses to specific stimuli. It has called a halt to the age old mechanical memorization, drill and practice work which lacks in basic understanding and use of thinking and creative mental powers.

It emphasizes that the learner must be given opportunities for using his mental abilities. Instead of telling him how to do a work, or solve a problem, he should be placed in the position of an independent inquirer and discoverer. He should himself collect the information and discover the knowledge. The teacher should not engage himself in spoonfeeding but help the children in acquiring knowledge and skill through their own attempts by using their mental powers. Scientific and progressive methods like. heuristic method, analytic and problem solving, which advocate learning by insight, should be kept in vogue.

Motivation of Humanbeings

In psychology, motivation is one of the most fascinating and important areas. If we can understand the motives of a child, we can understand and even predict his behaviour. Why is this true? Because motives are the dynamic force that energises behaviour. It is motivation that compels the child to act. And motives are persistent—they keep him acting until he finds satisfactions for them. Not only do motives keep him acting, they direct his actions toward specific goals.

As you can see, you have a professional need for understanding motivation. You will want to master both the theory (the 'why') of motivation and the methods (the 'how') through which you can use motives to guide behaviour and to promote learning.

There are certain basic motives or needs that every person—child and adult—strives to satisfy. So long as our present behaviour and knowledge are adequate to satisfy all our needs, we do not change our behaviour or acquire new knowledge. We modify our attitudes, interests, and personalities, and we acquire new knowledge, only when our present behaviour and knowledge do not satisfy our motives. The only things that appeal to us, the only goals that we desire to attain, are those that will help us to satisfy some strongly felt motive.

To learn something new, then, there must be (1) a *goal* that attracts us and (2) some *obstacle* that keeps us from attaining that goal. For if no obstacles stood in our way, our present behaviour and knowledge would take us directly to our goals and we would have no need to learn.

We learn only when there is no other way for us to reach the goals that our unsatisfied motives create. When we feel a need for learning, for example, it is because we are convinced that we can satisfy some motive only by acquiring learning. This felt need is a far more important element in the effective learning situation than is the simple physical presence of materials to be learned.

Let's look at why we learn from another angle. You want to be a successful teacher. That is a goal that appeals to many of your psychological needs. You want the esteem of your pupils, their parents, your fellow teachers, and your supervisor. And you want to feel a pride in your own professional skill. In addition, you want to be secure in your position as a teacher. Thus, professional skill and knowledge become very real goals to you. Are there any problems that must be solved before you attain these goals? You can see that there are numerous problems. Somehow you must learn a great deal about boys and girls as well as about general teaching methods and materials. You suspect that to reach your goals you must learn about the motives of children and how you can appeal to these motives.

Have you ever noticed how much a child learns when he sets out to raise a calf or a pig, to plant a garden, or to build a radio, a soap-box automobile, a telegraph set, a telescope, or a club house?

Although few of the conditions are present that we like to think are essential to an effective learning situation, he learns more on his own than he does when he attacks some of our well-planned classroom problems. When he feels a strong enough need, the child reads instructions that under ordinary circumstances are far beyond his reading level, and he obtains information from his elders without any forcing on their part. No record of attendance is required—no routine of examination is needed to keep him at the task. Yet in our clean, well-lighted, and well-equipped classrooms, we find that we must force information on this same child, and we find it difficult to teach him to solve tasks that appear far simpler than the extracurricular and freely chosen learning activities that he handles with ease.

Why is this true? Why does a child who must collect money for newspapers learn to make change correctly? Why does a child find it easy to remember what movie is playing at any theater at any time? Why does he have no trouble learning how to travel from one part of a large city to another and yet encounter extreme difficulty in learning to follow the simplest directions for cleaning his room or preparing a theme?

The answers to these questions lie in the fundamental needs of children. We can provide children with every opportunity to learn, but, if they feel little or no need to learn what we want them to, their learning will be slow and meager. Since need arises only when motives demand satisfaction, we must try to identify the basic motives that affect both children and adults.

Because a study of the 'why' of human behaviour contributes so much to our understanding of effective learning situations, we shall devote this whole chapter to motivation. We shall look at the specific effects that motivation has on classroom learning. In a sense, then, this chapter will introduce you to the remaining chapters, and will help you integrate the materials you have studied in the preceding chapters. In this chapter we shall study *why children learn* in both the classroom and in life outside the school.

Motives themselves do not vary greatly from person to person. Differences in behaviour from one person to another result primarily from differences in the obstacles they encounter as they seek to satisfy their motives. So first let us examine the motivational forces that form the central core of human nature— the rules that govern the learning of all; and second let us look at the problems that make one child or one adult different from another.

Motives are the drives that energise all behaviour. Every learned act that we perform—simple or complex—and the manner in which we perform it are the results of our attempts to satisfy motives. The child's learning, both in the classroom and in informal activities, and the personality traits that he exhibits are but symptoms of his strivings to satisfy his motives.

The motives that energise human behaviour can be divided into three broad groups: (1) physiological motives, (2) psychological motives, and (3) habit motives.

Physiological motives. These are the motives that insure the preservation of life for the individual and for the human race. They include hunger, sex, fatigue, elimination of body wastes, thirst, avoidance of pain, and the desire to maintain a proper bodily temperature. These motives are present in all animal life, but in man their method of expression becomes so interwoven with his learned social customs that it is exceedingly difficult to isolate them. The same pattern of behaviour may be aroused at different times by different motives, and any single pattern of behaviour is likely to be caused by numerous interacting motives. Our methods for satisfying our physiological motives are often intimately related to psychological motives and habit motives.

Psychological motives. Psychological motives (sometimes called 'ego' motives) are extremely important determinants of human behaviour. In lower animals these motives are of little importance, but in man they often exert a stronger pressure than the more basic physiological drives. The cave man's direct approach to the problems of securing food or winning a mate has long since been modified by the forces of law and social custom.

Our desire to maintain and bolster our self-esteem and our feeling of esteem in the eyes of others and our needs for security and for new experiences, are the important psychological motives.

Many different terms have been used in referring to these motives. Some psychologists, for example, believe that man has a psychological need to conform and to master. But we can consider conformity and mastery as parts of man's basic drive for security and esteem.

Situations involving a conflict between psychological motives and physiological motives give us some idea of how strong psychological motives really are. Probably no physiological motive is stronger than the desire to live. But we know that men in battle have volunteered to hold a position protecting others even when they knew that they were going to almost certain death. Self-preservation could motivate them in but one direction—retreat. Yet some military units have been able to build a tradition so strong that every man will volunteer for any mission, regardless of its danger. All the physiological motives urge them toward self-preservation, but the psychological motives alone are powerful enough to make them comply with the tradition.

Why are psychological motives so powerful? One reason is that we can seldom satisfy them completely. We may enhance our security, but we are never secure in a final and complete sense. Our feelings of security can be nurtured but never satiated. And so it is with self-esteem and our feeling of esteem in the eyes of others. We work and strive for ever greater conquests. As soon as we have attained one goal, we set up a new, more difficult one. There are probably few men who, once they have been elected governor or senator, do not dream of extending their authority and prestige over the whole nation. And kings and dictators have often thought longingly of ruling the whole world. Physiological motives, on the other hand, can be completely satisfied—at least temporarily. And in our culture the goals that satisfy our physiological motives are more easily attained than are the goals that fulfil our psychological needs.

Most of the behaviour problems that you encounter will result from threats to the child's feeling of security, self-esteem, or the regard of others. These threats occur in the home, on the playground, and in the classroom. A problem exists for. the child whenever he is blocked in his attempts to satisfy his psychological motives. He has a constant need for security and esteem that he actively seeks to satisfy. As a skillful teacher, you will want to construct problem situations that offer the child an opportunity to satisfy his psychological drives. Because these motives are so powerful, attempts to satisfy them lead to the most effective learning.

Habit motives. A habit once it is well established, furnishes its own source of motivation. Originally, it may have been formed in an attempt to satisfy needs based on a physiological or psychological motive. We learn to comb our hair or brush our teeth because it increases our security, self-esteem, or esteem in the eyes of others. However, once the habit is established we retain it. It acts as a motive in its own right long after the original source of motivation has become satisfied in other ways. Smoking, chewing gum or tobacco, cleanliness, following a certain route to school, posture, pitch of the voice in speaking, and application to the job at hand are other examples of such habits.

Various Problems

In many respects, the problems that we meet in life are even more important than our motives, because it is the problems that compel us to change our behaviour – that make us learn. The psychologist often refers to these problems as frustrations, and to the tense feeling that arises when problems are encountered as a feeling of frustration. Figure 1 shows us the three general types of frustration that can block our motives.

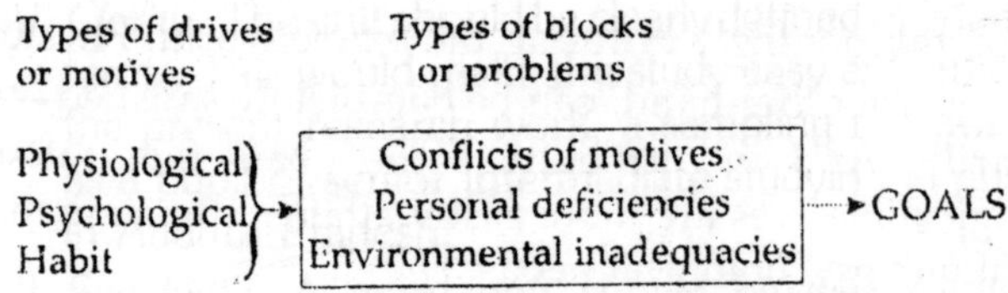

Fig. The motivations and frustrations in human behaviour.

Conflict between motives. As you have often been told, "You cannot eat your cake and have it too." You have to resolve the conflict between two or more motives. You want to save your money for future needs, but a new suit of clothes or an evening at a night club seems desirable too. You want to attend school during the summer to prepare yourself for a better position, but travel or a summer at a resort offers more opportunity for new experiences. The child in the classroom wants to win your approval, but he finds that in order to do so he must earn the disapproval of some of his fellow students.

Personal deficiencies. Personal deficiencies make up a second general class of frustrations. Because of insufficient size, strength, or agility, a child is unable to compete successfully with his fellows in rough-and-tumble play. Because of some lack of attractiveness, such as being too large or having a poor complexion, a girl is rejected by members of either her own or the opposite sex; because of insufficient intellectual ability, a child fails to attain success in the classroom; because he has suffered the loss of an arm or a leg, or is afflicted by muscular paralysis or some other disability, a child may lose both security and self-esteem.

Environmental inadequacies. Our third class of frustrations includes those that arise from a deficiency in the environment. A sailor is unable to obtain fresh drinking water. An explorer cannot find enough game to live on. A boy cannot secure spending money or clothing that meets the standards set by his fellows. A girl is ashamed of her clothes, her home, or the neighbourhood in which she lives. Frequently the home, the school, and the peer group make social, intellectual, or emotional demands on the child that he is unable to meet. A personal defect that would be insignificant in one environment poses an insoluble problem in another. The race, nationality, and religion of the child become serious problems in one group and highly acceptable characteristics in another.

The Response

As long as we are able to satisfy our motives, we have no real need and are faced with no real problem. If we can eat when we are hungry, drink when we are thirsty, receive the praise of our fellows, feel secure in our job and family, and brush our teeth if we are in the habit of so doing, we are scarcely aware of the potential power of our motives.

But when we are unable to satisfy our motives immediately, our contentment vanishes and we become tense. Mentally or physically, we spring into motion. Motion is typical of all animals in problem situations. We may learn to suppress physical motion by finding that mental activity is more likely to lead us to a solution of our problems, but the tendency to move remains with us. This tendency appears to arise from a heightened muscular tension that is typical of our behaviour whenever we encounter a problem that we cannot solve immediately. This type of reaction has had survival value through the long period of animal and human development. If our ancestors had felt contented and relaxed when they grew hungry, they would have starved and we would not have been born. If they had become sleepy when their motives were frustrated, they would have failed to avoid pain or to seek warmth. In short, the restlessness, aggression, and wakefulness that we experience when we are frustrated are natural responses, and, at least until recent times, have contributed to the preservation of the individual and the survival of the species.

As we move about in our search for a solution, our behaviour may be based on trial and error, or it may progress through a planned series of attempts to investigate the various possibilities for solving the problem.

But we can plan and carry out an intelligent campaign only if the present obstacle resembles one that we have overcome in the past. Our physical tension mounts and our search for a solution becomes more random when we feel that we are faced with a problem that is really insurmountable. The tension may lead to digestive disturbances and to acts of aggression toward individuals or other objects in our environment. Problem-solving behaviour is a highly active process.

This pattern is typical of human behaviour. The problems that stand between us and the satisfaction of our needs compel us to search actively for solutions. If a high-school girl feels that she needs a new party dress, she may be willing to take a job to earn extra money even though she has to sacrifice sleep and recreation. In the classroom, this same need for social approval may compel a child to sacrifice play time so that he can keep up with his classmates in spelling or algebra.

Personality is shaped by the problems encountered and by the individual's solution to those problems. If the girl who felt the need for a new party dress had chosen instead to pinch money from her mothers purse, or if the school child had copied from his neighbour's paper, and if these actions had resulted in general satisfaction, each child would have taken a serious step toward developing an unsavory personality. Thus motives are the life force, but the problems encountered shape life's course.

Fortunately, our civilisation forbids the use of physical force to compel children to learn. The teacher is not permitted to block physiological motives intentionally in order to force a child to master a mathematical problem or the parts of speech. Instead, we rely almost exclusively on psychological motives and on habit motives to encourage learning in the classroom.

And these are important motivational forces. The child needs the approval of both his teacher and his classmates. He wants to receive good marks to show to his parents and to convince himself of his own adequacy. By guiding and rewarding his curiosity, which is primarily a desire for new experiences, we can encourage him to move on from one valuable learning experience to another.

The habits of work and attention that we help the child to develop will carry him through many tasks for which he feels no immediate need. Once developed, correct habits of learning are perpetuated by two very strong forces: (1) the motivational value possessed by all habits and (2) the efficiency and ease of effort that they carry with them.

A general principle of behaviour is that the individual tends to eliminate unnecessary motion. As he practices a task, he becomes more efficient. For example, if a child attempts to find information in a book, he flounders about. But after he is taught to use the index, he goes directly to the proper place and finds what he wants. With practice, he forms the habit of using the index and, since this leads him most directly to his goal, he has an added reason for retaining his habit. We must consider this factor of efficiency when we seek to break habits that have become well established. If we have learned to operate the typewriter by the hunt-and-peck system, we are not likely to change to the more effective touch system without considerable motivation and instruction. To make a change would interfere with our existing habits and would result, at least for a time, in a loss in efficiency. However, once we do make the change and grow competent under the new method, our efficiency supplements the force of our new habit to guarantee that we will maintain it. Thus, though it is difficult to discard old habits of work and to adopt new ones, if we can once find better methods and practice them for a time, they will be retained.

The relative value of various goals. In a sense, striving toward goals is nothing more than an attempt to satisfy motives that have been blocked by obstacles or problems. Once we have reached our goal, we tell ourselves, the tension created by our present failure to overcome our problems will be reduced.

The effort that we expend to achieve a given goal is determined by a number of factors, some of which are more powerful than the importance of the goal itself. We strive harder for a small satisfaction that we can attain now than for a much larger goal that we can attain only at the end of a long period of time. A dime held near to the eye appears to be larger than the sun; a small reward attainable now may loom larger, and may induce more effort, than a great reward that can be obtained only in the indefinite future. When we set out on a 20-mile hike, the thought of arriving at our destination hours later furnishes us with little immediate satisfaction. Instead, we pick out a tree or a hill a mile or so away and then watch as our footsteps make the distance dwindle.

And so the child strives far harder for a gold star or a word of praise that he can get this morning or this afternoon than he does for a Ph. D. that will not be within his reach for twenty years. But notice that the higher his level of intellectual development, the longer he is willing to wait for rewards. The mature student is quite content to work for goals that are in the far-distant future. He is able to break his major goals down into the smaller steps of a book read, a paper completed, a few pages written, or a semester of study accomplished.

But immature students have not yet learned that the only way to reach important goals is by moving forward a step at a time. As a matter of fact, since their experience is so limited, they may not even be aware of the existence of distant goals. So one of your big jobs in working with these pupils is to break down the large but relatively unattainable goals of life into small, attainable goals. At the end of each small unit of accomplishment, you will want to provide opportunities for reward through a sense of accomplishment, through a satisfaction of curiosity, or through a feeling of teacher or group approval. The child cannot work for a mastery of arithmetic simply because he may need it when he becomes an engineer many years later. Each small step in the long-range plan must prove rewarding to his curiosity, his security, his self-esteem, his esteem in the eyes of others, or to some other motive.

Only by making sure that every unit of work will satisfy some need of every child, can we create a good learning situation. Pupils are more likely to strive toward vital goals when they themselves feel that the goals are important than when they are prodded by a taskmaster.

When the school provides for the satisfaction of needs, pupil motivation soars to the same high level that exists in out-of-school, informal, child-directed learning situations. What is more, the learning is directed toward a planned end. To the values of out-of-school learning, we add adult assistance and planning, the facilities of the library, well-lighted classrooms, and carefully chosen laboratory equipment.

But here is where our thinking about education so often goes astray. True—the tasks to be performed must fulfill a felt need of the child. But this alone is not enough. The tasks must also point toward definite and wisely chosen goals that possess social utility and that prepare the child to meet future problems of life. The school must be child-centered, but the child must not be deserted by the teacher and the curriculum maker and left to chart his course unassisted. Since he cannot appreciate how great his future need will be for certain-skills and knowledge, he is entitled to the very best guidance that educational experts can offer him. It will be your duty, as a teacher, to see that the child's activity takes him in a desirable direction and at the same time fulfills needs that he feels at the moment. As you grow in experience, you will discover that goals with high social utility can be made as rewarding to the needs of the child as goals with little or no utility.

Levels of aspiration. Different persons aspire to different levels of attainment. If we are to make an accurate estimate of how valuable a goal is to a specific child, we must think not only of how important it seems to us as adults, or of how soon the child can attain it, but also of how attractive it seems to the child. Goals that seem to us to have the same apparent size and to be the same distance from attainment may differ greatly in attractiveness from child to child. One reason is that individual children have individual needs. Some children are most in need of security, others of self-esteem, and still others of new experiences. These needs arise from the life problems that the child is encountering at the moment and from the level of aspiration that has been determined by himself, his family, and his associates.

His race, his religion, his family, his teachers, and his friends have taught him what values to place on various goals. One family places a high value on scholarship and assumes that its children will do well in school and will enter a profession. A child from such a family will need high marks to maintain his security, self-esteem, and esteem in the eyes of others. Another family places a higher value upon material possessions and urges its children to get a good job as soon as possible. The members of a minority group who have had few educational and cultural opportunities may expect relatively little from their offspring, whereas the members of another group may expect a great deal. One religious group may place high value on conformity to moral codes; persons who do not belong to any religious group may emphasise the importance of attaining a large share of worldly goods. A child's friends may be interested in music, art, and books, or in baseball and fishing. All these and many other aspects of the child's experience and of his present environment help to determine how attractive various goals will seem to him.

If the child sets up goals that are in proportion to his abilities he will probably succeed in reaching them. But if his goals are so high and his abilities so low that his efforts are not rewarded, he will be forced either to set a lower goal for himself or to choose quite different goals—goals that may even be socially unacceptable.

You will want to help each pupil to set his levels of aspiration low enough to guarantee some measure of success as he strives toward them, yet high enough to produce enough frustration to call forth effort and to stimulate learning. The level of aspiration is one determinant of how much frustration he will encounter. Since we find little or no motivation without frustration, and since no learning occurs without both motivation and frustration, the level of aspiration must not be too low. On the other hand, if the goal seems unattainable, the child may be driven into despair, unhappiness, random activity and aggression. Ideally, the goal should be attainable but high enough to be difficult. Such a goal fosters high motivation and stimulates the child to make logical exploratory efforts.

How the "personality" determines values. Each of us behaves with some degree of consistency and stability. Our individual pattern of behaviour is controlled by our habits, by our levels of aspiration, and by our past experiences in achieving success or suffering failure. This pattern is a major portion of what we call "personality."

Though we usually think of our personality as affecting others, its effect upon our own behaviour is no less important. One person—through habit, level of aspiration, and successful experiences in the past—places a high value on honesty; another seeks immediate successes without regard for the methods that he must employ to attain them. One child must aim for the praise of parents and teachers; another for the attention of his peer group. And still another must find his successes and excitement in a dream world. One adolescent may feel the need of having a camera, a coin collection, or the security and prestige of a good job; another needs a fast car or flashy clothes.

Thus, when you make an assignment, show a film, or give a demonstration, each pupil views this classroom experience from an entirely different vantage point from that of every other pupil—each seeks different goals. In reading a story, one child's past experiences and levels of aspiration make him identify himself with the hero, another with the heroine, and still another with the villain. One child gains his greatest pleasure from the wealth or physical traits of the hero (or the villain), another from his romantic successes or power over others.

15

Social Development

Human being is the best creation of God, but he does not receive the best education by the study of science or religion, philo-sophy or political science, education or Psychology, Art or litera-ture or by earning a Ph. D. or a D. Litt degree from a recognized university, but by the study of truth about how to live and how to be socialized. Sociability not only establishes his superiority over other animals but also provides him with capability of making sound adjustment and maintaining effective and influential social relations. Traits, habits and instincts come into being during childhood. Then they provide the criterion for the characteristic reaction of man to his environment. The child's respect for his elders, love for the youngsters, co-operation with peers and hospitality towards strangers, etc, depend on the process of the development of his personality in the environment of school and family. The more he learns sociability in this stage, the more he becomes sociable in his later life and the less he faces problems. So both the school and the home play an important role in the social development of the child.

Man is a social being. He comes in contact with the society and starts his interaction with it from the moment of his birth. The span of social relations gradually increases and continues till death. So it is a process from womb to tomb. Considering from social point of view, the childhood is the most valuable phase in human life. Real socialisation starts from childhood. The social habits along with the social instincts that he gains and his interaction with different persons and environment shapes his personality for the whole of his life. Hence it is a prime necessity on the part of a teacher to have the knowledge of how the social personality of a child develops and what are its main constituents.

At the time of birth, the child is neither social, anti-social nor unsocial. It depends upon the environment and experience of his life. His personality is shaped accordingly. At the time of entering the school, the child does not have egocentrism. Rather he expresses interests in the persons, objects and events of his surroundings. He takes part in group-activities. Qualities like distributing things among friends, co-operation, friendship, social interaction and leadership are the main characteristics of his behaviour at that time. With the increase of his experience with other elements of the world, these qualities become the traits of his personality.

Social development is a multi-faceted process in which children acquire talents and behaviour that allow them to function, within a social environment, in a manner that is mutually beneficial to their well-being and that of others. Through social development, children and youth establish inter-personal relationships, acquire a sense of sex-role identity, and develop social standards and a sense of conscience.

Social development is influenced by many different socialisation forces. These affect children's acquisition of the habits, values, and knowledge that facilitate their attainment of goals and enable them to function satisfactorily as members of society. In other words, children learn a complex network of clues that indicates the appropriateness of their actions for specific situations. For example, students' behaviour in one teacher's classroom may be very different from their behaviour in another classroom or on the playground.

A variety of social agents, or determinants, influence the socialization process needed for effective social interaction. These social determinants may include biological factors, social structure and cultural-group membership, the unique social interactions that children and adolescents have with parents and other, cognitive and situational determinants.

Children are not just passive recipients in their acquisition of social behaviour; rather they are active participants in their environments through their social interactions. Students actively incorporate the standards of external social agents and they process those mental structures that enable them to construct schemes or programmes that facilitate appropriate behaviour in other social situations.

Cultural System and Society

Social development varies with children's social and cultural system. Children are encultured differently based on their cultural backgrounds and on parental beliefs related to the nature of children and how they should behave as adults. For example, American-Indian, Oriental, and Anglo-American children are encultured to have different values and behaviour. However, it appears that children's acquisition of social traits and skills is independent of culture and that the process of social development is similar across cultures and social systems.

Importance of the School

School or any educational institution occupies a special position among the various factors that influence the social development of a child. School is basically a social institution. It can be called a society in miniature. So it can serve as a model of society with all the social characteristics. The amount of influence that school can have on the child depends on the caliber and will of the teacher.

Along with the discussion of child's physical, perceptual and cognitive development, psychologists are highly interested in infant's social and moral attachments. The reasons are many.

Firstly, the human beings are highly social and a child's birth is a social event in itself. Then as he grows he is influenced and shaped by the social and moral behaviour of people surroun-ding him. He also influences others. So it is a two way relationship and needs a good understanding among those involved.

Secondly, during early years an infant's behaviour is not clear but confusing as it does not have any uniqueness. Without a proper examination, we can't find out the possible psychological roots as causes of such behaviour.

Thirdly, there is the question of nature and nurture of the child. Different aspects of child's personality should be known to us. We must know about the inherent aspects and the factors that change due to influences of circumstances. Here social experiences take an important place in the child's life.

Finally, the effect of early deprivation trauma should be studied. The factors that produce a well-adjusted and balanced child and the cause that produce a permanent scar in an individual's psychology, must be properly studied.

Different methods and ways are open for the experimenter to study early sociability of human beings. Simple cases can be studied by mere observation. Then there longitudinal studies continuing for many years and experimental studies. We may conduct cross-cultural studies to know the difference in sociability of human beings caused by different social backgrounds. Then there are the studies of child's social behaviour in different socio-economic set-ups. Sociability of upper class, middle class and lower class children tend to be different and its cause and effect is to be properly studied.

Society under Development

Various thinkers have defined social development in the following way:

1. Garrett: "Socialisation or social development is a process whereby the biological individual is converted into a human person.

   This definition is based upon the distinction between the term individual and person. We cannot name each and everybody as person. The person always possesses some personality. The personality is the product of social interaction between him and his social environment. Socialisation and social development-the process of social interaction-helps the individuals to attain personality characteristics.

2. Sorenson: "By social growth and development we mean increasing ability to get along well with oneself and others".

   In this way Sorenson explains that during the process of social development there is a progress in the social abilities or skills of an individual. With these increasing abilities he tries to bring improvement in the maintenance of social relationships. He tries to mould his behaviour and seek adjustment and harmony with others.

3. Freeman and Showel: "Social development is the process of learning to conform to group standard mores and traditions and becoming imbued with a sense of oneness, intercommunication and co-operation."

This definition lays stress on the following:

(i) Social development refers to the process by which a person acquires the necessary knowledge, skills and dispositions that make him an acceptable member of his own group.

(ii) It develops group loyalty and encourages mutual dependence, co-operation and cohesiveness.

(iii) It is the process which helps an individual to behave in accordance with social traditions and mores and thus makes him able to adjust to his social environment.

In the light of all these views we can come to the conclusion that social development or socialisation is a process

(i) which begins with the infant's first contact with other people and continues throughout life.

(ii) it is the net result of his constant interaction with his social environment.

(iii) it helps in learning and acquiring various social qualities and characteristics, and

(iv) with the result of such learning the individual becomes adjusted to his social environment and can maintain proper social relationships.

Development of Babies

The child's attitude, social relationships and pattern of behaviour are to a great extent determined by his early social experience. In the beginning all these are "home-grown" and the foundation of sociability is laid in the homes.

Sociability is not innate and it must be learnt. Every social behaviour is an acquired trait. The period between six weeks to six months, is said to be a 'critical time' in the development of attitudes. For a sound and organised social development both "the types of opportunity" and "number of contacts" are important. Mothers, in upper and middle socio-economic families can give favourable opportunities to their children for contact with the members of their families while those who belong to the lower groups lack such opportunities. So their social immaturity is shown in a quiet, retiring and disinterested attitude towards people and social activities.

At birth the infant's perception is non-distinctive. He wants his physiological needs fulfilled. It does not matter who fulfils them. She may be his mother or a caretaker, it may be a soft pillow or a hot water bottle. When the child is six weeks old, the first social smile appears and between second and third months of life, the baby's ability to distinguish people from inanimate objects develops. He then becomes more attached to people and shows different types of emotional behaviour when detached from them. But still he is unable to distinguish people. Some psychologists call this stage as "discriminating responsiveness to people". It is the beginning of true social behaviour.

The baby, between the second and third months becomes interested in people. He tries to attract his attention towards him or watch his facial expression. He shows special relationship with his mother.

When the baby is four or five months old, he wants to be picked up and to be given a soothing and warm touch. He smiles, in response to the person who speaks to him. After one month he can distinguish between scolding and smiling, friendly and unfriendly voices. At the age of six or seven months he differentiates between familiar and strange persons. He smiles at friends and shows anxiety towards unfamiliar persons.

During this period "attachment behaviour" shown towards the mother is intensified. He smiles at her and tries to vocalise a word to her.

The age of eight or nine month is a period of imitation for the child. He imitates the speech, simple motor activities and gestures of others. When he is one year old, elders can refrain him from doing a thing by uttering the word 'No'.

When the child is one and a half years old he shows "Negativism". It means stubborn resistance to requests and demands of adults. The resistance may be physical or the child may remain silent or even tense.

At the end of second year a state of equilibrium is seen in a child. He co-operates with adults in many simple daily activities and follows their directions. Now he becomes more social in his behaviour. He plays with others and especially with the children of his own age. He even shares his playing materials with them.

Most babies become interested in viewing coloured pictures, television and listening to radio. Though they cannot understand the meaning of the subject matter, still they observe and become fascinated by the constant change in light, colour and pictures on the screen of the television or on the pages of the comic books.

Development of Children

Childhood consists of two phases known as early child-hood and late childhood. Pattern of socialisation changes from one phase to another. Early childhood has been charactc ised as tne "first stage" of socialization. At this stage he gathers training and experience to be a member of gang in late childhood. Area of relationship of the child increases every year and his talking, playing, etc, increases accordingly. The importance of social development during early childhood lies in its qualitative aspect rather than quantitative aspect. That means, it is not important to count the number of social relationships the child has, rather it is important how he develops intimacy with his environment. His future socialization depends upon the pleasurable social contact at this stage.

Early childhood is a crucial time, so far as social development is concerned, because the child during this time, learns the basic social attitudes and the pattern of social behaviour. From two to three years of age, the child's level of social relation is generally low. After three years of age his socialization shows the prominent symptoms of conversational interactions, dominance, leadership, dependent submissiveness, conformity or compliance with the wishes of others, etc. He also shows some unsocial or antisocial behaviour, but they are also important to the socialization of the child. Some prominent social traits develop during early child-hood, which are discussed below.

Firstly the child shows negativism or resistance to adult authority which reaches its peak between the age of three and four years. After that it declines. According to Macfarlane, "Negativism is an interesting combination of self-assertion, self-protection and of resistance to excessive pressures. Children learn that resistance is their best defence in the face of erratic training or when quick tempered persons push slow tempered persons too fast. The child's negativism takes the form of verbal responses and silence. They sometimes do not hear or understand an order or request or they try to neglect them".

Another trait of socialisation of the child is imitation, which implies that the child becomes interested in other children in and around him and tries to imitate their speech, action and emotions. By doing this he tries to prove himself a member of the group. The child does not imitate at all. He chooses the person or persons from whom he gets warmth and affection and imitates their behaviour. At times the child develops a desire to excel or outdo others. This results in rivalry and he tries to brag about his possessions. This is common in case of siblings in a home. When the child is frustrated he expresses aggression. By showing aggressive behaviour he tries to establish his dominance over others. From rivalry and aggression quarreling starts and the child takes away the toys of another child, distracts his work, screams, cries, kicks, hits and bites. These outbursts are short in duration and easily forgotten. At the age of three years such quarreling is frequent and after that improved social adjustments bring about a decrease in the frequency and intensity of quarrels. Children of the lower socio-economic levels quarrel more than those of the higher. Boys are more quarrelsome than girls.

Upto the age of four years, the boys and girls play together, without any specific preference for a particular sex. After four the discriminating attitude begins and it becomes prominent after five years. Then they play different games. In the opinion of Marshall it is a kind of aggressiveness shown by the boys towards the girls. The girls are also antagonised by this.

Between the age of two and three years the child plays alone without any interest in other children. Then comes "Associative play" and "Co-operative play" in which he is a part of a group. At the age of four years he starts team play. He becomes conscious of other's acceptance or rejection of his play activities. He starts playing 'neighbourhood-games' such as tag, hide-and-seek, cat and mouse, cops-and-robbers, etc. Games at this age are simple, involving few rules and lack any type of competition.

Late childhood has been named as "gang age" in view of an increasingly strong desire of the child to be a member of the gang. During this stage, social-development is rapid and the child is no longer a selfish, self-centered individual. He is a well-adjusted, cooperative member of his peer-group. Child's behaviour shows more maturity than before. When the child reaches the age of six, his negativism decreases, though again at the age of ten and eleven they show a type of rebelling attitude against adult authority by which they try to establish their self appropriateness.

The circle of friends of the child widens as he does not want to be confined to his home and family members. When the child enters the middle school, his puberty begins and boys as well as girls spend more time outside the home. Generally a gang consists of children of same sex. They form teams not only to play but also for other activities like stealing fruits, smoking and some other socially unacceptable behaviour.

By forming gangs they raise money for charity, make things or act out plays depending upon the nature of the community they belong to.

The child learns to compete with others, to co-operate and work as a member of a team, to accept responsibilities and to see them through, to take the part of others when mistreated or neglected and to be a good sport in adversity as well as in success. During the childhood, boys and girls prefer the companionship of the individuals of their own sex. The girls think themselves more matured than the boys of their age but at the same time they see them enjoying more social independence. So they develop antagonistic and unfavourable attitude towards the boys. Boys and girls of this age develop an attitude of hero worship towards someone who possesses qualities they admire. The children select a member of their gang as leader, who must be superior in most respects to the rest of the group especially in intelligence, dependability, diplomacy, self-confidence, emotional stability, athletic ability and awareness of the wishes of the others. Again the leader must be an extrovert.

Collective Impact

Late childhood is also called 'play age' because during this period overlapping of play activities is the characteristic of the younger years and those of adolescence of different social class backgrounds differ, qualitatively and quantitatively. Bright children are generally more solitary and take part in fewer activities. Within the play activities of boys construction of tools, drawing, painting and clay modelling are marked, while girls prefer sewing, drawing, painting and singing. The child who fails to establish good social relations spends more time in day dreaming than the socially well-adjusted child.

During late childhood the child develops interest in understanding people and things which formerly hold little or no meaning for him. After the child enters the school he becomes aware of his racial group and religious-group membership and tries to follow the attitude of elders. He develops a self-concept and understands his social class. He defines his social class status in terms of the occupation of his parents. The self-concept of boys and girls is different. The boys think that they should be able to run fast, play rough games, need to be smart, climb, swim carry things and above all they must have more ability than girls. On the other hand, the girls think that they must stay close to the houses play quietly and gentler than boys; sitting and talking about dresses; they need to know how to cook, sew and take care of children.

Additional Reading

Bhaskara Rao, Digumarti (1994). *Scientific Aptitude*, New Delhi: Ashish Publishing House. ISBN 81-7024-658-X.

Bhaskara Rao, Digumarti (1995). *Animal Kingdom*. New Delhi: Discovery Publishing House. ISBN 81-7141-274-2.

Bhaskara Rao, Digumarti (1995). *Batracology*. New Delhi: Discovery Publishing House. ISBN 81-7141-279-3.

Bhaskara Rao, Digumarti (1997), *Scientific Attitude*. New Delhi: Discovery Publishing House. ISBN 81-7141-308-0.

Bhaskara Rao, Digumarti (1996). *Scientific Attitude vis-à-vis Scientific Aptitude*. New Delhi: Discovery Publishing House. ISBN 81-7141-308-0.

Bhaskara Rao, Digumarti, Editor (1996). *Encyclopaedia of Education for All*, 5 Volumes. New Delhi: APH Publishing Corporation. ISBN 81-7024-759-4 (set).

Vol. I *Education for All: The World Conference*. ISBN 81-7024-760-8.

Vol. II *Education for All: The EPA-9 Summit*. ISBN 81-7024-761-6.

Vol. III *Education for All: Quality Education for All*. ISBN 81-7024-762-6.

Vol. IV *Education for All: Planning and Monitoring*. ISBN 81-7024-763-4.

Vol. V *Education for All: The Indian Scenario*. ISBN 81-7024-764-0.

Bhaskara Rao, Digumarti, Editor (1996). *Global Perceptions on Peace Education*, 3 Volumes. New Delhi: Discovery Publishing House. ISBN 81-7141-319-6.

Bhaskara Rao, Digumarti, Editor (1996). *National Policy on Education*. 2 Volumes. New Delhi: Anmol Publications Pvt. Ltd. ISBN 81-7488-323-1.

Bhaskara Rao, Digumarti, Editor (1997). *Care the Child*, 2 Volumes. New Delhi: Discovery Publishing House. ISBN 81-7141-394-3.

Bhaskara Rao, Digumarti, Editor (1997). *Education for the 21st Century*. New Delhi: Discovery Publishing House. ISBN 81-7141-389-7.

Bhaskara Rao, Digumarti, Editor (1997). *Reflections on Scientific Attitude*. New Delhi: Discovery Publishing House, ISBN 81-7141-319-6.

Bhaskara Rao, Digumarti, Editor (1997). *Success Story of a Primary Education Project*. New Delhi: APH Publishing Corporation. ISBN 81-7024-850-7.

Bhaskara Rao, Digumarti, Editor (1997). *World Food Summit*. New Delhi: Discovery Publishing House. ISBN 81-7141-386-2.

Bhaskara Rao, Digumarti, Editor (1998). *Adolescence Education*. New Delhi: Discovery Publishing House. ISBN 81-7141-432-X.

Bhaskara Rao, Digumarti, Editor (1998). *Community and School Nutrition Education*. New Delhi: Discovery Publishing House. ISBN 81-7141-435-4.

Bhaskara Rao, Digumarti, Editor (1998). *District Primary Education Programme*. New Delhi: Discovery Publishing House. ISBN 81-7141-396-X.

Bhaskara Rao, Digumarti, Editor (1998). *Earth Summit*, 2 Volumes. New Delhi: Discovery Publishing House. ISBN 81-7141-435-4.

Bhaskara Rao, Digumarti, Editor (1998). *National Policy on Education: Towards an Enlightened and Humane Society*, New Delhi: Discovery Publishing House. ISBN 81-7141-426-5.

Bhaskara Rao, Digumarti, Editor (1998). *Reforming School Education*. New Delhi: Discovery Publishing House. ISBN 81-7141-403-6.

Bhaskara Rao, Digumarti, Editor (1998). *Teacher Education in India*. New Delhi: Discovery Publishing House. ISBN 81-7141-406-0.

Bhaskara Rao, Digumarti, Editor (1998). *World Summit for Social Development*. New Delhi: Discovery Publishing House. ISBN 81-7141-420-6.

Bhaskara Rao, Digumarti, Editor (2000). *Education for All: Achieving the Goal*, 3 Volumes, New Delhi: APH Publishing Corporation. ISBN 81-7648-152-1.

Vol. I *The Global Consensus*. ISBN 81-7648-155-6.

Vol. II *Mid-Decade Review Reports of Regional Seminars*. ISBN 81-7648-154-8.

Vol. III *Issues and Trends*. ISBN 81-7648-155-6.

Bhaskara Rao, Digumarti, Editor (2000), *International Encyclopaedia of AIDS*, 11 Volumes in 13 Parts. New Delhi: Discovery Publishing House. ISBN 81-7141-6 (Set).

Vol. 1 *Introduction to HIV/AIDS*. ISBN 81-7141-523-7.

Vol. 2 *HIV/AIDS—Issues and Challenges*, 2 Parts. ISBN 81-7141-524-5.

Vol. 3 *HIV/AIDS—Socio Economic Realities*. ISBN 81-7141-524-3.

Vol. 4 *HIV/AIDS—Law Ethics and Human Rights*, 2 Parts. ISBN 81-7141-526-1.

Vol. 5 *AIDS and NGOs*. ISBN 81-7141-527-X.

Vol. 6 *AIDS and Home Care*. ISBN 81-7141-528-8.

Vol. 7 *STD Case Management*. ISBN 81-7141-529-6.

Vol. 8 *HIV/AIDS Prevention and Care—Teaching Modules for Nurses and Midwives*. ISBN 81-7141-530-X.

Vol. 9 *HIV Prevention Education for Education for Educational Institutions*. ISBN 81-7141-531-8.

Vol. 10 *Instructional Modules for AIDS Education*. ISBN 81-7141-532-6.

Vol. 11 *School Health Education to Prevent AIDS and STD—A Package for Curriculum Planners*. ISBN 81-7141-5338-4.

Bhaskara Rao, Digumarti, Editor (2000). *International Encyclopaedia of Science and Technology Education*, 11 Volumes. New Delhi: Discovery Publishing House. ISBN 81-7141-548-2 (Set).

Vol. 1 *Science and Technology Education*. ISBN 81-7141-568-7.

Vol. 2 *Science Education in Developing Countries*. ISBN 81-7141-570-9.

Vol. 3 *Organisational Structure of Science*. ISBN 81-7141-570-9.

Vol. 4 *Science Education in Asia and the Pacific*. ISBN 81-7141-571-7.

Vol. 5 *Science and Technology Education for All*. ISBN 81-7141-572-5.

Vol. 6 *Values, Ethics, Talent and Girls in Science and Technology Education*. ISBN 81-7141-573-3.

Vol. 7 *Popularization of Science and Technology Education*. ISBN 81-7141-574-1.

Vol. 8 *Science, Power and Society*. ISBN 81-7141-575-X.

Vol. 9 *Information Technology*. ISBN 81-7141-576-8.

Vol. 10 *Teacher Training in Science and Technology Education*. ISBN 81-7141-577-6.

Vol. 11 *Teacher Training in Science and Technology: A Curriculum Framework*. ISBN 81-7141-578-4.

Bhaskara Rao, Digumarti, Editor (2001). *Distance Education in Different Countries*. New Delhi: APH Publishing Corporation. ISBN 81-7648-229-3.

Bhaskara Rao, Digumarti, Editor (2001). *Decentralised Management of Education (Management of Education in Panchayati Raj and Municipal Bodies)*. New Delhi: Discovery Publishing House. ISBN 81-7141-617-9.

Bhaskara Rao, Digumarti, Editor (2001). *Electrochemistry for Environmental Protection*. New Delhi: Discovery Publishing House. ISBN 81-7141-619-5.

Bhaskara Rao, Digumarti, Editor (2001). *Global Educational Studies*. New Delhi: Discovery Publishing House. ISBN 81-7141-616-0.

Bhaskara Rao, Digumarti, Editor (2001). *Global Synthesis of Educational Assessment*. New Delhi: Discovery Publishing House. ISBN 81-7141-613-6.

Bhaskara Rao, Digumarti, Editor (2000). *International Encyclopaedia of Human Rights*. 7 Volumes in 13 Parts. New Delhi: Discovery Publishing House. (Royal Size). ISBN 81-7141-567-9 (Set).

Vol. 1 *International Instruments of Human Rights*, 2 Parts. ISBN 81-7141-595-4.

Vol. 2 *Regional Instruments of Human Rights*. ISBN 81-7141-604-7.

Vol. 3 *Human Rights and the United Nations*, 2 Parts. ISBN 81-7141-605-5.

Vol. 4 *Fact Files of Human Rights*, 3 Parts. ISBN 81-7141-605-3.

Vol. 5 *Study Stories of Human Rights*, 3 Parts. ISBN 81-7141-607-3.

Vol. 6 *International Meetings on Human Rights*, 2 Parts. ISBN 81-7141-608-X.

Vol. 7 *Professional Training in Human Rights*. ISBN 81-7141-609-8.

Bhaskara Rao, Digumarti, Editor (2001). *Jomtein Decade of Education*. New Delhi: Discovery Publishing House. ISBN 81-7141-618-7.

Bhaskara Rao, Digumarti, Editor (2001). *Nuclear Materials: Issues and Concerns*, 2 Volumes. New Delhi: Discovery Publishing House. ISBN 81-7141-611-X.

Bhaskara Rao, Digumarti, Editor (2001). *World Conference on Education for All*. New Delhi: APH Publishing Corporation. ISBN 81-7141-274-9.

Bhaskara Rao, Digumarti, Editor (2001). *World Conference on Higher Education*, New Delhi: Discovery Publishing House. ISBN 81-7141-610-1.

Bhaskara Rao, Digumarti, Editor (2001). *World Conference on Science*. New Delhi: Discovery Publishing House. ISBN 81-7141-612-8.

Bhaskara Rao, Digumarti, Editor (2003). *Inspiring Experience in Teacher Education*. New Delhi: Discovery Publishing House. ISBN 81-7141-656-X.

Bhaskara Rao, Digumarti, Editor (2003). *International Studies in Education*, 3 Volumes, New Delhi: Discovery Publishing House. ISBN 81-7141-647-0.

Bhaskara Rao, Digumarti, Editor (2003). *Military Conversion: Impact on Science and Technology*, New Delhi: Discovery Publishing House. ISBN 81-7141-578-4.

Bhaskara Rao, Digumarti, Editor (2003). *United Nations Millennium Summit*. New Delhi: Discovery Publishing House. ISBN 81-7141-632-2.

Bhaskara Rao, Digumarti, Editor (2003). *World Assembly on Aging*. New Delhi: Discovery Publishing House. ISBN 81-7141-637-3.

Bhaskara Rao, Digumarti, Editor (2004). *World Conference on Human Rights*. New Delhi: Discovery Publishing House. ISBN 81-7141-661-6.

Bhaskara Rao, Digumarti, Editor (2003). *World Education Forum*. New Delhi: Discovery Publishing House. ISBN 81-7141-639-X.

Bhaskara Rao, Digumarti, Editor (2004). *Education Employment and Human Resource Development*. New Delhi: Discovery Publishing House. ISBN 81-7141-681-0.

Bhaskara Rao, Digumarti, Editor (2004). *Successfully Schooling*. New Delhi: Discovery Publishing House. ISBN 81-7141-677-2.

Bhaskara Rao, Digumarti, Editor (2004). *European Education and Teachers*. New Delhi: Discovery Publishing House. ISBN 81-7141-702-7.

Bhaskara Rao, Digumarti, Editor (2004). *Teachers in a Changing World*. New Delhi: Discovery Publishing House. ISBN 81-7141-694-2.

Bhaskara Rao, Digumarti, Editor (2004). *Learning to Live Together*, 4 Volumes. New Delhi: Discovery Publishing House.

Vol. 1 *International Conference on Learning to Live Together.*

Vol. 2 *Globalisation and Living Together.*

Vol. 3 *Curriculum for Learning to Live Together.*

Vol. 4 *Science Education for the Contemporary Society.*

Bhaskara Rao, Digumarti (2004). *International Guidelines on Open and Distance Education*, New Delhi: Discovery Publishing House.

Bhaskara Rao, Digumarti, Editor (2004). *Adult Learning in the 21st Century*. New Delhi: Discovery Publishing House.

Bhaskara Rao, Digumarti, Editor (2004). *Educational Practices: Research and Recommendations*. New Delhi: Discovery Publishing House.

Bhaskara Rao, Digumarti, Editor (2004). *Chernobyl: Never Again*. New Delhi: APH Publishing Corporation.

Bhaskara Rao, Digumarti, Editor (2004). *Virology and Immunology*. New Delhi: APH Publishing Corporation.

Bhaskara Rao, Digumarti, C.A.P. Swami and B.S.V. Dutt (1997). *Self-Evaluation in Student Teaching*. New Delhi: Discovery Publishing House. ISBN 81-7141-374-9.

Bhaskara Rao, Digumarti and B.S.V. Dutt, Editors (2003). *Education: Programmes and Policies*. New Delhi: APH Publishing Corporation. ISBN 81-7648-470-9.

Bhaskara Rao, Digumarti and D. Naresh Kumar (2004). *School Teacher Effectiveness*. New Delhi: Discovery Publishing House.

Bhaskara Rao, Digumarti and D. Sridhar (2002). *Job Satisfaction of School Teachers*. New Delhi: Discovery Publishing House. ISBN 81-7141-652-7.

Bhaskara Rao, Digumarti and Digumarti Pushpa Latha (1994). *Achievement in Biology*. New Delhi: Discovery Publishing House. ISBN 81-7141-264-5.

Bhaskara Rao, Digumarti, C. Sridevi and K. Vijaya (1995). *Achievement in Social Studies*. New Delhi: Discovery Publishing House. ISBN 81-7141-281-5.

Bhaskara Rao, Digumarti and Digumarti Pushpa Latha (1995). *Achievement in English*. New Delhi: Discovery Publishing House. ISBN 81-7141-283-1.

Bhaskara Rao, Digumarti and Digumarti Pushpa Latha (1994). *Achievement in Science*. New Delhi: Discovery Publishing House. ISBN 81-7141-280-70.

Bhaskara Rao, Digumarti and Digumarti Pushpa Latha (1995). *Achievement in Mathematics*. New Delhi: Discovery Publishing House. ISBN 81-7141-278-5.

Bhaskara Rao, Digumarti and Digumarti Pushpa Latha, Editors (1998). *International Encyclopaedia of Women*. 5 Volumes. New Delhi: Discovery Publishing House. ISBN 81-7141-410-9.

Vol. 1 *Status of World's Women*. ISBN 81-7141-494-X.

Vol. 2 *Women, Education and Empowerment*. ISBN 81-7141-498-1.

Vol. 3 *Women Challenges and Advancement*. ISBN 81-7141-497-4.

Vol. 4 *Women and Family Health*. ISBN 81-7141-497-4.

Vol. 5 *Women and International Action*. ISBN 81-7141-498-2.

Bhaskara Rao, Digumarti, Digumarti Pushpa Latha and Digumarti Harshitha, Editors (2001). *Biological Warfare*. New Delhi: Discovery Publishing House. ISBN 81-7141-597-0.

Bhaskara Rao, Digumarti, Digumarti Pushpa Latha and Digumarti Harshitha, Editors (2001). *Women as Educators*. New Delhi: Discovery Publishing House. ISBN 81-7141-602-0.

Bhaskara Rao, Digumarti and Digumarti Harshitha, Editors (2001). *Education in India*. New Delhi: APH Publishing Corporation. ISBN 81-7141-207-2.

Bhaskara Rao, Digumarti, Digumarti Pushpa Latha and Digumarti Harshitha, Editors (2001). *Assessing Learning Achievement*. New Delhi: Discovery Publishing House. ISBN 81-7141-601-2.

Bhaskara Rao, Digumarti, Digumarti Pushpa Latha and Digumarti Harshitha, Editors (2001). *Energy Security*. New Delhi: Discovery Publishing House. ISBN 81-7141-598-9.

Bhaskara Rao, Digumarti, Digumarti Harshitha and K.R.S.S. Rao, Editors (1999). *Advanced Biotechnology*. New Delhi: Discovery Publishing House. ISBN 81-7141-516-4.

Bhaskara Rao, Digumarti and K.R.S. Sambhasiva Rao, Editors (1996). *Current Trends in Indian Education*. New Delhi: Discovery Publishing House. ISBN 81-7141-311-0.

Bhaskara Rao, Digumarti and K. Vijaya (1995). *A Text Book of Evaluation*. Ambala Cantt: The Associated Publishers.

Bhaskara Rao, Digumarti and N.V.M. Mohana Rao (2002). *Problems of Mentally Handicapped Children*. New Delhi: Discovery Publishing House. ISBN 81-7141-645-4.

Bhaskara Rao, Digumarti and S. Chandra Mohan (2002). *Sports Management*. New Delhi: APH Publishing Corporation. ISBN 81-7648-467-9.

Bhaskara Rao, Digumarti and Sk. Johni Basha (2004). *Teachers' Population Education Awareness*. New Delhi: APH Publishing Corporation.

Bhaskara Rao, Digumarti, V.V. Rao, V.V. Lakshmi and V.V. Krishna, Editors (1999). *Status and Advancement of Women*. New Delhi: APH Publishing Corporation. ISBN 81-7648-169-6.

Babu, P.C., Author and Digumarti Bhaskara Rao, Editor (2004). *Flowers of Wisdom*. New Delhi: Discovery Publishing House. ISBN 81-7141-695-0.

Bhagya Lakshmi, Lingineni, Author and Digumarti Bhaskara Rao, Editor (2000). *Reading and Comprehension*. New Delhi: Discovery Publishing House. ISBN 81-7141-543-1.

Bhuvaneswara Lakshmi, Gadde, Author and Digumarti Bhaskara Rao, Editor (2000). *Attitude Towards Science*. New Delhi: Discovery Publishing House. ISBN 81-7141-541-6.

Devraj, T.A.S., Author and Digumarti Bhaskara Rao, Editor (1997). *Trace Analysis of Uranium and Thorium*. New Delhi: Discovery Publishing House. ISBN 81-7141-375-7.

Durga Rani, K., Author and Digumarti Bhaskara Rao, Editor (2000). *Educational Aspirations and Scientific Attitudes*. New Delhi: Discovery Publishing House. ISBN 81-7141-555-55.

Dutt, B.S.V. and Digumarti Bhaskara Rao (2001). *Empowering Primary Teachers*. New Delhi: Discovery Publishing House. ISBN 81-7141-615.2.

Ediger, Marlow and Digumarti Bhaskara Rao (1996). *Science Curriculum*. New Delhi: Discovery Publishing House. ISBN 81-7141-321-8.

Ediger, Marlow and Digumarti Bhaskara Rao (2000). *Teaching Mathematics Successfully*. New Delhi: Discovery Publishing House. ISBN 81-7141-552-0.

Ediger, Marlow and Digumarti Bhaskara Rao (2001). *Teaching Science Successfully*. New Delhi: Discovery Publishing House. ISBN 81-7141-600-4.

Ediger, Marlow and Digumarti Bhaskara Rao (2001). *Teaching Social Studies Successfully*. New Delhi: Discovery Publishing House. ISBN 81-7141-596-2.

Ediger, Marlow and Digumarti Bhaskara Rao (2002). *Philosophy and Curriculum*. New Delhi: Discovery Publishing House. ISBN 81-7141-631-4.

Ediger, Marlow and Digumarti Bhaskara Rao (2002). *Improving School Administration*. New Delhi: Discovery Publishing House. ISBN 81-7141-633-0.

Ediger, Marlow and Digumarti Bhaskara Rao (2002). *Elementary Curriculum*. New Delhi: Discovery Publishing House. ISBN 81-7141-658-6.

Ediger, Marlow and Digumarti Bhaskara Rao (2003). *Language Arts Curriculum*. New Delhi: Discovery Publishing House. ISBN 81-7141-657-8.

Ediger, Marlow and Digumarti Bhaskara Rao (2004). *Teaching Language Arts Successfully*. New Delhi: Discovery Publishing House. ISBN 81-7141-678-0.

Ediger, Marlow and Digumarti Bhaskara Rao (2004). *Teaching Mathematics in Elementary Schools*. New Delhi: Discovery Publishing House. ISBN 81-7141-687-X.

Ediger, Marlow and Digumarti Bhaskara Rao (2004). *Teaching Science in Elementary Schools*. New Delhi: Discovery Publishing House. ISBN 81-7141-709-4.

Ediger, Marlow and Digumarti Bhaskara Rao (2004). *School Curriculum and Administration*. New Delhi: Discovery Publishing House. ISBN 81-7141-709-4.

Ediger, Marlow and Digumarti Bhaskara Rao (2004). *Modern Elementary School*. New Delhi: Discovery Publishing House.

Ediger, Marlow and Digumarti Bhaskara Rao (2004): *Relevancy in Elementary Curriculum*. New Delhi: Discovery Publishing House. ISBN 81-7141-751-5.

Ediger, Marlow and Digumarti Bhaskara Rao, (2004). *Teaching Social Studies in Elementary Schools*. New Delhi: Discovery Publishing House.

Ediger Marlow, B.S.V. Dutt and Digumarti Bhaskara Rao (2004). *Teaching English Successfully*. New Delhi: Discovery Publishing House. ISBN 81-7141-707-8.

Harshitha, Digumarti and Digumarti Bhaskara Rao, Editors (2004). *Educational Innovations*. New Delhi: Discovery Publishing House.

Indira Devi, Author and J. Prasanth Kumar and Digumarti Bhaskara Rao, Editors (2004). *Values in Language Text Books*. New Delhi: Discovery Publishing House.

Jayasree, Kandi, Author and Digumarti Bhaskara Rao, Editor (1999). *Correlates of Socialisation*. New Delhi: Discovery Publishing House. ISBN 81-7141-517-2.

John Babu, Chikati, Author and T.J.R. Prasad, G.M. Madhukar and Digumarti Bhaskara Rao, Editors (1996). *Problem Solving in Mathematics*. New Delhi: APH Publishing Corporation. ISBN 81-7648-273-0.

Lalitha, T., Author and K.S. Prabhakaram, D.S.N. Sastry and Digumarti Bhaskara Rao, Editors (2004). *Educational Philosophic Beliefs*. New Delhi: Discovery Publishing House. ISBN 81-7141-765-5.

Madhu Bala, Jampala, Author and Digumarti Bhaskara Rao, Editor (2004). *Adjustment Problems of Hearing Impaired*. New Delhi: Discovery Publishing House.

Marja, Talvi and Digumarti Bhaskara Rao, Editors (1996). *Educational Leadership and Social Changes*. New Delhi: Discovery Publishing House. ISBN 81-7141-320-X.

Nirmala Jyothi, M., Author and Digumarti Bhaskara Rao, Editor (2003). *Non-detention Systems in School Education*. New Delhi: Discovery Publishing House. ISBN 81-7141-654-3.

Prabhakaram, K.S., Author and Digumarti Bhaskara Rao, Editor (1998). *Concept Attainment Model in Mathematics Teaching*. New Delhi: Discovery Publishing House. ISBN 81-7141-424-9.

Prasanth Kumar, J., Author and Digumarti Bhaskara Rao, Editor (1998). *Effectiveness of Distance Education System*. New Delhi: Discovery Publishing House. ISBN 81-7141-437-0.

Prasanth Kumar, J., Author and G. Sundara Rao and Digumarti Bhaskara Rao, Editors (2000). *Open University Student Support Services*. New Delhi: Discovery Publishing House. ISBN 81-7141-550-4.

Ramatulasamma, K., Author and Digumarti Bhaskara Rao, Editor (2002). *Job Satisfaction of Teacher Educators*, New Delhi: Discovery Publishing House. ISBN 81-7141-655-1.

Rama Krishnaiah, D., Author and Digumarti Bhaskara Rao, Editor (1998). *Job Satisfaction of College Teachers*, New Delhi: Discovery Publishing House. ISBN 81-7141-438-9.

Rama Kumar Ratnam, M., Author and Digumarti Bhaskara Rao, Editor (1998). *Dukka: Suffering in Early Buddhism*. New Delhi: Discovery Publishing House. ISBN 81-7141-653-5.

Rathaiah, Lavu and Digumarti Bhaskara Rao, Editors (1996). *International Innovations in Education*. New Delhi: Discovery Publishing House. ISBN 81-7141-359-5.

Ramesh, Ganta and Digumarti Bhaskara Rao, Editors (1998). *Environmental Education: Problems and Prospects*. New Delhi: Discovery Publishing House. ISBN 81-7141-423-0.

Rathaiah, Lavu and Digumarti Bhaskara Rao (1997). *Achievement Correlates*. New Delhi: Discovery Publishing House. ISBN 81-7141-385-4.

Reddy, Sudhakar Y., Author, and Digumarti Bhaskara Rao, Editor (2003). *Creativity in Adolescents*. New Delhi: Discovery Publishing House. ISBN 81-7141-659-4.

Reddy, M.S., Author and Digumarti Bhaskara Rao, Editor (2004). *Creativity in College Students*. New Delhi: Discovery Publishing House. ISBN 81-7141-697-7.

Radramamba, B., Author and Digumarti Bhaskara Rao, Editor (2003). *Problems of Teaching*. New Delhi: APH Publishing Corporation. ISBN 81-7648-462-8.

Sanjeeva Rao, P.C., Author and Digumarti Bhaskara Rao, Editor (1996). *A Text Book of Geology*. New Delhi: Discovery Publishing House. ISBN 81-7141-313-7.

Satya Narayana V., Author and Digumarti Bhaskara Rao, Editor (2001). *Physical Education, Social Attitudes and Leadership Qualities*. New Delhi: Discovery Publishing House. ISBN 81-7141-593-8.

Srinivasulu Reddy, M., and K.R.S. Sambasiva Rao, Authors and Digumarti Bhaskara Rao, Editor (1999). *A Text Book of Aquaculture*. New Delhi: Discovery Publishing House. ISBN 81-7141-482-6.

Srinivasa Rao, Mandalapu, Author and Digumarti Bhaskara Rao, Editor (2004). *Achievement Motivation and Achievement in Mathematics*. New Delhi: Discovery Publishing House. ISBN 81-7141-674-8.

Vanaja, M. Author and Digumarti Bhaskara Rao, Editor (1999). *Inquiry Trnining Model*. New Delhi: Discovery Publishing House. ISBN 81-7141-515-6.

Vanaja. M. and N. Sneha Latha, Authors and Digumarti Bhaskara Rao, Editor (2004). *Student Shyness*. New Delhi: APH Publishing Corporation.

Valeri V. Koustiouk, Author and Digumarti Bhaskara Rao, Editor (2002). *A Text Book of Cryogenics*. New Delhi: Discovery Publishing House. ISBN 81-7141-642-X.

Valeri V. Koustiouk, Author and Digumarti Bhaskara Rao, Editor (2004). *Refrigeration and Environment*. New Delhi: APH Publishing Corporation.

Veena Kumari, Balusu and Digumarti Bhaskara Rao (1996). *Operation Black Board*. New Delhi: Ashish Publishing Corporation. ISBN 81-7024-711-X.

Veena Kumari, Balusu, Author and Digumarti Bhaskara Rao, Editor (2000). *Psycho-Social Correlates of Achievement*, New Delhi: Discovery Publishing House. ISBN 81-7141-547-4.

Vanaja, M., Author and Digumarti Bhaskara Rao, Editor (1999). *Inquiry Training Model*. New Delhi: Discovery Publishing House. ISBN 81-7141-515-6.

Venkata Rao, P. and Digumarti Bhaskara Rao (1989). *A Text Book of Zoology—Junior Intermediate*. Guntur: Vignan Publishers.

Venkata Rao, P. and Digumarti Bhaskara Rao (1989). *A Text Book of Zoology—Senior Intermediate*. Guntur: Vignan Publishers.

Venugopala Rao, K., Author and Digumarti Bhaskara Rao, Editor (2000). *Teacher Morale in Secondary Schools*. New Delhi: Discovery Publishing House. ISBN 81-7141-551-2.

Vidya, C., Author and Digumarti Bhaskara Rao. Editor (1996). *A Text Book of Nutrition*. New Delhi: Discovery Publishing House. ISBN 81-7141-309-9.

Vidya Bharathi, D., Author and Digumarti Bhaskara Rao, Editor (2000). *Educational Philosophies of Swami Vivekananda and John Dewey*. New Delhi: APH Publishing Corporation. ISBN 81-7648-309-9.

Books in Telugu Language

Bhaskara Rao, Digumarti (1986). *Dhrushya Sravana Bodhanapakaranalu* (Audio Visual Teaching Aids). Guntur: Nagarjuna Publishers.

Bhaskara Rao, Digumarti (1993). *Jeevasashtra Bodhana* (Teaching of Biology). Guntur: Nagarjuna Publishers.

Bhaskara Rao, Digumarti (1995). *Vignanasasthra Bodhana* (Teaching of Science) Guntur: Nagarjuna Publishers.

Bhaskara Rao, Digumarti (1997). *Vidya Manovignana Seshtram* (Educational Psychology). Guntur: Creative Press.

Bhaskara Rao, Digumarti (1998). *DSC Study Material*. Guntur: Nagarjuna Publishers.

Bhaskara Rao, Digumarti (1998). *Upadhyayudu Vidya*. (Teacher and Education). Guntur: Nagarjuna Publishers.

Bhaskara Rao, Digumarti (1998). *Vidya Drukpadalu* (Prespectives of Education). Guntur: Nagarjuna Publishers.

Bhaskara Rao, Digumarti (1999). *EdCET Teaching Aptitude*. Guntur: Nagarjuna Publishers.

Bhaskara Rao, Digumarti (2001). *Bharata Samajamulo Upadyayudu Vidya* (Teacher and Education in Emerging Indian Society). Guntur: Nagarjuna Publishers.

Bhaskara Rao, Digumarti (2001). *Bhoutika Sastra Bodhana Paddathulu* (Methods of Teaching Physical Science). Guntur: Nagarjuna Publishers.

Bhaskara Rao, Digumarti (2001). *Jeeva Sastra Bodhana Padhathulu* (Methods of Teaching Biology). Guntur: Nagarjuna Publishers.

Bhaskara Rao, Digumarti (2001). *Vidya Manovignana Sastram* (Educational Psychology). Guntur: Nagarjuna Publishers.

Bhaskara Rao, Digumarti (2003). *Patsala Yajamanyam/Paripalana* (School Management and Administration). Guntur: Nagarjuna Publishers.

Bhaskara Rao, Digumarti (2004). *Vidya Sanketika Sastram mariyu Computer Vidya* (Educational Technology and Computer Education). Guntur: Nagarjuna Publishers.